Australian Cultural Studies

AUSTRALIAN POPULAR CULTURE

Edited by
Ian Craven
with Martin Gray and Geraldine Stoneham

Published in association with *Australian Studies*
and the British Australian Studies Association

CAMBRIDGE
UNIVERSITY PRESS

Published by the Press Syndicate of the University of Cambridge
The Pitt Building, Trumpington Street, Cambridge CB2 1RP, UK
40 West 20th Street, New York, NY 10011-4211, USA
10 Stamford Road, Oakleigh, Melbourne 3166, Australia

First published 1994

Printed in Great Britain by Antony Rowe Ltd, Chippenham, Wiltshire

National Library of Australia cataloguing in publication data applied for

Library of Congress cataloguing in publication data applied for

A catalogue record for this book is available from the British Library

This book is published simultaneously as *Australian Studies* No. 7

ISBN 0 521 46667 9 paperback

CONTENTS

Introduction: Australian Culture as Popular Culture

IAN CRAVEN

One of the most noticeable phenomena evident to students of popular culture in the past ten years has been the increasing audibility of an Australian 'accent' amongst the languages and discourses that compose the field of their study. In domains more usually characterised by the anonymity of their national reference, Australian popular culture has made a quite remarkably self-conscious incursion into the everyday lives of shoppers, cinema-goers, TV-watchers and domestic consumers in general whose impact and significance this collection of essays begins to examine. Undoubtedly the Australian 'invasion' of international popular culture has involved a remarkable proliferation of images and references that have shifted perceptions of Australia throughout the world. The instance of the television soap opera, displacing the narrative environments of bush and outback by those of suburbia, offers only perhaps the most conspicuous example of the much broader process of re-imaging that has taken place. Given the continuing insistence of these Australian 'presences', it seems appropriate that serious attention should start to be given to the current transmission of Australian culture through popular media and other everyday contexts. For with Castlemaine XXXX behind the bar, Yakka in the department stores and *Neighbours* on the television, it is very much through popular culture, rather than the loftier icons of the Australian 'tradition' that most overseas people now make their first contact with the Australian experience.

One of the abiding fascinations of popular culture lies of course in this mobility, which involves the circulation of texts, fashions, styles and even 'attitudes' across widely differing cultural spaces. But popular texts and other cultural forms also of course move through their immediate 'home' territories, with the domestic market usually as crucial to their continued production as sales deals on behalf of more distant consumers. The same popular forms accepted so enthusiastically overseas also circulate within Australia, where they are understood in relation to that immediate setting, forming an apparently 'natural' part of the everyday landscape. It is of course this 'double circulation', the 'transportability' of popular cultural meaning across states and nations which has long troubled those commentators concerned about the erosion of indigenous cultures, the economic viability of culture industries and ultimately the loss of 'imaginary' senses of cultural identity itself. For Australian consumers of 'its' popular culture, the role of particular elements may well have much less of a sense of national 'projection' attaching to it than it does in overseas contexts, but its potential for meaning-making is no less reduced by its reduced exotic or curiosity value.

Some of the essays collected here attempt to consider the most routine and casual elements of Australian cultural production, and their uses and meanings for both Australian and overseas consumers. Practices as well as texts are scrutinised, for popular culture is not only a matter of objects and purchases, but also of course a matter of lived relations and phenomena, a 'whole way of life' in which popular cultural commodities are transformed into cultural 'resources' to be used in the expression of experience, meaning and pleasure. A number of the essays included here examine such 'lived' rather than 'produced' texts, to borrow a suggestive distinction from Fiske, Hodge and Turner's *Myths of Oz* (1987), and in doing so contribute to the study of the 'politics' of consumption which has emerged as a central issue in recent theoretical work on popular culture such as John Fiske's *Understanding Popular Culture* (1989). Through its analysis of both popular texts and the lived relations which exemplify popular 'use', the volume aims to suggest a range of possible responses to the paradox of a culture produced out of economic interest but 'possessed' by its consumers and deployed as a mark of their identity. The focus on the popular culture of a single nation such as Australia then seeks to contribute something to the understanding of popular culture in general. But the narrowing of the sample produces no unified conclusions. In interrogating the idea of 'the popular', these essays reach very different positions on the possibility—or desirability—of constructing a 'culture of the people' through the commercialised forms whose 'popularity' may be as much a symptom of ruthless marketing as audience discrimination and approval.

The relatively recent penetration of Australian reference into other cultures through the increasingly global media makes many of the examples and issues discussed here highly topical ones. More critically, the analyses offered represent something of a belated recognition that Australia has long been defined in terms of its popular culture. Myths of Australian leisure and consumption have always been juxtaposed in our imaginations with all those images of the unforgiving outback and the digger struggling for survival. Through its successive re-inventions, Australia has always been an 'antinomic' sign, bearing connotations of abundance as well as scarcity; of escape as well as imprisonment; and of the environment overcome by the sporting superhero as well as dominating and terminating tentative acts of nation-building.

There has always been a certain national pride in the recreational potentials of the Australian environment, and perhaps more so than any other nation, Australia has presented itself to the outside world as a country that has perfected cultures of leisure as well as those of struggle. For many, the dance-energy of Kylie Minogue and Jason Donovan ultimately only reiterates very common-place assertions that Australians 'know how to enjoy themselves'.

Cultural historians may debate whether Donald Horne's celebrated description of Australia as a 'lucky' country should or should not be taken ironically, but for many the very idea of Australia does promise degrees of self-realisation unavailable elsewhere, not just through a 'standard' of living defined in terms of the availability and accessibility of commercial commodities, but precisely in terms of the opportunities for productive use that such an enhanced range of commodities makes possible. For overseas observers Australia still often figures rather more as spectacle than narrative: the land of the long weekend, the barbecue and the perfect suntan. Apparently eternal myths of climate and landscape conspire to naturalise senses of Australia as almost inevitably a context for the elaboration of enjoyment 'skills'. For many Australians too, their country is still a place to earn more and consume more, a *mise-en-scène* whose seductive power plays against contending everyday realities. Locals have invested heavily in this dream of Australian possibility, and its export helps to ease the acceptance of Australian popular culture internationally, where it serves a curious function of authentication, helping to guarantee if not the universal verities of *Neighbours*, then at least its status as a product of the most truly popular of *all* popular cultures.

This association of Australia with notions of popular culture has tangible and contradictory outcomes of course, and ones which reach well beyond the domains of 'cultural politics' considered by several of the essays here. The articulation of Australia with and through the supposedly 'lowliest' of discursive practices can serve to reinforce conceptions of Australia as a zone free of more 'elevated' cultural discourse. The evidences of popular culture can all too easily be invoked by post-imperialists at home and cultural-cringers abroad to confirm ossifying stereotypes, in whose preservation both Australians and others can have considerable interest. So long as Dame Edna Everage reminds overseas TV viewers that, for example, Australian sporting excellence can be attributed to a lack of local 'intellectual' distraction, the association of popular culture with devaluation will be reinforces, and 'popularity' will refer only to a substitute culture of repetition, facility and immediate gratification to which Australians will be constructed as peculiarly susceptible. For this reason, if for no other, 'the popular' needs to be framed within new discourses, and broken free of the binarism which fixes it as the *other* of true culture. Such a project acquires particular resonance in the Australian context.

Questions of popularity and value figure in all of the essays included in this volume and remain the key issues around which the study of popular culture has turned both inside and outside Australia for over thirty years.

There has been much work 'for' and 'against' of course, but whether
motivated by a desire to 'innoculate' against the stupifying excesses of the
'merely' popular, or to validate the (usually proletarian) practices which
could provide senses of community and continuity for large groups of
people, the debate has been extended with a force and a sense of immediate
relevance rarely witnessed elsewhere in the humanities. The comprehensive bibliography provided by Alan McKee at the end of this volume
records how a trickle of studies through the 1960s and 1970s became a
flood in the 1980s and 1990s, and at the time of writing the demand for
an academic study of popular culture still seems limitless. Given the
argument being made here, it is surely no coincidence that Australian
writers and Australian examples have played such a central role in the
debate over popular culture in recent years. As anglophone culture's
definitive recreational space, Australia is uniquely equipped for the
provision of this new discipline's canonical texts.

The Everyday

Popular culture seems to be everywhere and opportunities for its analysis
seem endless. Yet it is one of the abiding ironies of the study of popular
culture that the *omnipresence* of its object proves one of the greatest obstacles
to its interpretation; everyday availability ensures popular culture's taken-
for-granted quality (suggesting that analysis would be a redundant
activity) whilst its familiarity questions its susceptibility to traditional
aesthetic approaches (which place an emphasis on the novel, the original,
the different or the surprising). The continuing presence of a popular text
or icon in commercial culture further frustrates attempts at defining it as
an object suitable for criticism, and therefore as a finished entity available
for evaluation. Unlike 'true' art which is inaccessible and rare, operating
autonomously against the concerns of everyday life, popular art surrounds
and seems to engulf us as the raw material of everyday life itself. The
experience of popular culture is thus often one of an excess—more soap
operas, more fast-food chains, more dance music than we can possibly
give attention to—which may thrill with postmodernism's 'ecstacy of
communication' but which will leave focus on any particular instance of
that culture feeling impossibly relative. The critic of popular culture usually
drowns in data, struggling to identify the boundaries of his or her object of
study, which is revealed as ever more inter-connected with chain after
chain of distracting 'inter-texts', themselves thoroughly enmeshed with
the warp and weave of everyday life. Popular culture is thus non-
autonomous: not so much deeply embedded in the life of a people so much
as ever present on its surface; a transient and often ephemeral experience,
which frustrates the establishment of critical distance in its stress on
sensation and immediacy.

These emphases are particularly suggestive of the difficulties involved in the study of popular foodstuffs or cuisines. The semiotics of taste (would such a discipline be conceivable?) seems utterly undeveloped. How would one begin the study of culture taken in through the mouth rather than the eye or ear? Robert White's paper engages these issues of proximity and affectivity head-on in his account of the origins and cultural inscriptions of Vegemite. No other foodstuff has become so identified with Australia than this dark brown sandwich spread, whose mythical properties White explores with insight and considerable wit. Probably no other product is seen as more specifically Australian, or more unproblematically 'possessed' by the nation whose identity it is seen as expressing. Yet White's analysis soon reveals a vast complex of social and ideological forces at work behind this most innocent of consumables, and soon underlines once again, the folly of conceiving any national culture (popular or elite) in unitary terms. Historical research reveals Vegemite as far from a 'uniquely' Australian element, some spontaneous culinary expression of local authenticity, but as a simulation of British-made Marmite, now marketed and part-owned by Americans. The fragile bases on which popular culture may be claimed as a culture 'of the people'—which will be apparent throughout the volume—are exposed. Even so secure a national icon as Vegemite apparently offers at best only another instance of the Australian 'accent' audible within a more global narrative of production and consumption, and at worst a marketing strategy designed to ease its introduction into Australian and overseas shopping trolleys.

George Seddon also seeks a uniquely Australian reference, this time outside rather than inside, the Australian kitchen. Considering as prosaic a feature of the urban and suburban environment as the back yard, he argues that the space in Australia from the 1930s 'had no equivalent in any Italian city, or inner London or Dublin or Tokyo'. Seddon's is an unashamedly aesthetic move in relation to popular culture, painstakingly cataloguing detail as a foundation for comparison and celebration. In restoring a history to the back yard, he shows how its altering form and function index changing aspirations and practicalities which themselves mark complex shifts in the everyday lives of millions of Australians. Despite signifying a drift from self-sufficency to a dependency on centralised services, which is linked to commodification and consumerism ('Gardening has become a conspicuous element in the consumer society...') the contemporary yard remains for Seddon a site for popular, but less specific-ally Australian, expression. Its transformation from utilitarian to display and recreational space in recent decades may represent a continuing sign of struggle for respectability especially charged by the convict inheritance, or evidence of a persisting fear of environment long associated with

Australianism, yet it simultaneously represents the coming-of-age of the Australian consumer.

The transience of the popular cultural form, and the variety of scales on which it demands analysis is well illustrated by Xavier Pons's essay, in which he reads—almost microscopically—postage stamps as national fictions, drawing attention to their work as official representations of Australian identity. In detailing decisions about what to include and exclude from the Bicentennial Commemorative collection, he draws attention to the highly selective nature of the representations offered, and the organisation of the images around the principal of an accommodation, offered in the interests of avoiding controversy ('it is not possible to decide whether the stamp is in praise of genetic engineering or its opposite'). Pons's deeper point is however that these highly ordered and mediated images of a 'new' Australia still operate in relation to a still 'colonial' mythic core around which Australian identity is perenially organised. In this sense their importance is less that they may offer false images, but that they are ambiguously effective; appealing to a supposedly shared national heritage they may foreground narratives that speak not of collectivity but of difference. By the same token, the omission of an explicitly multicultural or Aboriginal reference from the set of stamps, for example, may in practice further focus debate on those topics rather than cancelling it. As unconsidered an object as a postage stamp is revealed as redolent with Australian meanings, and for Pons, disappointingly conservative ones.

No study of Australian popular culture could be complete without serious attention to the national sporting life. Stephen Alomes's study of Australian Football contributes to the burgeoning literature of Sport Studies and offers fresh perspectives on this surely specifically Australian phenomenon. The perspective here is both nostalgic and optimistic. Australian football is approached not primarily as a commodity for consumption, but as a credo for expression, still almost a 'folk' culture of the people despite its appropriation by television and marketing interests which for others index 'a larger sense of loss...of grass roots spirituality'. Alomes still finds amongst football's devotees a commitment akin to religious faith, which he links to secularism and materialism in a new society. Football is thus seen as offering the possibility of 'transcendence' of the routine and everyday in moments of bliss and ecstacy; the 'high mark' as epiphany. Alomes exemplifies clearly how popular culture supplies metaphor within which wider realities are understood, whilst also drawing on metaphor as a way of confirming its deep significance. The many strands of his argument illustrate particularly clearly the function of popular cultural forms as sites for the articulation of disparate ideologies and aspirations, in the case of football, particularly in terms of class and region as well as ethnicity and gender. As a reminiscence about the past and a sign of continuity and community for the present, Alomes argues that footie remains a vital reference point in the contemporary culture, 'in its frequent penetration of the workplace, it is simply part of life, impacting more or less on everyone'.

The Media and Popular Culture

If popular culture can be understood positively, that is as a network of practices binding a people together in patterns of recognition as it 'impacts' upon them, then it is clear that a society's information and entertainment media will play key roles in nurturing and shaping those practices. Not surprisingly therefore it has been writing around the media that has stimulated some of the most critical reflection upon the meaning and character of the popular.

Television has of course come to represent the limit-case in discussions of the merit or even 'salvageability' of popular culture. Positions around television seem particularly polarised. With its technological—and capital—intensive base, TV poses perhaps the ultimate challenge to advocates of the popular as a kind of carnival for a late-industrial society, whilst supplying some of the most convincing instances of resistant and subversive reading. Television thus illustrates especially graphically the energising axis between 'spontaneity' and 'commodification' which seems so characteristic of truly everyday culture. As a means of dissemination, television's aesthetic of 'liveness' seems to offer the ultimate possibility of a shared and simultaneous experience; at the same time, its predominantly commercial organisation within Australia seems to illustrate all too perfectly the harnessing of a medium to capital interests which seem remote from those of the people.

Jim Walter provides an important reminder that questions of organisation and control are at stake here, rather than social imperatives implicit in the technology of television itself. Anticipating Nicholas Brown's study of the 'management' of the popular as a *concept* within post-war critical discourse, Walter considers the moment of the introduction of television to Australia, as a point at which the possibilities of TV as a 'people's' medium were initially discussed, but then traces a subsequent history which leads him to doubt that 'a people's culture can survive within a free market'. He illustrates convincingly how struggles for the ownership and control of the fledgling networks were bound up with debates around the definition of the 'popular' itself, in which distinctions between popular culture as 'vernacular culture, resonant with the concerns of specific local communities' and popular culture as an 'international phenomenon' or kind of global 'consumer preference' battle for acceptance and definitional power. For Walter, it is the process by which these definitions are 'naturalised' which forms the true history of popular culture, rather than any list of canonical 'popular' texts, which may or may not allow resistant postmodern readings. More polemically, Walter suggests that from 1949 to 1972 the latter definition of popular TV (consumer preference) slowly gave way to the former (vernacular culture) within new forms of broadcasting regulation. This shift has arguably been qualified in the 1980s by the growing involvement of overseas interests in Australian TV, indicating further that television remains a prime site for contesting and enforcing definitions of the 'people's' interest.

It is perhaps the internationalist connotations of the concept of popular culture that have most troubled those who would control TV in the Australian 'cultural' interest in recent years. Australian broadcasting policy since the early 1970s has often operated with a defensive posture geared towards the preservation of Australian 'content' against the imperialist force of overseas-controlled interests. Ian Craven confronts such questions of Australian control in the context of a particular television programme and a particular style of production. Arguing that the international co-production poses possibilities as well as problems for the political development of both British and Australian national conscious-nesses, he questions the identification of such co-production with the erasure of vernacular resonances, and points to the productive comparative element that such industrial collaborations may introduce at the level of representation. International co-production is thus seen as potentially enhancing the diversity of Australian TV drama in ways that are important for viewers both within Australia and in Britain.

For many years the guiding paradigm for research in the English-speaking world into popular culture and evaluation of its texts was provided by the Frankfurt School whose cultural pessimism placed popular culture in the service of dominant ideology and the consumer of popular culture as its subject. Echoes of this paradigm are audible as Ruth Brown engages perhaps the single most visible icon (internationally) of Australian identity in the 1980s, in the formidable shape of Mick 'Crocodile' Dundee, whose first cinema-vehicle in 1986 became at its point of release the highest-grossing foreign film in US cinema history. Brown's emphasis is less upon the movie as a mis-representation of Australia, than on its utility for American audiences reconsidering their own national imaginaries in the mid-decade. American dominance in the field of commercial cinema is seen here, despite the film's Australian origins, as leaving little space for more indigenous Australian discourse, with the film capitulating to overseas interests in general and the attractions of the US box-office in particular. Little escapes the power of the market 'which has enough money, power and technology to produce its own version of reality' and indeed the film is seen as endorsing fundamentally elitist ways of seeing.

Its appropriation of popular forms, and generic (the western) and social (US foreign policy) inter-texts does little to modify its basically hegemonic functions. Brown's essay provides an important reminder that the appropriation and activation of a text's meaning can cut in a wide variety of political directions. Subversive reading need not be the prerogative of the Left.

National rather than class readings are the focus of Stephen Knight's study of crime fiction. The concern here is with the ways in which popular forms are modified in different national cultures, as he explores the inflections produced by Australians within the inherited narrative structures of the English popular detective story. Sampling some 200 or so Australian crime-writers from the early 1800s to the present, he traces the shifting tropes of the genre. He describes the changing character of the literary detective from police officer to private eye and a range of other contemporary variants, and accounts for manifest preference in terms of local Australian conditions and attitudes, as well as the dictates of the commodity form in which the narratives circulated: 're-positioning in terms of market and class do not seem enough to explain the disappearance of the police'. Knight concludes that specifically Australian mythologies of national identity conspired against the representation of the police as valued detectors, and encouraged the subsequent proliferation of 'zero-detection' crime fiction felt more appropriate to Australian conditions. Interestingly he associates the one major recent example of police-centred Australian crime fiction, the work of John Cleary, with his 'international reputation'.

Kevin Foster and Christine Higgins shift the emphasis from questions of intertextuality to those of mediation. Both consider the treatment of actual crime stories by press, radio and television and show how dominant mythologies colour 'nonfiction' constructions of contemporary Australian news stories. Foster's examination of British press coverage of the Spycatcher trial finds it drawing on fictional antecedents in the thriller novel, which reinforce notions of British pre-eminence at a point of national decline and refurbish nineteenth-century literary constructions of Australia as 'moral and geographical other' for the 1990s. Amply fulfilling definitions of newsworthiness that privilege 'the elite, the negative and the unexpected', the trial provided the opportunity for a restatement of Australian stereotypes that allowed Australian perspectives on British legal principle to remain wholly unexamined and 'politically neutered'. Foster's crucial point however is that Australian protagonists in the trial resisted construction in these typed forms, and the unsettling this produced within established Australian realisms encouraged strategies of evasion. These were for Foster most apparent in the popular press, where the trial was constructed through the sporting metaphors discussed by Stephen Alomes earlier in this volume.

The role of fictional genres in framing readings of nonfictional events is also explored in Christine Higgins's account of the Lindy Chamberlain case's inscription into the news media. In this instance the figures and tropes of horror narrative are deployed to enable readers to decode the case 'in accordance with pre-existing and known cultural meaning systems'. As one might expect, the story provided an opportunity to re-express familiar Australian mythologies of landscape, but also to indicate their connection to wider western—often religious—mythologies, within which 'patriachal, racist and conformist attitudes were privileged' and which assigned culpability in advance of the verdict for the popular consciousness. Once again, the text of popular culture seems primarily to amplify rather than to challenge existing 'common senses' about national and social relations, although Higgins does note that some shifting of received wisdoms may be triggered by the very voraciousness of the media for more and more 'copy'. An examination of the 'secondary' texts generated by the original Chamberlain 'event' intensifies its polysemic quality, and encourages further proliferation of new versions. Faced by this ever-expanding textuality, Higgins concedes only a relative signific-ance for the case: 'meaning finally rests with the culturally and historically situated reader'.

Theorising Popular Culture

The study of popular culture is of course a major academic growth-industry in the 1990s, and the archaeology of the everyday is well under way. A number of essays in this volume contribute to that work. The terms of the intellectual's engagement with the everyday, ordinary and routine manifestations of that culture also itself possesses a history. The Australian version is in process of construction in recent volumes such as *Myths of Oz* (1987) and *Post Pop* (1991). Conspicuous on all fronts is a shift from an emphasis on recuperation, in which the values of elite culture are unearthed from the most unpromising of grounds, towards a variety of theoretical paradigms whose indebtedness to structuralism works to refuse the elite/popular opposition, in its concentration on the mobility of signifying systems across forms of widely varying social status. Paradox-ically, the very 'lowest' of popular culture has increasingly attracted attention from the very 'highest' of theoretical positions, and the final essays in this volume attempt in different ways to examine some of the approaches that have come to characterise work in the field of popular culture in recent years. From the wide range of models available, three principal areas of theoretical initiative are represented here: feminism, discourse theory and postmodernism.

Kay Ferres's essay questions what is seen as an inherent masculinism in the intellectual traditions which have defined Australian cultural value, and contrasts this bias with an account of more feminine cultural heritages and the potentially empowering experience of popular culture for Australian women. This entails a turn evidenced in much writing on popular culture which seeks to qualify the assumed passivity of consumption as a more dynamic activity which 'involves complex manipulations of symbols for many purposes'. As illustration, she examines the ways in which popular magazines in the 1920s became spaces within which questions of feminine sexual pleasure could actively be taken up, and through whose columns editors could both entertain and stimulate the political development of their readerships. Her accounts of moral panics induced around 'jazzing' amply demonstrate that discussion through these magazines possessed a highly tangible political charge and that the magazines were already developing an analysis of the expressive potential of leisure activities for women in Australian society.

Undoubtedly, the most commonly posed challenge to academics studying popular culture is to account for the 'popularity' of a particular personality, lifestyle accessory or craze. Graham Seal attempts a reasoned response to this deceptively straightforward question as he considers the 'pan-anglophonic appeal' of the Australian ballad 'The Wild Colonial Boy'. For Seal, the taking up of the ballad in Britain and elsewhere, instances an early example of the re-transmission of Australian culture 'back into the matrices of the tradition from which it arose'. For Seal the ballad draws upon the mythic connotations of a 'pan-anglophonic' outlaw tradition that pre-exists it, and its appeal is that of the 'historically ungrounded hero' who can be adapted to meet the needs of local circumstance rather than a matter of its broad exoticism or any more specifically Australian reference. Seal's implication is that the internationalism of popular culture is well-defined prior to the advent of both the modern media of mechanical and electronic reproduction and more theoretical accounts of the universalism of mass forms.

Concepts of popular culture are also discursively produced. Nicholas Brown traces another pattern of re-transmission in his essay dealing with the distillation of the concept of popular culture by Australian intellectuals in the post-war period. For Brown the term is significant within a discourse that addresses and constitutes a politically viable sense of belonging for the members of the Australian state. He sees an investment in the term, and an attendant, if limited, validation of a cultural life associated with 'the people', as a strategic response to threatening notions of 'mass mentality' which would concede individualised rights to centralised authority. In what is seen as a peculiarly conformist and Australian intellectual turn, notions of 'the popular' are seen to resolve potentially threatening social contradiction by mediating 'between evocations of a collective integrity on the one hand and fears of an amorphous, selfish mob on the other'. His revelation that the organisers of Australian Adult Education in the period policed a distinction between 'the merely popular, which might slide into the selfishness of the mass, and the refined popular culture of the self-improving community' provides in particular a fascinating pre-echo of much to come in cultural theory in the 1980s, whose re-definition in terms of postmodernity still seeks to negotiate and lend political resonance to this boundary.

It is perhaps the development of theories of postmodernism which has done most to raise questions about the positive and creative possibilities of popular culture in recent years, indeed to shift the very terrain of debate about everyday practice from concern with mass consumption to questions of popular discrimination and engagement. As a glance through any comprehensive bibliography on popular culture indicates, theories of the postmodern and theoretical analyses of popular culture from its perspective have proliferated in Australia to a quite remarkable extent. Graham Seal's suggestion that in the 1950s concepts of the 'plain Australian' encouraged 'a peculiarly normative approach to the popular' implies that a considerable sea-change has in fact occurred in Australian intellectual culture in the past twenty-five years or so. Indeed the Australian academy's embrace of postmodernism has contributed much not only to the study of Australian popular culture, but—as a major export—also to that of its overseas counterparts.

Andrew Milner confronts this enthusiasm for postmodernism, and traces its acceptance to specifically Australian sensibilities. Postmodernism, he argues, has been embraced not only as a theory of the popular as a domain of pleasure, emancipation and enfranchisement but also as a theory of Australia itself. The coincidence of postmodernism's 'apocalyptic hedonism' with Australia's self-definition as anglophone culture's definitive play-space (somehow also terminal), has ensured that the new theory would gain a firm grounding in Australian contexts of all kinds, whilst Australian lifestyles themselves (especially life on the beach) would increasingly provide the 'lived texts' for postmodern analyses in every direction. Much of Milner's account of the theory seems to echo predispositions (the scepticism of authoritative 'metanarrative', an anxiety around the threat of extinction, culture as transgression) already firmly encoded elsewhere in the Australian national narrative. As such, postmodern culture becomes a 'culture which remains peculiarly visible from a New World, extra-European vantage point' such as Australia. If Milner is correct, then Australian cultural criticism perhaps represents a no less significant re-transmission of inherited discourse than that discussed by Graham Seal in his account of 'The Wild Colonial Boy'. As much a commodity form as a content, postmodernism does indeed emerge from Milner's account as critical theory's own variety of blockbuster. It remains to be seen whether it is also an apocalyptic moment for the study of popular culture.

Acknowledgements

No introduction to this volume would be complete without an acknowledgement of the support that the British Australian Studies Association (BASA) continues to receive from the Sir Robert Menzies Centre for Australian Studies (SRMCAS) at the University of London. The Association has enjoyed a long and very productive relationship with the staff of SRMCAS, whose visiting professors and lecturers serve on the Association's Executive Committee and contribute time and expertise to BASA's various initiatives. In recent years BASA has been particularly well-supported by Jim Walter and Richard Nile, whose joint efforts have helped BASA to become established as a central focus for British work on all aspects of Australian experience and endeavour. The success of the Popular Culture Conference—these essays have been chosen from among those papers delivered at the event—was particularly attributable to the investment of Richard Nile in its organisation, his last of many initiatives before a return to Australia which prevented his more direct participation in the editing of this volume. I am very pleased to have this opportunity to record our thanks to Richard and his colleagues for their continuing contribution to BASA's development. The study of Australia from the distance of London or Glasgow can often seem a very solitary experience: Richard's efforts did much to banish that particular 'tyranny' of distance.

POPULAR CULTURE AS THE EVERYDAY

A Brief Cultural History of Vegemite

R.S. WHITE

At the outset I should make it clear that, to coin a phrase, Vegemite studies is not my bread and butter job. I am a Shakespearian scholar. The colourful tale of my sortie into yeast extracts will be told a little later.

In the beginning there was Marmite. Who invented or discovered it is the subject of a frosty correspondence in *The Guardian* between two English families (27 April and 4 May 1992). The date of its inception is also in doubt, but certainly lies in the late nineteenth century. The Sanatarium Health Food Company which markets the product at least in Australia, has kept an inscrutable silence in the controversial debate. This reticence may have something to do with the fact that the company is run by a teetotal Seventh Day Adventist Church which may not wish it to be widely known that Marmite is, to put it bluntly, made from a waste product from beer. Marmite made inroads into the Australian market in the early twentieth century, aided by substantial advertisements in major outlets such as *The Sydney Morning Herald* and *Australian Home Journal*. These advertisements took advantage of the relatively recent discovery of vitamins, for -mite products are indeed rich in the Vitamin B complex. But they sail a little close to the wind in calling this yeast extract a 'pure vegetable extract' and invoking the old-fashioned call to 'eat plenty of greens'. The advertisements also tend to overstate the versatility of Marmite, advocating its use as a sandwich filling, ready to spread on biscuits and to enrich all manners of soups, stews and savoury dishes, appropriate for 'a refreshing and invigorating "cup"', and—more surprisingly—suitable for making a 'piquant' tasting custard which is said to make a refreshing change from sweet custard. In the apparently heavily patriarchal society of 1920s Australia, Marmite is also advertised as 'a man's drink, with the advice 'It is very economical in use—Ask your wife to buy the Large Jars'.

Since these expensive advertisements were appearing from 1923 onwards, it would appear that Marmite had realised that an upstart crow from the colony could in the long term pose a threat. Enter Vegemite. Fred Walker and Company was a firm whose main activity was processing cheese and preserved meats, servicing country areas in the eastern states of Australia. Flushed with success at simulating British Bovril with Bonox, on a fateful day in early 1923, Fred Walker passed a jar of Marmite to his brilliant chemist Dr C.P. Callister, asking 'Could you produce a product like that?' Callister had never seen it before, but courageously said 'yes'. With no information to go on, he researched the chemical makeup of Marmite and discovered it was made from brewer's yeast from the Burton-on-Trent Breweries. Callister's research was written up into a thesis which was awarded a DSc from Melbourne University, which at the time was a rare achievement. Fred Walker used supplies from Carlton Breweries in Melbourne to simulate Marmite, and thus began Vegemite, sold under this name, which had won a competition, in small amber jars. In 1929 it was sold in opal jars, and in 1934 the suppliers of raw materials were joined by Tooth and Company Breweries. Various centres were investigated, including Adelaide and Ballarat, as potential factory sites.

Something of a false turn was made in 1928. Disappointed by sales of Vegemite, Fred Walker, renamed the product Parwill. If Ma might, then Pa will. The change proved a flop, and Vegemite returned, together with Toohey's Brewery as supplier. In the Depression years of the thirties, it was still, however, losing the battle with Marmite for markets in Australia and New Zealand. The cultural cringe dictated that any product from the old country must be superior to those from the colonies. The company employed heavy-duty promotion techniques in 1935–6 by offering with every sale of a Kraft-Walker product a coupon which could be redeemed with a jar of Vegemite. This was the real launch of the product as a mass commodity. By this time, the once and future great Australian product, was part owned by Kraft, the United States company. Such is colonisation that in 1950 Kraft Foods Limited took over the whole company and advertised it with images of Walt Disney cartoon figures.

The Second World War changed many things in relations between Britain and its colonies. During the War period, supplies of Marmite from England were cut off, because it was considered a central part of the British war effort. There might be an argument to mount that Marmite and the Queen Mother won the war. In Australia, restrictions to the civilian population of Vegemite became a problem to the manufacturers. Michael Symons in *One Continuous Picnic: A History of Eating in Australia* (1982) quotes an advertisement of the time: 'if you are one of those who don't need Vegemite medicinally [a curious phrase, to which we shall return], the thousands of invalids and babies are asking you to deny yourself of it for the time being' (p. 165). Apart from the invalids and babies, the Department of Supply wanted it all for the Australian armed forces, in a choice of seven pound tins, eight ounce tins or half-ounce ration portions. The demand was *not* a problem but rather an opportunity for the producers, who, no longer able to produce enough from brewer's yeast, set up a factory producing baker's yeast. Today it is made from a blend of brewer's and baker's yeast, augmented by vegetable extract which softens the taste. In 1947 a huge supplier of pure alcohol from sugar in northern Queensland at Sarina guaranteed Vegemite its yeast waste. This enabled Vegemite production to expand and diversify into other states and other breweries in Australia and New Zealand. The enormous amount of Vegemite supplied to the Forces undoubtedly contributed to the creation of a giant market when they all returned. This generation in turn gave birth to those politicised in 1954 by the jingle:

> We're happy little Vegemites as bright as bright can be.
> We all enjoy our Vegemite for breakfast, lunch and tea.
> Our mummy says we're growing stronger every single week.
> Because we love our Vegemite, we all adore our Vegemite,
> It puts a rose in every cheek.

Competition with Marmite had been rejoined, for Vegemite beat Marmite to a contract with a brewery in Auckland by pledging to start operations within three months. The old colonies were beginning to club together against the old seat of empire.

The competition still goes on. I found on a packet of Weet-Bix distributed by Sanatarium Foods in Australia an advertisement claiming 'Our Mite is better than their Mite' which almost concedes defeat by breaking the cardinal rule of all companies not even to acknowledge the existence of rivals. Meanwhile, Vegemite in Britain has moved with the stealth of guerilla warfare, quietly entering major supermarkets, exclusive delicatessens and corner shops, with the unobtrusively effective colonising strategies of the tandoori restaurant, Clive James and Richie Benaud. The Empire bites back indeed.

Other countries have not proved so receptive to the product. I recall seeing a couple of years ago on television a report of an attempt to market Vegemite in Japan, on the theory that it resembles soy sauce. The sample consumers were neither convinced nor amused. They found it inedible. Apparently, United States citizens, unaware that they owned it, did not take to Vegemite when many hundreds of them stayed in Fremantle for the Americas Cup in the late 1980s. An article in the *Toledo Blade* published on 23 January 1987 reported back from Perth to America that Vegemite has the thick consistency of 'axle grease'. The reporter, Steve Pollick, Toledo Blade's Outdoors Editor, continues:

> It smells like a can of rusty nails, and tastes salty and yeasty—at best—or maybe like a bloody lip or an inadvertently bitten tongue. It definitely is an acquired taste, yet 15 million Australians consume something like 4,500 tons of it a year...Now the stuff supposedly can be found in 9 out of 10 Australian households.

The Outdoors Editor concludes 'Maybe the motto Down Under should be, "Vegemite—don't leave home without it"', and in fact he has stumbled onto a truth. In my fieldwork for this paper, it was remarkable how many people attested to having a relative abroad who regularly demanded large quantities of Vegemite to stave off withdrawal symptoms, and as many witnesses have told of Australian travellers in unlikely places producing their pot at mealtimes. I myself saw a young man at breakfast in a modest hotel in Rome produce it to have with his Italian rolls and strong coffee which he diluted with a lot of milk. There is an outpost for the desperate expat in the USA, for Olivia Newton-John sells Vegemite in her Californian boutique, Koala Blue, and an exclusive but eccentric shop in Dallas, Niemen Marcus, is rumoured sometimes to stock it. I have not checked Harrods, but would not be at all surprised to find a supply there, beside the potted quails and gentleman's relish.

Curiously, the original subject of my paper inhabits something of a vacuum. For a product which commands such fantastic loyalty from the Australian populace and its expatriate body, and which is making insidious inroads into Britain, the cultural inscription of Vegemite is strangely absent. There is indeed a pictorial genre called Vegemite painting alive and well at least in Western Australia. Diluted or undiluted, Vegemite can, on butcher's paper or card, applied with fingers or spatula, have an effect of sepia and charcoal. This, maybe Australia's only indigenous 'white' art form was, I presume, generated in country areas which lacked access to ready supplies of paints. But where is the great Australian Vegemite novel, the poems whose theme is this national institution?

My research for this paper was originally foreseen as focusing on the cultural inscriptions and influences of Vegemite. For something which is familiar to every single Australian, there are surprisingly few cultural references. However, it is heartwarming to the Australian republican how affectionate these are. A heavy metal rock band refers to it in the track 'Down under' on their album called *Business as Usual*. The singer, finding himself in Brussels, asks a muscular man of 6 feet 4: '"Do you speak-a my language?" He just smiled and gave me a Vegemite sandwich'. Julian Croft in his volume *Confessions of a Corinthian* has a poem called 'Strangeness and Charm' which has the verses:

> I've been back along those north coast beaches
> on and off, in and out of seasons,
> for twenty years and twenty different reasons:
>
> My nose making bread out of golden banksia,
> storing up radiant blue for sea and sky
> in beach heath, brought back in sprigs to dry
>
> into the faded blue of sailors' dungarees,
> stuck in vegemite jars in frosty

> tableland kitchens, their water rusty
> with age and neglect, like myself...

A writer contributing to the recent *Directory of Australian Authors*, edited by Mary Lord, announces that she 'hates Vegemite sandwiches', so the subject must be one which has some relevance to creative people. An outsider's confirmation of this fact comes in a patronising introduction by a famous American science fiction writer, Harian Ellison, to a book by a promising Sydney writer Terry Dowling:

> Not easy being an admirer of the Author...The Introducer has a vested interest, of course. I know the Author as a mate, chum, pal, buddy; he tricked me into actually tasting Vegemite...

In a short story by Georgia Savage, 'The Spider', published in *The Bulletin Literary Supplement* on 30 June 1981, reprinted in *The Illustrated Treasury of Australian Stories*, edited by Geoffrey Dutton, we find the line 'To find her waiting for me with what looked like an entire jar of Vegemite on her eyelashes...'. Apart from these rather scanty quotations (and I have to admit that my research is barely on the threshold of this immense subject), other cultural references are confined to children's books such as *Possum Magic* by Mem Fox and the alphabet book, *A is for Australia* which, like Vegemite itself, is marketed by an American company rather than an Australian. They may not know what is good for them, but they know what sells.

Speaking of what is good for us, many claims have been made for and against Vegemite on health grounds. Indeed, its significance for health issues is the area in which it really reveals cultural priorities of the Australian nation. Ever since sporting and fit young men were made part of the propaganda war effort in 1914–18, Australians have been little short of obsessed with the subject. If a product can be marketed to the fitness-conscious it is sure to succeed. Undoubtedly this is so of Vegemite. I shall spare you the details of the process of autolysis which alchemises spent yeast into our prized paste, and I shall spare you the various water soluble protein derivatives such as peptones, peptides and amino acids, the glycogen and mannan, the potassium and magnesium phosphates. Suffice it to say that Vegemite does seem proven as a dietary source of protein, minerals and the vitamin B complex. One of the ironies is that of the vitamin trio, Thiamin, Riboflavin and Niacin, Thiamin, the one that maintains the nervous system, is notoriously depleted by heavy drinking, and a recent argument was mounted that it should be added to beer. Before this is done, presumably the answer is to eat equal quantities of Vegemite after every binge.

Armed with these scientific facts, the producers of Vegemite have predictably stressed the healthy effects of eating it. It also has no fat whatsoever, very few kilojoules, no added sugar, no animal content and no gluten, all valuable factors for the health-and-fitness-conscious Australian. The cult of the young, healthy and beautiful body is served by advertising for children ensuring them thriving brain cells, fully toned nerves, healthy skin, efficient digestion, and sparkling eyes, if they eat Vegemite. I have also been informed from a variety of sources that Vegemite cures mouth ulcers, that it is used in the bush for insect bites—to cure them, that is, not to attract them—and it can reduce swelling. It is said that its folic acid content protects against spina bifida, that it can cure muscular dystrophy, and dyslexia by increasing learning and memory capacities. Witnesses from the Second World War tell some remarkable stories of Vegemite's curative and reviving properties. Prisoners of War from Changi who were seriously debilitated were treated with Vegemite for vitamin deficiency. Another story related to me is that an experiment conducted by Colonel Bonnin of Adelaide showed that Vegemite led to faster progress for starving POWs and Internees than vitamin supplements, liver injections and iron tablets respectively. (This experiment was said to have been written up in the *Australian Medical Journal* but cannot be found.)

There is, however, a dark underbelly to the curative claims. A twilight world of dedicated researchers has tried to penetrate the monolith of uncritical enthusiasm. The first attack was from the anti-salters. For example, Dr Mark Legatt and Susan Leggatt in *The Australian Food Report* in 1989 found both Marmite and Vegemite massively above the guideline levels for sodium. Rather tartly, they add '[Vegemite's] savouriness is, we felt, somewhat harsh, and unmellowed by the sugar content that helps make Marmite palatable' (p. 190). This preference, based unashamedly on personal taste, of course, opens up a huge area of contention between the Australians and the British. Vegemite at least has recently countered this attack by drastically reducing the salt content. However, other maverick researchers are pursuing the line that pure, concentrated yeast is not good for anybody, let alone children, particularly when it coincides with the huge postwar expansion in consumption of sugar. Apparently feeding yeast with sugar causes some kind of explosion which, enacted in the human body can—it is alleged—weaken the immune system and lead to allergies, thrush and asthma, all of which do indeed seem to have increased in Australia. The argument is that something which before the War was a good thing has, because of the social context which introduced more sugar, pasteurised milk, preservatives in food and so on, now changed into a dangerous thing. Could we have here in the 1990s cultural revelation given to us by Vegemite studies? As in former times the sun was our friend, and now it has become our enemy, so perhaps we are witnessing the first stirrings of an anti-Vegemite movement, which may lead to the classic Australian habit of lopping the tall poppies, and finding the hero has clay feet. The age of green revisionism may be upon us and even Vegemite may not be a safe icon.

Just how powerful is the social embeddedness of Vegemite in Australia, and now in Britain, I discovered through experiences in researching this paper. Having offered a title to the British Australian Studies Association I then thought I would tap my colleagues' brains and entered in our departmental newsletter (circulation 30) a request for information about literary references. This was spotted by the editor of the University's newsletter (circulation about 1,000), who reprinted it there. From there it was spotted by the editors of both *The West Australian* and the Western Australian Sunday paper (circulation about two million in all). After this, the switchboard at the University of Western Australia was jammed for three days with callers for Professor White proffering information. I was rung by three Western Australian radio stations for interviews, by ABC National for a national phone-in, by *The Age* for an interview and more recently by Channel 9. I was also rung by small suburban Perth free newspapers. Life became hell for me, a giant black hole of Vegemite which seemed to swallow up my past and future. I fled to the medieval sanctuary, Oxford University, to avoid it.

The consequence, however, is that this paper has been not just an academic exercise but a life-experience which has left me sadder and wiser. I am the lonely repository of tales of disaster and tragedy involving Vegemite, which cannot be told because they threaten national security, or at least would invite libel suits. But it has given me a perverse taste for the kind of oral research that brings us in touch with people beyond our books and academe. And so, I dedicate the paper now to my army of informants: among them, especially Ian Kiely, bus driver from Wembley Downs; Jean Blake of Kraft Foods; Carol Bower; Lyn Broad of Marawa; Michael Day of *Campus Review Weekly*; Loraine Dragosavic; Lilian Dyke; Betty Foster; Mrs P. Heming of Cadaux (?); Dr Van Ikin; Nola Kellow of Ferndale; Joe of *The Sunday Times*; Carmel MacAuslan from Ocean Grove Victoria; Ms McKenzie; Betty Masterson; Jean Knight (connections with Carlton Breweries); Andrew Nielson; David and Judy Ray; Patricia Roberts of Wanneroo; Lorna Robertson; Christine Stephens; Kate and Ron Shepherd; Julie Stout; M.G. Suter of Mandurah; a lady sea-scout from Cottesloe Beach; C.F. Symonds of Shoalwater; Julie Turner; the Reverend Ted Witham; Chris and Anne Wortham; a man who rang from Meeka-tharra petrol station; and more recently the *Guardian*, Channel 9, ABC News, Celandine Television London and the BBC.

The Australian Back Yard

GEORGE SEDDON

When I was young in the 1930s, and for several decades on either side, the function of the typical Australian back yard in the cities and country towns could be known easily from a list of its contents. It had all or most of: a woodheap, often with rickety woodshed with a low roof of galvanised iron, and a fence for the back wall; a wash-house, with two tubs and a copper with a grate beneath it to heat the water and a wire rack to hold the Velvet soap and Reckitts blue; a clothes line; one or more tanks on wooden tankstands, with mint and parsley under or near the dripping tap in a cut-down kerosene tin; a dunny against the back fence, so that the pan could be collected from the dunny lane through a trap-door; there might be a kennel for the dog, although he often slept under the verandah; there was sometimes a crude incinerator, often a old oil drum, although rubbish was also burnt in an open bonfire. There might be chooks, usually in a chook-house along the back fence, and sometimes a sleep-out, usually a verandah enclosed with fly-wire, but sometimes free standing. A lemon tree was nearly universal; other trees varied with climate—almond trees in Adelaide and Perth, plums and apples in Melbourne, choko vines and bananas in Sydney and Brisbane, a mango in Cairns, figs and loquats almost everywhere. For a few weeks, there was gross overabundance of fruit, and much trading ('I'll take some of your plums if you take some of my apples next month'). Blackbirds, Ceylon crows and starlings grew fat (except in Perth). They didn't mind the fruit fly grubs and codlin crawling in the apples. In the country towns, there was a good chance of a pepper tree (*Schinus molle*), which left a grubby latex film on your hands and clothes when you climbed it. In Kalgoorlie, where water came in a pipe from the Darling Scarp, the shower water was drained out to a banana plant. Sometimes there was a patch of coarse grass, couch or buffalo, for the kids to play on, but there was rarely any special provision for the young, who played under the tankstand, in the wood shed, in the back lane, or in the driveway—which was good for cricket. Swings and sandpits all came later, as did swimming pools and barbecues.

I don't think there was much regional variation, and not much change either, over a period of fifty years or more. Wooden slatted fern and orchid houses were fairly common in Brisbane, and staghorn ferns were common even as far south as Melbourne. In Tasmania, the wash tubs might be made of Huon pine, in Victoria, concrete. Drier places like Mildura might have two tanks for rainwater rather than one, and Melbourne none. Some people had vegetable gardens—onions, peas, beans, cabbages, lettuce—

and a compost heap to go with it. There was often junk piled up somewhere in the yard, since councils did not come round to collect it. From the late 1930s onwards, there was sometimes an old car body, enlisted by the young as play equipment. The advent of the car was a major change, adding a driveway, perhaps a garage, and a new activity (washing the car). In the last thirty years, changes have come thick and fast. The basic functions of the back yard have changed, but we will come to that later.

Not all back yards were the same, of course, but the variations were not so much regional as a reflection of differences in social standing and ethnic background. The Italians grew tomatoes, onions, oregano and tarragon, zucchini, fennel, olives and wine grapes, and sometimes 'rolled their own'. So did the Greeks, who also grew tomatoes, and two or three different kinds of basil, although any but the most common herbs (mint, parsley, thyme and sage) were hard to get in Australia before the Second World War, and the fashionable herb garden of today's fashionable middle-class suburban cook was unheard of. The Chinese, as always, cultivated every inch of ground available to them; Tom Hungerford (1977) gives a good account of such a garden in South Perth in the 1930s. Greeks and Italians to this day often grow vegetables in their front yard as well as their back, in inner city suburbs like Richmond in Melbourne and Leichardt in Sydney. The back yards of the German settlers in the Barossa were more orderly and better cared for than the Australian average, but not essentially different in function.

The vegetable garden probably showed the greatest variation. A raised bed was made for growing vegetables in many areas, but not all, reflecting the regional practice in the British Isles from which the settlers came. This neat raised bed, bordered with wood, brick or beer bottles gave good drainage. Narrow rectangles with gravel paths between gave good access. The bed itself was built up with compost, and mulched with straw and horse dung. I have seen survivors in Port Fairy in Victoria, an Irish town, and in Hobart, but the formal plots are not now so common; although vegetable beds are still often mounded, they are rarely bordered.

The other variation was social. Rich people had much bigger back yards, often with stables, a tennis court on the double block beside the house, more fruit trees, a bigger vegetable garden, a cutting garden for flowers for the house. Yet rich or poor, most of the domestic functions still had to be met.

Function is the key word. The back yard, equally in the town and the country, was complementary to the house in providing resources for living: storage, water, fuel, washing facilities, food input, and food output (by way of the dunny and the compost heap). It also served as a male domain, while the house was female. The women did the washing, perhaps the flower garden, if there was one, and kept an eye on the children, but the men chopped the wood, usually lit the copper on wash-day, and looked after the vegetables, washed up in the wash-house, as country men still do. The bathroom inside was for the women, and men continued to use the outhouse long after a toilet was installed inside. Glen Tomasetti (1976) faithfully records all these rituals and uses in *Thoroughly Decent People*, in which she is describing East St Kilda in 1934:

> Schooled to the remote privacy of the outhouse, no sewerage would induce Bert to have or use a lavatory in a bathroom. He continued to use the wash house for shaving and scrubbing in preference to the bathroom which, unless he needed something from the medicine chest, he entered only twice a week to have a bath (p. 24).

> Bert was up at half-past six and Lizzie at seven. She didn't have tea in bed on Monday morning because it was washing day. Bert had filled the copper with water and, since he had lit the fire under it for so many years, he now lit the gas (p. 22).

> While the men and boys played cricket in the drive with a kerosene tin for stumps, a good old bat and a tennis ball, the girls went inside to help Lizzie get the tea (p. 4).

So the suburban back yard served as a play space, and for imaginative children, a magic carpet that could become many things. But that is not what it was *for*. In being a necessary adjunct of the house serving domestic needs, it was essentially *rural*, a gesture towards functional self-sufficiency, not complete, but not totally dependent on a web of urban services as we are today. The suburban back yard was not fundamentally different from the country back yard in Australia. Indeed the main difference was only that the country back yard usually had more junk—because it was harder to get rid of. The suburban Australian back yard had no equivalent in any Italian city, or inner London or Dublin or New York or Tokyo, nor does it today. They never had the space, and the domestic functions had to be served in more compact ways. In London, there was no wood to heap in the tiny 'area', as the space was called, but coal in the cellar, reached directly from the street. In Rome or Hong Kong, washing hangs from upstairs windows. The cities that have something like the suburban Australian back yard are those that have grown in the last one hundred years or so, swelled by a migration of rural people to the city: cities of countrymen and women. Some are rich, some are poor; Los Angeles is a rich example, but full of Dust Bowl farmers who walked off the land in the Depression. Port Moresby is an example of a poor city, made up of villagers who have to keep up a degree of self-sufficiency because urban services have not kept pace with their arrival, and who need and want to keep up a degree of self-sufficiency because they are culturally attuned to it: certain foodstuffs that must be fresh, or that cannot be readily obtained, or that should not be touched by other possibly malign hands. Most squatter settlements on the outskirts of the Third World cities have these characteristics—because the squatters come from a culture of self-sufficiency, and because in any case, there is no choice; similar forces applied in our suburbs. The dream of almost every immigrant was to acquire land of his own, no matter how little, but production on the quarter-acre block was also a product of living conditions characterised by poor supplies, no refrigeration, indifferent urban services—and recurrent poverty and shortage, as in the depressions of the 1890s, the 1930s, and much of the Second World War.

But if there is a functional continuum from country back yards to suburban back yards on the quarter-acre subdivision, there is a break as we move in to the inner city. These areas have a different history, especially in Sydney and Melbourne—although they now represent only 2 per cent and 1 per cent respectively of the housing of those two cities, they represent a distinctive urban form and culture (Neutze, 1977, p. 5). They spring from rapid population growth in the second half of the last century.

In some inner city areas, especially in inner Sydney, densities were very high. By 1891, the 3,500 people of Darlinghurst were housed in 672 five-to-six roomed houses built on 62 acres. The density per acre was 61.88, but this is less than the density of habitation, because it takes no account of space used for shops and offices, and therefore not available as residential. Paddington had 44.11 persons per acre, and Redfern 46.86. Several wards of the City of Sydney had a high average of persons per inhabited dwelling. In the ward of Bourke, there were 8.2 persons per dwelling (often of only four rooms) in 1891. 'In Long's Lane, off Cumbernauld Street, seven houses shared one water tap' (Kelly, 1978, p. 74, from whom these data are drawn). The back yards were minuscule and filthy, with a water closet at the back door.

They were lucky. A court in the Rocks—Miller's Buildings—of fourteen houses, each of two rooms less than 3 square metres, had four closets for the fourteen houses, which were estimated to house about sixty people. In 1889, the investigating committee 'found on the doorstep, a heap of human excreta, covered with an old straw hat' (quoted in Kelly, 1978, p. 76). In 1900, 303 people contracted bubonic plague, and 103 of them died. This at last brought these conditions into the limelight, and led to slum clearance and better sanitation in inner Sydney.

In 1890, however, working-class housing in Sydney was thought by those few who had studied it, to be worse than that of London, which was generally agreed to be worse than anywhere else. Rapid growth in population and the loss of inner residential land to industrial and commercial use led to a growing population, trapped by poor public transport, crowded into a diminishing area, served by an incompetent local government, in a steep sandstone terrain that of itself made the provision of adequate urban services difficult.

Water supply and sanitation had been difficult in Sydney from the outset: in 1851, only about 1,000 houses of an approximate 8,000 in the Sydney Corporation area were connected to mains supplies. Many houses in the 1850s had wells and cesspits side by side. A report in the *Sydney Morning Herald* (7 March 1851, p. 2, quoted in Clark, 1978, p. 57) said of the inhabitants of Paramatta Street that 'they cook in dirt—they eat in dirt—and they sleep in it, they are born, bred and they die in dirt; from the cradle to the grave, they pass through life in filth—society tolerates it, and they look upon it as their inheritance'.

'Marvellous Melbourne' was little better than Sydney in the colonial years. Bernard Barrett (1971) has given a detailed account of the slums of Collingwood, and the uses to which back yards were put there. 'In the mid-nineteenth century privy out-houses were usually constructed over or near a cesspit. Cesspits were of varying degrees of sophistication. In the 1850s and 1860s the typical cesspit on Collingwood Flat tended to be at the primate end of the scale—a mere hole dug in the ground. It was probably never emptied; when it became filled with solid matter, it might be covered over with earth, and the timber superstructure would be moved a few yards away to a new hole' (Barrett, 1971, p. 75—in a chapter with the title: 'From Cesspits to Cesspans'). They grow good tomatoes in Collingwood back yards today.

The Board of Works was created in 1890, with the responsibility of providing water and developing a sewerage system. Melbourne had already established a clean, continuous and publicly owned water supply by 1853, while London's system did not reach this stage until 1899, but Melbourne was well behind in establishing a sewerage system. London had made cesspools illegal in 1847, although it then ran its sewers into the Thames. Adelaide began constructing a sewerage system in 1878, and Sydney shortly afterwards. Hobart and Melbourne constructed their major works in the first years of this century. The inner suburbs of Perth were sewered at a leisurely pace, as befits the more relaxed lifestyle in the West, between 1906 and 1920, with the main outlet at Claise Brook on the Swan in East Perth. 'Some wealthy households installed their own septic tanks. Most made do with the double-pan system and dry-earth closets until the sewerage pipes reached them' (Stannage, 1979, p. 278).

Brisbane was the last of the capital cities, on a timetable like that of most country towns. The construction of Brisbane's first sewerage project began in 1916, but did not proceed until 1923, so that 'pan closets were still operating in central Brisbane in 1923—and they still operate (along with septic tanks) in many Australian country towns and outer suburbs today. In 1960, it was estimated that half a million people lacked mains sewerage in the Sydney metropolitan area alone' (Barrett, 1971, p. 137). Perth in 1988 was 73 per cent sewered; septic tanks in the Darling Ranges are causing concern, and led to an official *Report of the Select Committee appointed to enquire into effluent disposal in the Perth Metropolitan Region*, chaired by Ian Alexander, MLA. Thus if one of the prime objectives of today's town planning is to connect bums to oceans, their success is not yet complete in Australian cities, and the back yard often continues to perform one of its most basic functions. The unsewered subdivisions today are not, however, in the inner city, which has different problems and prospects. They are in the outlying suburbs, especially those in the hill areas that adjoin all of our capital cities. These are expensive to service adequately, but suburbia continues its low-density invasion. Not, however, on the legendary 'quarter-acre block', which was common enough, but never standard—there was great variation in subdivision size both in and between cities.

The 'classic' quarter-acre was 100 links (or one chain) by 250 links (or two and a half chains), with a frontage of 66ft and a depth of 165ft (roughly 20m x 50m—1000 square metres). This was the standard subdivision in Dalkeith and Nedlands in Western Australia, for example, but blocks in South Perth were subdivided at the same time (1916 onwards) at 32 perches, which represented four-fifths of the Dalkeith standard. In Claremont, an older suburb than Dalkeith, frontages were generally narrower (often 55ft) but many blocks were deeper, 180 or 200ft. The critical point is that most suburban houses everywhere in Australia other than the innermost cities had big back yard spaces by world standards. The measurements and their names—chains, links, perches—are alien and bizarre to those brought up with a decimal system, but they were so important in the production of Australian suburbia with all the values and design habits this form has engendered, that they are worth a footnote in themselves. The measurements have an ancient and practical origin. An acre, for example, was the land that one man could plough with one horse in one day; as a strip of cultivated land, it could be conveniently measured out by two chains in width, five chains in length. The system lasted because it was familiar and convenient. The 'chain' was valued, culturally because it was the length of a cricket pitch, practically because it was both Imperial and metric—66 feet, but 100 links. In short, it was a magic number. Roads, for example, were commonly one chain wide. When they curved, the width had to vary. The surveyor could then use trigonometrical tables to calculate the variation from 100 links by shifting a decimal point. It was a physical measure until well into this century—first the Gunter chain, later a steel band. Many country towns, especially in New South Wales, were laid out in 10 chain square blocks, and then subdivided into housing blocks that were one chain wide and five chains deep. half an acre, and very deep (for example, Tumut). The system began to be metricised in the Eastern states from the 1920s—the ACT, for example, used a metric foot—but it persisted in Western Australia until the introduction of the metric system in the late 1960s. And that is why so many of us now live, in a city, on a block of land the length that a man with a horse could plough a straight furrow, and the area that one man could plough with one horse in one quarter of a day.

Australia is often described as one of the world's most urbanised nations, but this is misleading. For most of our history, most of us have been living in a suburb. Our culture still has a semi-rural flavour, although things are changing, and our back yards reflect it. In fact, our back yards faithfully reflect the history of the word 'yard', on which the Oxford English Dictionary has a long entry. First, there is a range of Teutonic words (OS. *gard*, yard, farm, MHG. *garte*, G. *garten*, garden, Goth. *garda*, enclosure) and so on. It goes on to say that 'close affinity of sense is exhibited by the words derived from the Teutonic root ...'. The primary sense is that of 'enclosure'—of which the circle is the most economical form, used by cattlemen from the Bantu to early Australian bush-drovers, whose roughly circular corrals can still be found in quiet decay south of the Monaro. The basic enclosure was either to keep cattle in, or keep them out. It was sometimes qualified by a prefix—farm yard, vineyard, orchard. In short, the word was used for a multifunctional enclosure, generally attached to a house, basically rural in origin. There is a similar set of words 'derived from an Indo-European root *ghort*, viz, Gr. *Xopros*, farm-yard, feeding place, food, fodder, L. *hortus*, garden, *co-hors*, enclosure, yard, pen for cattle and poultry ...; but there are phonological difficulties in the way of equating both groups of words'. Whether they can be equated or not, it is interesting that both sets of words have a similar range of meanings.

So there is something primitive about the Australian suburban back yard, both word and thing. Indeed the word itself is faintly archaic, more used, at least unqualified, in North America and Australia than in the British Isles. The verb form, used as in 'yarding cattle', is given as '*colonial and U.S.*,' with a quotation from Kingsley's novel, *Geoffry Hamlyn*, 'Well, lad, suppose we yard these rams'. There are few rams to be yarded nowadays in St Kilda or Double Bay, few outhouses or wood heaps or chooks or coppers, and not many vegetable gardens, either, although the lemon tree seems to be assured of eternal life. Self-sufficiency is no longer desirable to most people.

Does the suburban back yard described go back to founding days? Denis Winston, the Foundation Professor of Town and Country Planning at the University of Sydney until his retirement in 1974, emphasised both space and function as follows:

> With wide streets went large building plots; even the town-lands in Adelaide had originally one acre plots: horses, cattle, hens and pigs had to be provided for so that good yard space and extensive out-buildings were general. Even today Australians expect that a family home should accommodate the two cars, with trailer or caravan, and have room for the children's tent as a summer sleepout; and many home sites relatively close to the centres of the main cities are still big enough for this. (1976, p. 188)

In Perth, there was a fine debate in council in 1876 on pigs. The Medical Officer thought they were injurious to health and the Attorney-General proposed that no one should keep a pig within 50 yards of his neighbour's house—which would have had the effect of allowing them on the large blocks of the wealthy while forbidding them on the small blocks of the poor—but George Shenton and James Lee-Steere defended the poor man's right to keep a pig, and they won the day (Stannage, p. 174). Pigs were finally banned for ever in 1886 as insanitary, to be replaced by far more insanitary rubbish tips. This was part of the move towards centralised services that has characterised the growth of cities everywhere.

It is this that has deprived the back yard of its utility, or, more accurately, changed its functions. First, the coming of sewerage, then the advent of the motor car brought significant change, the car, requiring a garage, also used for storage. There was sometimes an entry from the back lane (the dunny lane) into the garage in the back corner; if not, there was a long drive from the front, eventually paved, usually with two concrete strips and a well trimmed grass median. The garage was usually behind the house. Later it grew in size, to accommodate two or three cars (and a trailer, and a boat, in homes that are more affluent but not necessarily wealthy); and it moved forward flush with the frontage, of which it became an integral part, rather than an afterthought.

In the late forties and fifties, the old clothes line went and was almost universally replaced by a horizontal windmill of steel and galvanised wire, known as the Hills Clothes Hoist (which began production in 1945); later, electric driers and retractable washing lines replaced the Hills Clothes Hoist in design conscious back yards—or, rather, back gardens, because this is what they were becoming. I asked a middle-class, middle-aged English friend to describe the back yard of her childhood home in Surrey; she replied, with mild affront, that they did not have a back yard, they had a garden behind the house. This was a class distinction that applied in Australia also to a degree, but as the nation has become more uniformly suburban and middle-class, the distinction is blurred. Perhaps it is more accurate to say that people make statements of various kinds by the way they use the land around the house. Especially in country towns, the old back yard lives on. Others still use their back yard as a functional space, still primarily male, for working on the boat, maintaining the vehicle, fixing the trailer, stripping the paint off doors and mantelpieces—it is still a service yard, although the services have changed. The atmosphere is casual, male, untidy, relaxed, spontaneous, and in its way, creative. It is emphatically for use, not for display—and it is still common. I have seen some prime examples in South Fremantle recently.

However, the trend is all the other way. The back yard has become back garden, for recreation, adult-dominated family use, and for showing off to one's peers. The following advertisement (from the real estate advertisements, *Sunday Times*, Perth, 18 December 1988) is typical of middle-range homes now being offered in the new suburbs. It is *not* in the exclusive, luxury class of Claremont or Peppermint Grove, but is able to offer many of the same 'features', because the land is cheap:

> At the rear of the home there is a large and shady patio area, complete with gas barbecue. The rear garden is terraced and leads up to a paved area and a sparkling free-form swimming pool.
> The area is beautifully landscaped with palms and shrubs, being sheltered by a shade covered pergola.

In becoming display space (entertainment), the back yard has added a public function to its private one, and thus acquired a characteristic of the front garden. We have not looked at that yet, but front and back are a dialectical pair, defining each other negatively, and to understand either, we must look at both. Once again, Glen Tomasetti sets the background with her Bert and Lizzie in East St Kilda, 1934. First, what Robin Boyd called 'arboriphobia':

> An enemy on one boundary, inoffensive people on another and friends at a short distance was a pattern repeated in the suburbs. The Larkins fulfilled the requirements for enmity. Their garden was neglected. Their flowering gums, planted right on the fence, dropped leaves and nuts on Bert's drive. Hanging low after rain, they wet his head when he parked the Vauxhall beside the house (pp. 7, 8).

With this enmity to trees goes a mania for pruning, which is still alive and well:

> Arthur didn't believe in pruning soft-fruit trees. Bert did. He loved pruning, cutting back and lopping. He often walked round the garden working a pair of secateurs in his right hand, looking for dead flower heads and wayward twigs. When the day came to prune a tree, he started the job joyfully, cutting back to the last possible spot from which new growth might shoot. The sight

of a tree, just after he'd pruned it, was as painful to Lizzie as the sight of her
was to him, after she'd had a new permanent wave (p. 4).

By implication, Tomasetti later attributes both these behaviour patterns
to a pioneering mentality by showing Bert's reaction to natural bushland:

> They were passing through bush and it depressed him. He could see no
> beauty in it, no beauty at all. It represented only back-breaking labour. He
> thought of fire because he'd really like to put a match to it and see it swept
> away, leaving the land for man's use. That didn't happen after a fire of
> course. The bush recovered. The grey-green leaves of the gum trees with
> their ragged bark and the spindly wattles not yet in flower all filled him with
> dull melancholy; work, monotony, work. The bush had nothing to do with
> Bert's understanding of the glories of nature (pp. 130–1).

This hatred of trees is still common. The following letter from a
suburban newspaper (*Weekly Post*, Subiaco, W.A. 10 January 1989, p. 6)
is not unusual:

> Those damn box trees!
> I must admit I call them stronger things than that.
> Well, I've just spent another one and a half hours raking leaves.
> When are the Subiaco council going to do something about them?
> The streets and footpaths are an absolute disgrace.
> We know the council has a thing about cutting down trees but why not
> revert to pruning them to a nice round shape, every year, on both sides of
> the street, not just on the side with the telephone wires?
> Surely in the long run it would be cheaper than the major job it will be one
> day.
> I thought I would try if you can't beat them join them, but we like a tidy
> yard and a drive and the road sweeper would need to come every day to
> sweep them away.
> Subiaco and Shenton Park would certainly never win a tidy city or street
> award.

Mechanical sweepers which suck up leaves from roads, footpaths and
grass are common in Perth, used by councils, public institutions and home-
owners. Although the hungry sands of the Perth metropolitan area are
notably deficient in organic matter, the leaves so collected are rarely
composted, even in educational institutions.

A passion for neatness is the most striking characteristic of Australian
display gardening, either institutional or private. Edges are trimmed, leaves
are raked, flowers are staked, concrete hosed down, shrubs trimmed and
clipped, trees pruned. The bounteous, brimming, rambling, over-blown
careless garden is still rare—with reason, in that it is actually harder to

maintain in Australia, where growth is rapid, and the overgrown garden soon becomes no garden. But the driving forces behind this mania for neatness are highly conjectural. It is not peculiar to Australia—it is to be found in New Zealand, parts of the north of England, parts of Canada, less so in the USA. It may in part represent the pioneering spirit, but it is clearly also a cultural inheritance, as its distribution shows. There is a strong component of what is variously described as 'keeping up with the Jones's', 'peer group pressure' or 'civic pride'. In the pre-Second-World-War Australia, ordinary, decent people kept up appearance, not without considerable effort, to maintain their self-respect; freshly ironed shirts for the school children and a tidy front yard kept the flag flying. Perhaps this concern with appearances, although a common human characteristic, was intensified in Australia by the awareness of the convict background. Respectability had to be fought for. Popular phrases reflect a fear of 'going under' or 'giving up', of *failing* 'to keep the flag flying'. Outward signs of disorder might signal the rule of chaos and old night come again. The working classes of industrial Britain must have shared these fears. Rural immigrants and the unskilled poor these growing cities attracted and bred could so easily be forced by sheer circumstance into what were called vice and crime, which began a nightmare of subhuman deprivation. Scrubbing and sweeping and raking may have helped to keep these fears at bay.

But the mania for tidiness also represents a discourse with the environment. Our house and its immediate surrounds are one of the few areas in our lives where we have real power, make decisions, and may put them into practice. Perhaps it is this sense of control, especially among those who have limited control of their own lives in the outside world, that leads Bert to prowl the garden, secateurs in hand, looking for something to 'manage' by imposing his will. If there is a distinctively Australian component in this behaviour, which on the whole I doubt, it is a rejection of the endless leaf litter and the asymmetry—the *untidiness*—of the Australian bush. Perhaps that fear of the red-back spider lurking under the toilet seat, waiting to strike when your defences are down, was seen as a malign outsider from the bush, a fifth column from that harsh natural Australia we have fought to control or exclude—since the fear was quite out of proportion to the occurrence.

Since it was always semi-public, a place to work in, but not for recreation or living, the front garden has changed less than the back yard, but it too has been subject to the vagaries of fashion. Some of the changes are shown in my last quotation from Glen Tomasetti:

'You look like having a good show of dahlias,' said Keith. 'They're always good after they've been lifted and you can stake them as you re-plant. You ought to have more dahlias instead of all those annuals and borders you plant: not worth the work.'

'Valerie likes them for picking,' said Keith solemnly. He wasn't interested in gardening but did what was expected of him, only declaring his independence by growing different plants from those favoured by the family into which he'd married. Instead of hydrangeas, standard roses, dahlias, snapdragons, a lemon tree and stag ferns for the shady side, he'd tried lupins, delphiniums, hollyhocks, begonias and his lawns were pure English grass, fine and soft. He'd just bought two azaleas for the south side of the house and he knew his father-in-law would disapprove of this unnecessary expenditure. Bert, the son of a gold-miner turned farmer, could spend happily only on essentials. When boots or chairs or a pocket-knife had to be bought, he went for quality because it was economy in the long run. But gardens were to be made from other gardens, from cuttings, corms, bulbs and roots of buffalo grass. You had to buy a lemon tree, standard roses and grass seed for bare patches (pp. 10, 11).

The azaleas and English lawn grasses mark the availability of a more abundant water supply, and a more reckless attitude to its use, with hose and sprinkler rather than bucket and watering can. The disciplines of scarcity are relaxed. Not only water is abundant and used wastefully. Fertilisers, pressure-pack sprays, pelleted snail-killer, all add to the convenience of gardening, as take-away foods, full of fat, sugar and salt, add to the convenience of eating. Gardening has become a conspicuous element in the consumer society.

The nurseries reflect this growth in consumerism, and promote it. They are now rarely places where embryo plants are nursed into being, but supermarkets which sell flowers—these showy sexual organs attract the customers, and the living organism from which they come is incidental. To turn the pot over to tap out the plant and so inspect its roots—the most important part of what you are buying—is 'unacceptable' behaviour.

A recent book (Fiske, Hodge and Turner, 1987, p. 30) asserts the following:

The gradual infiltration of native plants into our suburban gardens, and the corresponding withdrawal of European-styled gardens, suggests that a process of legitimation is being acted out that mirrors positive changes in the Australian's relation with the landscape. Certainly the low-maintenance factor recommends the native garden to the house-proud, but that recovery of leisure—the delivery from the garden's tyrannical domination of the weekend—also signifies a growing sense of accommodation with the land, through which culture and nature have been made to co-exist more harmoniously. While creative and adaptive, the highly stylised character of the versions of 'nature' found in the native garden is nevertheless controlled by an edging of old railway sleepers and a covering of woodchips, the latter suggesting how ambiguous the putatively harmonious relationship can be.

It is hard to know how to tackle assertions such as this, which are common enough in popular journalism. What is a European-styled garden? Is the 'style' of a garden necessarily dependent on the choice of plant material? Are gardens using Australian plants necessarily low maintenance? Why should an increase in leisure signify a growing sense of accommodation with the land? (Its most obvious outcome has been increasing pressure on natural resources.) How many 'native' gardens are either creative or adaptive? As for the 'old railway sleepers', most are new—cut for the garden trade. Ancient red-gum forests along our inland rivers are steadily and relentlessly felled to supply them. Is this harmony with the land?

I would myself like to see more use of local plant material, gardens that provide habitat for birds, gardens in which plants are chosen and sited with care so that they can thrive without excessive cosseting. Such gardens are rare, as they always have been. They are not generally a feature of popular culture today, except perhaps in the vegetable garden, and they were probably more common when manure was recovered in the wake of the milkman's horse, and water was too precious to be wasted.

So both back and front changed as the times changed. As Rob Ingram put it (Sydney *Sun-Herald*, 1 January 1989, p. 116):

> With seven-and-a-half million square kilometres of playground available, Australians have largely withdrawn to their own quarter acre. And why not? It's summertime and the livin' is easy...with the pool, the barbecue, and the old redwood setting. The suburban backyard has become the resort that we used to drag the caravan down the coast to.

This retreat to the back yard—or 'patio' behind the inner city terraces—doubtless reflects attitudes to congestion on the roads and over-crowding and high prices at the resorts. Despite the transformations in function, the standard subdivisions persist in their millions, and thus the back yard space itself remains, or has done so until very recently. The free standing house with space before and behind has been the Australian dream, but that too is now changing. Units, strata titles, duplexes, apartments, row housing, infill housing, penthouses, townhouses, all are names for denser living with reduced outdoor spaces. Australia, for better or worse, or both, is becoming urban, and the generous old back yard may become a threatened species.

Acknowledgements

I am grateful to several friends and colleagues whose critical comments helped me, especially Mike Bosworth and Warwick Forge.

References

Barrett, Bernard (1971), *The Inner Suburbs: The Evolution of an Industrial Area*, Melbourne University Press

Clark, David (1978), '"Worse than Physic": Sydney's Water Supply, 1788-1888', in Max Kelly (ed.), 1978

Fiske, J., B. Hodge, and G. Turner (1987), *Myths of Oz: Reading Australian Popular Culture*, Sydney, Allen & Unwin

Hungerford, T.A.G. (1977), *Wong Chu and the Queen's Letterbox: the First Collection of Stories*, Fremantle Arts Centre Press

Kelly, Max (ed.) (1978) *Nineteenth-Century Sydney: Essays in Urban History*, Sydney University Press

Kelly, Max (1981), *Plague Sydney, 1900*, Sydney, Doak Press

Neutze, Max (1977), *Urban Development in Australia*, Sydney, Allen & Unwin

Stannage, C.T. (1979), *The People of Perth*, Perth City Council

Tomasetti, Glen (1976), *Thoroughly Decent People*, Melbourne, McPhee Gribble

Winston, Dennis (1976), 'Nineteenth Century Sources of Twentieth Century Theories, 1800-1939 in George Seddon and Mari Davis (eds.), *Man and Landscape in Australia*, Canberra, AGPS

Stamp Duty

XAVIER PONS

Stamps are one of the mirrors in which a culture likes to see itself reflected, and usually glorified. Harold Ickes, a former United States Secretary of the Interior, once said: 'I conceive of a stamp being a fragment of history, a word in the annals of human experience, a picture of an ideal fresh from the human heart. The design impressed upon it signifies what the nation may be at the moment'.[1] This illustrates the ambiguous function of stamps, which may be taken to depict reality—the state of the nation—but also an ideal—what is not yet entirely translated into fact but hopefully will be. This ambiguity is very much apparent in the particular stamps with which I am concerned here and with which it is not always easy to draw the line between reality and the ideal.

To contribute its mite to Australia's bicentennial celebrations, Australia Post issued in 1988 a set of twenty-seven stamps carrying the official slogan 'Living Together', which was meant to promote both multi-culturalism and a conception of national harmony and unity. The stamps are supposed to illustrate the various component parts which make up the entity 'Australia', and each of them depicts, by means of a cartoon, some significant aspect of the assumed entity. The slogan, referring as it does to the policy of multiculturalism, defines Australia as a place where various communities coexist and interact in harmonious fashion, each having a recognised, legitimate individual identity and yet participating in the wider national identity—a kind of secular Holy Trinity: one nation with a plurality of faces. It should be recognised, though, that 'Living Together' is less a statement of fact than an exhortation or perhaps a pious wish. This fine phrase can be construed to mean a great many different forms of coexistence—that of men with women, or employees with employers, of citizens with politicians, and what not. But in practice the main reference tends to be to the multiple ethnic origins of the population, and these two innocuous-sounding words celebrate a turning point in Australian history: the official repudiation of Anglo-Celtic ethnocentrism, the demise of the old selfish attitudes, both arrogant and timorous, which went by the regrettable names of 'White Australia Policy' or 'assimilation'. Their adoption marks departure from traditional, race-imbued norms to redefine Australian identity on more imaginative, and more generous, lines.

Stamps, as Dennis Altmann asserted, 'are both miniature art works and pieces of government propaganda: they can be used to promote sovereignty, celebrate achievement, define national, racial, religious or linguistic identity, portray messages or exhort certain behaviour'.[2] The set under discussion clearly fits this bill. Its artistic dimension is quite real—at least in places: the stamps, eschewing the narrowly realistic mode which is traditional in this medium, are meant to be humorous. They were designed by Australia's best known cartoonists—Bruce Petty, Ron Tandberg, Jim Russell, etc.—and they certainly portray a message, embodied in the phrase 'Living Together' which they all carry. But what sort of national identity do they in fact illustrate? Their ostensible purpose is to celebrate multiculturalism, which is an important—and controversial—aspect of government policy in Australia. Multiculturalism is a worthy goal, though one difficult to reach. As with Asian immigration, not all Australians are convinced that it is in the best interests of the country[3] and no doubt an educational effort is required in order to persuade them. In a sense, it was the duty of the bicentennial stamps to contribute to this effort and, if not actually 'sell' multiculturalism to the country, at least to popularise it. But how well does the 'Living Together' set acquit itself of this duty? Not as well as one might wish, it would appear.

It should be acknowledged that, given the constraints under which the individual artists laboured, the task was far from easy. To begin with, the cartoonists were given a tall order. 'It was a baffling brief', Patrick Cook said of his commission—a stamp which was to illustrate trade unions: 'It was not to be flippant, political or topical, and it had to represent both genders, all colours and creeds and ethnic groups. The problem was how to represent this rich tapestry of Australian existence on a postage stamp'.[4] Besides, there was the problem of supervision—or censorship: the cartoonists were given a fairly free rein, but their designs, if found unsuitable, had to be amended—Australian Post candidly confessed that Geoff Cook 'was one of the few participants in this issue to have his cartoon accepted without alteration'. If still unsatisfactory, they could always be definitively rejected, and in a number of cases were. Sometimes the censoring was done by Australian Post, as in the case of a design for 'Parliament' by Matthew Martin: his cartoon showed an aggressive arm and fist emerging from the mouths of two opposing parliamentarians, smashing one's nose and giving the other the finger. Given the low esteem in which politicians are held in Australia, it may have been wiser indeed not to make a further contribution to their negative image by reducing political debate to blows and insults. Sometimes the veto came from the bodies concerned and was rather less understandable: the ACTU objected to Cook's and Tandberg's designs for 'Trade Unions' because it thought it showed the workers in a bad light; unnamed 'industrial interest groups' rejected Gaynor Cardew's design for 'Industry', while the Victoria Police disapproved of a design by John Spooner depicting Ned Kelly, whom, well over a century after the facts, they do not seem to have forgiven yet. The weaknesses of the set as a whole can therefore be traced in part to official supervision of the artists's work which resulted in blandness, in a watering down of the more subversive approaches to the theme. This is in itself a disturbing counter-illustration of the 'Living Together' theme: cultural diversity is tolerated, but only within bounds, and transgression of unwritten but influential norms is frowned upon.

True, the stamps do illustrate a number of ways in which people 'live together', that is, cooperate for the common good of society. But a more important preoccupation seems to be the presentation of certain basic features of a 'modern' society, without any reference to what we might loosely call the philosophy of Living Together, to show, as Australia Post put it, 'the fabric of our society, portrayed with a light hand to avoid an overwhelmingly ponderous general effect'.[5] Those features can be gathered under three broad headings: the economy (banking, commerce, mining, industry), to which about one-third of the stamps are devoted, which is not without some irony since the state of the Australian economy would seem to offer little cause for celebration; politics and institutions (parliament, law, armed forces, police), society and culture (welfare, rescue and emergency, religion, the performing arts). The stamps, or at least the headings which they illustrate, show a high degree of political bi-partisanship which is quite laudable—one would not quite have expected a Labor government to commission a stamp in praise of banking. Taken as a whole, the set does present important facets of Australian society, of which it offers a vibrant and often attractive picture. This is consistent with the traditional image-making function of postage stamps, which by their very nature tend to look mostly at the bright sight of life. A number of the stamps perform this duty wittily—witness 'Postal Services' which shows two postmen flying away on a magic carpet/stamp, with a flying dog in hot pursuit, or 'Visual Arts' with its sculpture of a hand, finger pointing towards the ceiling, giving an injunction eagerly followed by the spectators, as if the arts pointed to higher things. A similarly gentle irony is used to depict 'Transport': the truck, actually driven by a ram, is brought to a standstill by the mob of humans milling around it! But, as we have seen, designs which gave an unflattering image of the institution they were supposed to illustrate were rejected. Not all the officially approved stamps found favour in the eyes of the public, though, and some were criticised for setting a bad example: it was pointed out for instance that the cyclists on the 'Recreation' stamp are not wearing helmets! However, more substantive criticism is also called for.

One cannot help noticing that the set contains fairly glaring omissions, that some significant features of Australian society are not in any way illustrated by the stamps. Thus, what of the monarchy? Australia Post is not usually shy about paying homage to the Queen, and indeed in 1989 issued a stamp to commemorate her birthday. Considering the growing number of Australians who favour a republic, it may have been thought prudent to disguise by omission the country's political status. And what of federalism? Political life is represented by an image of Parliament House made to resemble a birthday cake, but this contains no reference to what is a very distinctive feature of the Australian political system—at least as distinctive as local government which is embodied by a Mayor in full regalia. Australia is undisputably a nation of immigrants, but one would not know it from looking at the stamps, none of which refers to immigration—but more of this later. 'Primary Industry' is illustrated by apple-pickers—not quite the mainstay of Australian agriculture. Besides, the heading itself is odd—'Agriculture' would have been better—since another stamp is devoted to 'Mining', which in economic parlance is also part of primary industry. If the visual and performing arts are represented, what of literature and the cinema, which both have considerably enhanced Australia's international reputation? And what of the beach culture which is often associated with the country? It may have been regarded as too trite a subject, like koalas, which are also absent (but not kangaroos!). Of course, one can argue that some twenty odd stamps are not enough to illustrate *all* significant aspects of Australian society, but this is all the more reason to make the selection as rigorously representative as possible, which is far from being the case. The deliberate avoidance by Australia Post, in the name of light-heartedness and whimsy, of controversial topics such as the monarchy or immigration results in a slightly biased overall picture.

Besides, some of the institutions which *are* illustrated by individual stamps are depicted in such a benign light that the image becomes positively misleading. Thus, in the wake of the Fitzgerald Commission or of the Darren Brennan and other incidents, who will believe that the main activity of the police consists in gently steering over-imbibed gentlemen towards their home? Who, having heard of the Third World's debt crisis, or having to struggle to repay a mortgage, can agree that the purpose of banking is to joyfully juggle money around the globe—and around the clock—so as to benefit all its inhabitants? The picture has a fairy-tale quality which is perhaps meant to illustrate the concept of 'economic rationalism'. Similarly, the smiling soldier, sailor and airman who stand for the armed forces hardly suggest the grim purpose which the forces are meant to serve. All suggestions of violence have been carefully avoided—even the rifle held by the soldier is made to look like some kind of telescope rather than the lethal weapon it actually is. And it is all very well to illustrate 'Industry' with a cartoon of worker, boss and (presumably) secretary all pulling together to boost productivity. But who is to pocket the profits? The idea of cooperation by all classes to lift the economy is a little glib. If this were reality, who would need unions? And, precisely, is the smiling face of unionism, as it appears on the relevant stamp, the most significant one?

This brings us back to the 'Living Together' motto which all the stamps should have illustrated since, according to Australia Post, 'The brief to cartoonists was a lighthearted, whimsical and friendly interpretation of the official bicentennial theme 'living together''. Few stamps actually do this, no matter what interpretation one puts upon the theme. If it is taken to refer to the sexes, it is clear that the whole set, mostly designed by men—among the accepted designs, twenty-two were made by men and only five by women—is tilted towards masculinity. Not only are there far more men than women depicted (cf. 'Industry' or 'Trade Unions'), but the men are shown in a more positive light: where women feature prominently, they tend to be reduced to caricatures as on 'Education' (represented by a severe-looking Victorian female teacher with four children peering out of the pockets of her ample dress), 'Primary Industry' or 'The Media'. Not for women the positive image given to men, for instance in 'Armed Forces', unless the women happen to be flanked by men! If 'Living Together' is taken to mean cooperation among the community, one finds few illustrations. 'Rescue & Emergency' is one example. Its suggestions of solidarity in the face of danger (here, a bushfire) are in accordance with the traditional Australian ethos of mateship such as Lawson expounded it. 'Welfare' is equally convincing: putting a roof over the heads of the homeless, in other words striving towards a more egalitarian society, trying to close the gap between the haves and the have-nots, is another relevant aspect of 'Living Together'. But these two stamps are the exception rather than the rule. Others are not merely inadequate—they actually go against the grain: the frenzied pack of journalists rushing to get an exclusive interview ('Media') hardly suggests solidarity, and neither does the sweet music of the cash register ('Commerce').

But the great loser is undoubtedly multiculturalism. It is this concept, or policy, which the words 'Living Together' call to mind most clearly, and yet hardly a single stamp suggests that it is of some relevance to contemporary Australian society. The lone exception is 'Religion', which features side by side a Christian church, a mosque, an Orthodox church and a synagogue as well as a Buddhist temple, thus illustrating the peaceful coexistence of a plurality of religious faiths, all sharing a spiritual purpose which is embodied by the angel hovering above all the houses of worship and which is meant to suggest a mood of inter-faith dialogue. By some fluke, this stamp has the lowest denomination of all (1c)... One might add the 'Sport' stamp, which shows fourteen children forming a living pyramid: one of them is black! There is nothing else on the stamps to suggest that all Australians are not Anglo-Celts: all the faces appearing on them are white—including that of the construction worker who is featured on 'Trade

Unions': his complexion is darker but that is only because his occupation gives him a deep suntan. Coloured minorities have been neatly obliter-ated—or should one say cancelled? Shades of White Australia... What is the point of touting multiculturalism on the one hand if on the other one consistently forgets the existence—and hence the needs and the rights—of the minorities which are part and parcel of Australian society today? To illustrate 'mining', one stamp shows a gold digger of the 1850s and 1860s who has just found a huge nugget shaped like Australia itself. A clever illustration indeed! But it also brings to mind the racial strife of that period (such as the Lambing Flat riots) which marked the beginning of institutionalised anti-Asian racism in Australia. Gold made Australia wealthy and, some say, democratic. It also ushered in a policy of racial exclusion and violence whose traces are still visible today. A student of mine suggested that the expression on the miner's face was panic, and that the Australia-shaped nugget's colour hinted at the fearful prospect of a Chinese invasion of the country and the latter's subsequent asianisation. Although this is clearly not what the cartoonist intended, she may not have been far off the mark... Even more glaring is the total absence of any reference to the Aborigines. One duly finds images of the original inhabitants of Australia—in the shape of three kangaroos ('Tourism', 'Law', 'Rescue and Emergency') and an emu ('Tourism')—but not a single Aborigine—they have been thoroughly eradicated from the stamps' version of Australia, which is rather disquieting and, in retrospect, justifies Aboriginal anger at the Bicentennial celebrations. Is this multiculturalism in action? It may be argued that those very omissions do reflect Australia's reluctance to adopt multiculturalism. But, if stamps are pictures 'of an ideal fresh from the human heart', they should promote desirable values, and from this point of view the 'Living Together' stamps do not do proper justice to their theme, nor do they do their educational duty.

One might ask what is particularly Australian about the stamps. Many of them have no distinguishing Australian feature at all: 'Religion', 'Industry', 'Sport', 'Commerce', 'Banking', etc. could have been issued in almost any Western country, as the activities they illustrate are depicted without any explicit reference to an Australian context. I'm not saying this is necessarily a bad thing: it just provides a point of comparison for those other stamps—less than one-third of the set—which proclaim their Australianness. From the formal point of view, the most striking feature of the stamps is that they are all cartoons—this is unusual in postage stamp, which usually prefer quasi-photographic representation and its associated dignity. Cartoon suggest a levity which is regarded as inappropriate in those 'paper ambassadors'. Australia Post deliberately chose a mode of representation which favoured the light-hearted and the whimsical,which is a welcome departure from the serious if not self-important spirit which presided over some other Bicentennial celebrations. The choice of cartoons is a way of signifying that Australia does not take herself too seriously, that she has a sense of humour. This is of course an endearing trait, and would be even more so if the humour was a little more corrosive. As it is, it lacks a critical dimension and in fact tends to conceal those aspects of Australian reality which are less than rosy. In choosing cartoons and a self-deprecating sort of humour over more 'dignified' or perhaps harder-hitting approaches, Australia shows a certain lack of self-confidence: she hesitates to proclaim her achievements in a more straightforward manner because she is uncertain about those achievements, and whether they are truly worth celebrating. The kind of humour displayed in the stamps recalls the 'silly quipping' which, in Murray Bail's *Homesickness*, is said to be an Australian characteristic, prompting a character to add: 'We're embarrass-ed. We're not as confident as we look... quips keep us going. Being so far removed and relatively alone... we seem to need encouragement. Quips help us along; things aren't all that bad. It's as if, in Australia, we're all in hospital. There's a lot of quipping in hospitals'.[6] 'Lighthearted whimsy' sometimes seems to be evasiveness in disguise.

To appreciate how meaning is conveyed, one should distinguish between two broad modes of representation—the mimetic and the iconic. The first tries to reproduce reality—a version of reality, at any rate—in a directly recognisable fashion. Because we are dealing with cartoons, the style is never quite that of 'photographic' realism, but some stamps, such as 'Trade Unions' or 'Housing', come close enough. But the mimetic mode accommodates caricature without difficulty: Michael Leunig's characters in 'Rescue and Emergency', for instance, have the distorted features—huge noses in particular—which are the artist's trademark, but the whole scene is nonetheless mimetic: distortions literally stretch the rules of realistic representation but do not break them. The iconic mode, on the other hand, results in a highly stylised and symbolical representation in which what is illustrated is not so much a slice of life as a concept: 'Industry', 'Welfare', 'Tourism' or 'Telecommunications' all show this. Sometimes the two modes appear to intermingle: in the one design mimetic and iconic elements coexist, complementing each other to produce a meaning which results precisely from this coexistence or fusion. Such is the case of 'Parliament', in which a still discernible Parliament House is covered in lighted candles to look like a birthday cake; in 'Postal Services' where the posties are sitting on a flying carpet which is also a stamp; or on 'Science and Technology', where the calculator is also Australia. The essence of this dual mode of representation is the dual function of the objects depicted—both literal and symbolical. This allows for greater conceptual complexity than with either of the 'pure' modes: although much depends on the individual artist's talent, the stamp's message may thus become more sophisticated.

What bearing does this have on the way Australia is represented? It leads to different degrees of representational sophistication. Mimetic representation is 'flat'—to borrow E.M. Forster's term. It leads to recognition—instant recognition, in most cases—but does not provide the mental stimulation of the iconic and dual modes because it requires little interpretation: the bushfire scene in 'Rescue and Emergency' will look familiar to most Australians, like the soldier's uniform and slouch hat on 'Armed Forces': they are very recognisable features of Australian life—chosen for that very reason—and do not require much further explanation. I'm not saying that they cannot be further interpreted—of course they can (I have tried to interpret some features of 'Armed Forces')—but, because they can be made sense of immediately, they do not for the most part produce the sense of defamiliarisation which Russian formalists regarded as essential to a work of art since, as Victor Shlovsky put it, 'Art removes objects from the automatism of perception.' With iconic representation, symbols must be interpreted and, thus, meaning has to be constructed, but this is even truer of the dual mode because of the encounter of two different types of representation which have to be sorted out, interpreted separately and then globally. Sometimes, of course, this complexity leads to a degree of obscurity. 'Law', for instance, is an iconic depiction of evolution by means of a line of ever-taller figures: a fish emerges from the ocean, following a dinosaur, a kangaroo, an ape and a barrister in full wig and gown. The apex of evolution, however, is not the barrister—as lawyers themselves might like to think—but a gigantic test-tube which suggests that science will help produce an even higher type of humanity, which does not seem all that difficult. The meaning, however, is not entirely clear and it is not possible to decide whether the stamp is in praise of genetic engineering, or the opposite. Besides, the connection between this and 'Law', the stamp's ostensible theme, is anything but obvious. True, laws apply to genetic engineering as to other human endeavours, but this remains a rather marginal province of the law, and hardly the one people would spontaneously associate with the words 'law'. In this particular case, the overlay of meanings obfuscates the stamp's purpose and is to that extent self-defeating.

Iconic representations of Australia on the 'Living Together' stamps are of three major types: the country's flag (as in 'Parliament'), its coat of arms (as in 'Tourism'), and its distinctive shape (as in 'Science and Technology'). The first two have long been institutionalised so that, no matter how controversial in another context, they also lead to instant recognition: they are familiar, and thus commonplace, at least if used in straightforward fashion. The Australian flag in 'Parliament' is more mimetic than iconic since it reproduces—though on a bigger scale—the real flag which does fly over Parliament House. The Australian coat of arms is used in a somewhat more sophisticated fashion because the emblem is modified and made to serve an additional purpose on top of its representative function. On the real coat of arms, the kangaroo and the emu face each other across the crest. Here, however, they both face the same direction which allows the crest to become a sedan chair carried by the two animals, and from which tourists take pictures of what lies around them. The stamp's overall design is iconic, but the graphic style is fairly mimetic. The interaction between the two modes defamiliarises the familiar symbol of Australia, makes it serve a new purpose which however does not replace the old, but complements it to create an allegory: Australia itself welcomes foreign visitors. The third icon offers a similar combination. Australia's stylised shape originates in the country's actual geographical outline, and to that extent is mimetic. But it is also used as an icon—it was for instance the Bicentennial Authority's logo and as such appears on the bottom margin of every stamp in the set. It thus partakes of the two modes, which makes it particularly suggestive. 'Science and Technology', which shows a man, according to his hat and checked shirt probably a farmer rather than an office worker or an engineer, holding an Australia-shaped calculator up to the sun, combines suggestions of science—the calculator as a scientific machine—modern non-polluting technology (the sun suggests sun-powered batteries) as well as their application to agriculture, which is a fair representation of Australian agriculture as underlined by the calculator's shape. The various elements of the design co-operate with one another to produce a coherent and relevant image of an important Australian reality. 'Mining' relies on a similar technique, with the Australian-shaped nugget—an iconic element in an otherwise mimetic design—firmly locating the scene down under rather than in, say, California or Brazil. 'Telecommunications' offers a somewhat different but equally successful design. The stamp is wholly iconic. It depicts a stylised character holding a kind of large phone one end of which is not only shaped like Australia but carries the Australian flag as well—a double assertion of nationality—while the other gathers in a bunch a number of buildings meant to represent various overseas cities. This design graphically suggests the electronic links between Australia and the rest of the world. The Australian element is clearly emphasised, though again in symbolic rather than realistic fashion.[7]

Altogether, not many stamps proclaim their nationality otherwise than through the word 'AUSTRALIA' and the bicentennial logo featured at the bottom of every stamp. This is, of course, enough for any stamp collector to know where they come from, and greater emphasis on Australianness might have resulted in ponderousness if not downright nationalistic propaganda. The recourse to twenty-seven different cartoonists made it practically impossible to achieve any great homogeneity of design—a homogeneity that was probably undesirable anyway.

Insofar as they had to illustrate the fabric of Australian society, the stamps' record is rather mixed: there are strong and weak points, and few glaring inadequacies except—but it is an important exception—where the 'living together' theme is concerned. The cartoonists had to provide 'a lighthearted, whimsical and friendly' interpretation of the theme.[8] The trouble with the designs is not that they do not fit the bill—it is rather that the bill was questionable in the first place because it discouraged the artists from looking at the more disturbing aspects of Australian society, and it did not explicitly emphasise multiculturalism as it should have done given the implications of the phrase 'living together'. Some, if not all, cartoonists were clearly aware of these implications—witness Patrick Cook saying that his cartoon 'had to represent both genders, all colours and creeds and ethnic groups'. Unfortunately, the vast majority of their designs just do nothing of the kind. However one might choose to describe the society thus illustrated, 'multicultural' is the one adjective which certainly does not apply, and to that extent the stamps perform well below the call of duty.

Notes

1. Quoted in Dennis Altmann, *Paper Ambassadors—The Politics of Stamps*, Sydney, Angus & Robertson, 1991, p. 37.

2. Ibid., p. 2.

3. See David McNicoll: 'So called multiculturalism, which has resulted in the setting up of ethnic enclaves, has also been a contributing factor in the recession' (*Bulletin*, 22 March 1988, p. 53).

4. Quoted in Lenore Nicklin, 'Elusive stamp of approval', *Bulletin*, 22 March 1988, p. 53.

5. *The Collection of 1988 Australian Stamps*, Australia Post, 1988, p. 32.

6. Murray Bail, *Homesickness*, Penguin, 1981, pp. 224–5.

7. Still another way of representing Australia appears on 'Performing Arts', where the jugglers' balls form the two letters OZ—another accepted symbol of the country and one that also works iconically rather than mimetically to add an unmistakable touch of Australian-ness to the theme.

8. *The Collection*, p. 30.

Tales of a Dreamtime: Australian Football as a Secular Religion

STEPHEN ALOMES

Every Sunday morning, a little after nine o'clock, three men in their sixties leave the suburban brick Gothic world of the Holy Rosary Catholic church in Gower Street in Melbourne's historically working-class Kensington to walk home. As they walk along McConnell Street—past my window—the conversation usually turns to football, particularly the successes (or occasionally the defeats) of North Melbourne in the Australian Football League (AFL), until recently the Victorian Football League (VFL). For them the worlds of religion, football and their suburb (Gower Street is a few torpedo punts from North Melbourne's Arden Street ground) are intertwined. For three boys—two of them Indo-Chinese—and a man in the North Melbourne library discussing the best five players of the last few years, whom I overheard while I was searching fruitlessly for a copy of the historian Richard Stremski's *Kill for Collingwood!* (most of them had been spirited away), the ranking of the players was a serious matter. For the blonde girl and the Vietnamese boy kicking a football in the grounds of the Errol Street primary school or for the local Vietnamese supermarket owner who has the Saturday afternoon football on the radio and a small Buddhist shrine at the front of the shop, there is more to multiculturalism than is heard of in the official philosophy.

In analysing some aspects of the social role of Australian Football (the semi-professional and amateur game dominant as the winter sport in the Southern states) I want to look beyond cliches and find the parts of them that are truisms. Accepting Donald Horne's observation that 'sport to many Australians is life and the rest a shadow', I want to reject a different cliche about Australia.[1] In Britain, despite the occasional endeavours of Channel 4 in showing Australian Football, many people believe—inspired by grey skies and by the expatriate fantasies of the theatre director Michael Blakemore and the journalist John Pilger—that Australia is all about surf and beaches. In fact—as I have remarked in the luminous world of TV, open learning style—the beach is an irrelevance for most Australians, despite the appeal of it as an idea. In the south it is too cold, in the north there are too many stingers, in Sydney there is too much of other substances and for many Australians from the western suburbs to Canberra and back of Bourke the beach is too far away.

It is football which inspires and stimulates. Consequently, religion and Australian Football are more closely intertwined than it might at first appear. Although Stremski has challenged the view that Collingwood and its players were both local and Catholic, religious forms and links are often profound.[2] In one recurring story, in 1966 when St Kilda, with strong Jewish support from that suburb, won its first premiership by one point over Collingwood on the Day of Atonement, many religious Jews forgave Ian Synman for being at centre half back rather than in the synagogue, while the transistor radio allowed the good news to be brought to the doubly faithful. A more mainstream popular story, told by the historian Ian Turner in his annual 'Barassi Memorial Lecture', concerned the Tasmanian full forward, Peter Hudson, the greatest goalkicker in the history of the VFL, playing with Hawthorn. A vicar had posted a notice outside a church in Hawthorn, asking:

> 'What would you do if God came to Hawthorn today?' A graffitist had written underneath it: 'Move Peter Hudson to centre half-forward.'
>
> The colleague who reported that to me said: 'When I tell the story outside Hawthorn, they say, "Who's Peter Hudson?", but when I tell the story in Hawthorn they say, "Who's God?" '[3]

For an Australian intellectual, cultural and political historian who went to the football before going to school—and has over the years put in thousands of hours of empirical research—and who has studied the meanings of cultural and political forms, from nationalism to festivals, the subject of Australian Football as a secular religion is particularly significant. It poses a number of questions: the nature of belief in the New World which lacks the complex legacies of custom and tradition of older societies; the role of sport in a society which—according to many writers on religion—lacks deep religious spirituality, despite the institutional strength of religion; the role of the many forms of popular culture in the contemporary era in which in all developed societies, materialism and secularism proceed apace, and consumerism offers new temples of worship; the relationship between ideas and realities of 'community' at a time of unprecedented everyday geographical social mobility and the simultaneity of mass communications; and the role of traditional beliefs in a changing world overcome by the pluralism of the mass media and consumer society.

Australian Football, the dominant winter sport in all states except New South Wales and Queensland, is particularly important in this context as it is also one of the greatest creations of Australian society after 1788. In a New World society, shaped in the era of the industrial revolution and the internationalisation of social and cultural institutions, this is significant. Although Australia has evolved a distinctive society and culture, within the parameters of Western liberal capitalist democracy and the modern city, it has originated few wholly original cultural forms which have survived the onslaught of the juggernauts of modernisation and internationalisation. The reason lies in the answer to the most profound question I have ever been asked about Australian nationalism, by the TV newsreader and interviewer Clive Robertson: 'how would it have been different if Australia had been settled or invaded several centuries earlier?' It is certain that Australia would have evolved in a more distinctive way—and with different forms of interaction between the Aboriginal inhabitants and the invaders/settlers—developing local customs and nuances but also more local technologies, cultural forms and social institutions.

Australian Football is one of the great achievements of Australian popular culture, a fusion of the creative and the physical, of speed and strength, of subtlety and endeavour, of the aesthetic and the practical, of courage and stamina, of the individual and the co-operative, despite its occasional moments of disfiguring violence on the field. In its different phases and forms—for like all sports it has changed over time—it represents a superior sporting achievement. Since its creation in Melbourne in the 1850s, building, according to different accounts, on early rugby, Gaelic football and Aboriginal football,[4] it has evolved to a higher form, leaving behind other codes, which the writer Oriel Gray termed 'necessary steps in the Ascent of Man'.[5]

Given its complexity and visual appeal, it is also relevant to ask why Australian Football has spread only modestly around the globe? As with other Australian achievements, relative isolation, Australia's colonial and contemporary lack of cultural clout (contrast the marketing of American grid-iron and basketball) and in Britain the elite prejudice against Australia as the place to which the working class got away, have limited the exportability of Australian Football, with the recent exception of television. More specifically, as James Bradley remarks, the problem was compounded by a marketing video prior to the October 1987 games in London which emphasised the more violent aspects of the game, inevitably arousing the historic prejudices noted above.[6]

Another general context is worth briefly noting here, the question of whether sport is particularly important in Australia. In the nineteenth century much of the debate about 'the Australian Type' focused on what James Hogan called in 1880 'an in-ordinate love of field sports', although other contestants in the debate suggested that 'young Englishmen [were] equally enthusiastic'.[7]

Is an excessive love of sport especially characteristic of Australia, the product of a colonial society with its fresh air, open spaces and temperate climate and its lack of older folk traditions? Or is it a product of the era of muscular Christianity? Or was it typical of an Anglo-Saxon society (e.g. the USA and Canada), contrasting with the less athletic (or more cultured) societies of Western Europe?

In this discussion, however, I want to explore three major aspects of football as religion: first, the elements of transcendence offered to its devotees; second, the association between football and ideas of shared community (and its rhetorical opposite, the forces of the sectarian enemy if not the Devil); and third, the extent to which as habit it has permeated everyday life in the more spiritual Australian states. Other aspects include the role of art in worship and the critiques of the corruption of the 'church' through the Faustian bargains with TV and commerce in a mass media society. Questions of ritual, of religious vestments of players and supporters and of the politically hegemonic implications of a sport which pervades all classes and transcends gender, can only be noted here.[8]

The idea of football as religion begins with metaphor—the 'hallowed turf' of Subiaco or the MCG, the theme of injustice ('we were crucified'), the *deus ex machina* (or perhaps 'devil *ex machina*') of the umpires, the divine powers of individual players, the religious trinket stalls which line the road to the temple, the symbols of devotion, the Heaven and Hell of victory and defeat, or, in Australian idiom, players who have made 'the best comeback since Lazarus'. In recent years divinity has been associated with the skills of Gary Ablett of Geelong while more indigenous religious traditions have been associated with the creativity of Aboriginal footballers.

Gary Ablett, short, balding and brilliant, received the sobriquet 'God', which as a convert to Christianity he felt understandably uncomfortable with. It also resulted in him having an unusual need to speak the truth before the disciplinary tribunal when being questioned about an on-field misdemeanour. His return from a self-imposed journey into the wilderness was hailed as 'the second coming' by a Geelong Catholic priest, Monsignor Murray, while more secular observers discerned 'a lift in the spirit of the community with Ablett's return'.[9] More recently, a 70 metre goal by Ablett brought back rhetorical comparisons with an earlier miracle man. The intuitive abilities of Aboriginal footballers, which extend the individual and team skills of the game, have been praised as magical or, sometimes more strangely, individual players have been dubbed not just 'magic' but 'black magic' by an older generation of commentators. In sport as in art the spirituality and subtlety of Aboriginal achievement is now being recognised.

As art has celebrated religion as well as nature and beauty, football is a theme in the Australian artistic canon. The achievement ranges from Arthur Streeton's painting of 'The National Game' to works by Noel Counihan, Albert Tucker and John Brack and the miniaturised cartoon dreaming of Michael Leunig; from Barry Oakley's fictional work *A Salute to the Great McCarthy* to David Williamson's drama *The Club*, in which the idea of a new world of achievement comes tumbling down under the pressures of ambition, faction and fantasy; from the desert fantasies of the film *Gallipoli* to Barry Dickins's play *Royboys* with its metaphors of sporting and social decay; from Bruce Dawe's 'Life Cycle' to songs and poems of

Collingwood by the Magpie poet laureate, Mark O'Connor, and the master of 'the club's music', Jan Wositzky, to the football sequence in Robert Helpmann's ballet *The Display*; from the high-flying rhetoric of Ian Turner's annual 'Barassi Memorial Lecture' to, in these days of artistic humour on radio, the 'Coodabeen Champions' 'talk-back callers', from posh Peter from Peterborough to the magical predictions of Guru Bob, the author of 'Thrashed in the Wet by West Tibet'; all of them aspire to the sublimity of the great aesthetic spectacle of the high mark, as in the artistry of the 1970s Nureyev of the high mark in football itself, Alex Jesaulenko.

The everyday links between religion and football as it grew in popularity and significance over the last century have been many. The strong Protestant links of northern suburbs Essendon—drawing many of its clean cut players of the 1950s and 1960s from the local Protestant churches league—which had its first ever Catholic coach in the former Collingwood player Des Tuddenham in 1972, and the mainly Catholic composition of the adjacent inner northern suburbs team, North Melbourne, both suggest conventional religious influences. Perhaps, in the tough world of the inner suburbs, Collingwood was both wiser and more ecumenical in its recruiting, despite the early twentieth-century links through the John Wren political machine to the Catholic Church.

The argument regarding football as a secular religion is more complex. It begins with the observation of many historians and sociologists of religion that religious spirituality in Australia has never been deep. Despite the extent of nominal adherence (census figures of up to 90 per cent to a Christian denomination),[10] despite the relationship between religion and respectability (and the former popularity of Sunday school as a child care agency—'it gets them out of our hair' as well as 'being good for them'), despite the role of religion in political conflict (sectarianism and education in the nineteenth century, conscription in the Great War, the 'Democratic Labor Party', or DLP, as a Cold War Catholic party) and the role of religion in wowserism (from low church and fundamentalist Sydney to sabbatarian Melbourne to nonconformist Adelaide) and in support for war, it has been argued that religion does not deeply permeate the 'sunburnt soul' of Australian life. That may or may not be changing in multicultural and 'New Age' Australia, and was not so before 1788, but a case can be made for the lack of deep religious traditions during most of the materialistic last two centuries.

In this argument, Christian religion with its derivative forms, colonial loyalties to mother churches and imported clergy never struck deep roots in the spiritually thin soil of the southern continent. Even with churchgoing figures in the 30–40 per cent range in the 1960s,[11] religion has been relatively unimportant. It has also been a mere footnote in many scholarly accounts of Australian society—for example the index to one recent text,

Keith Hancock (ed.), *Australian Society* (1989), has only three references to religion.[12]

In one traditional argument the religious spirit in Australian society was found in the 'Australian Legend' or 'Australian Dream' traditions with their roots in the Australian bush. The young Henry Lawson believed that unionism was 'new religion' which would lead to the 'great social reformation of the future', aiding not hindering 'the formation of a universal brotherhood'.[13] Ian Turner discerned a bush and city people rejecting imported religion more appropriate to a more ordered society, using it only as 'ceremonial for formal occasions'. Optimistically, he saw Australians—even those in cities who sang the praises of Mammon—believing that 'the building of a perfect society in Australia would redeem mankind'.[14] However, the utopian aspirations of Australian popular socialism would eventually merge into other views, at the service of nation, Empire and war.

In this sphere, and regarding the period around the turn of the century, questions of meaning in a new society and particularly in male society are significant. At this time when the bush was, in Lawson's words, 'tethered to the world' by the 'great iron rail', the agrarian utopian dream of independence on the land was declining; the dreams of the clerk in 'the dingy little office' of being with Clancy of the Overflow waxed as the numbers of drovers and bushman waned. As a consequence the aspiration for transcendence took several different forms. While many were inspired still by the Judaeo-Christian idea of linear material progress towards a better world (social, material or merely individual), others looked towards spiritualism, or still romantically wished for land, clinging onto the continuing dream of being a small farmer.[15]

In the United States, invaded and founded by the Pilgrim Fathers, the aspiration for transcendence was expressed in the fusion of religious and material aspirations, rural and urban. In Britain the socialisation into Empire, and at times into jingoism, through the invented traditions of the late nineteenth and early twentieth centuries offered a new sense of progress. In all societies individuals found purpose and significance in other aspirations and involvements—in the Industrial Revolution capitalist ideal of economic success and the status it brought, in the aspirations for power, in the sense of community offered by different groups, whether based in a suburb or area, in ethnicity or class, or in more personal and family aspirations and in the conventional consolation of respectability.[16]

In Australia the radical and romantic dream of transcendence would see 'Freedom on the Wallaby' or in the tramp, tramp, tramp of the faces in the street and the possibility that the tyrants would be removed by revolution. However in the disillusion faced by labour in the defeats of the 1890s, alternative dreams would appear. Henry Lawson, embittered by his struggle to make a living as a writer in Australia, turned to millennialist emotions and fantasies in the spirit of the late nineteenth century; increasingly, in his political poems, he saw meaning coming through the neo-Social Darwinism of the era of the new imperialism—through war. In a settler (as well as subject) colonial society which was accustomed to accepting decisions, technologies and ideas from elsewhere this would become a powerful idea in the ensuing decades. Henry Lawson's transition from a socialist to a militarist would have a strong populist element, at least in its poetic expressions. War would bring meaning (lifting life above the gossip in the public bar) and unity transcending class and region, it would bring together the boy from bush creek and town, from city slum and the home of wealth and pride. Realised in the South African or Boer War, those ideals would become an item of faith in that collective carnage, the Great War. C.J. Dennis' larrikin character, Ginger Mick, believed 'I know wot I wus born fer now, An' soljerin's me game'. Lawson's preface to the October 1915 edition of Dennis' book, *The Songs of a Sentimental Bloke*, asked rhetorically, in the early months of the Great War, 'How many men, in how many different parts of the world and of how many different languages—have had the same feeling—the longing for something better—to be something better?'[17]

The celebration of war as giving meaning in a modern society was reinforced by the deliberate association of war with sport. Along with the ideologies of Empire and nation, heroism and chivalry, and with the support of institutional Christianity, sport sent the troops to their deaths. From the football matches in Egypt to running onto the field at Gallipoli football helped give meaning to meaningless massacres, while at home the 'patriotic' John Wren sought to raise a 'Sportsmen's Thousand'.

In the Second World War, when the troops were fighting against a real evil and then fighting to defend Australia the war cry as many went into battle was 'Up there, Cazaly!'—the football cry of the inter-war years inspired by the high marking genius of Roy Cazaly. In more peaceful times it has often been observed that as Australian men have found meaning in overseas military service and the Anzac tradition they have also found it in sport, particularly in Australian Football.[18]

Today, when the search for transcendence takes many forms, football offers one possibility. Contemporary consumer society offers transcendent moments in the objects it sells as experiences—in the transports of fashion, of consumer durables, of music and its sexuality, and of tourism. The world of everyday work and daily life is transcended in the highs of rock music, in the exotic tourist environment, whether the vehicle is the cult of sun or the cult of exotic culture, and through entertainment, fashion and the world of private objects for the house.[19] In the late twentieth century when the Judaeo-Christian-derived teleologies of both material progress for the society and career progress for the individual have lost some of their paradisiacal sheen, other ideas of transcendence have become more important. Today, traditional religion can seem institutional and out of date and the 'tongues' of new sects appeal to only some from the legions of the working-class and lower-middle-class lost who have no longer a parish and a local community; the fantasies of 'New Age' spirituality also appeal only to a minority. In this situation it is perhaps inevitable that the more suburban transports of delight of football—even when mediated by television—will offer contemporary consolation for many. In the words of the Mike Brady anthem 'Up There Cazaly!':

> During the week you work to earn a living
> But at the weekend comes the time
> You can do whatever turns you on
> Get out there and clear your mind.

The song moves between the quietly spoken words of the spectator to the peak emotional expression which football offers, supported by the power of the crowd, triumphant, magical crescents and soaring high peaks. The religion militant meets the religion heavenly in the opening verse:

> Up there Cazaly,
> In there and fight,
> Out there and at 'em,
> Show 'em your might,
> Up there Cazaly,
> Don't let 'em in,
> Fly like an angel
> You're out there to win.

The afterlife is not after death but is found on the weekend and the transcendence is in the spirituality of the high mark ('fly like an angel') or in the collective community of the team (from Brady's 'the crowd's on your side'[20] to the abstract and communal 'we' of the world of football supporters). From the outer this can express self-satisfaction—'we were brilliant'—or, with a sense of the injustices of the world—'we were crucified!'.

In the holy book, Ross Fitzgerald and Ken Spillman's collection *The Greatest Game*, Manfred Jurgensen (ex-Carlton reserves, still personal chair, University of Queensland) writes of the spirituality and the aesthetics of football:

There were Saturdays when the game turned into poetry for both the team and the crowd. The ball was recited in a metre of inevitable beauty. For once there was precision, even among supporters. And I went home alone, kicking words, booed by the barracking of dusk.

'Not a game,' I began, 'but old dreams re-enacted. In its drama of endeavour, life became the ballgame it reflected. High marks in the Never-Never. Suddenly its meaning depends on a kick twenty metres out dead in front.'[21]

In contrast the poet and fellow exile in the desert of Queensland, Bruce Dawe, finds the religion not in the aesthetics of the game and the lifestyle but in the tradition. In one of the most prescribed poems in Australian schools, 'Life-Cycle', he celebrates the traditions from cradle to grave:

> When children are born in Victoria
> They are wrapped in the club colours, laid in beribboned cots,
> having already begun a lifetime's barracking.
> Carn, they cry, Carn...feebly at first

Other religions (ANZAC) and regions are noted in the reflection on the passing of time:

> They will not grow old as those from more northern states grow old,
> For them it will always be three-quarter time
> With the scores level and wind advantage in the final term.

Regeneration—individual and social—is found in football:

> That passion persisting, like a race-memory, through the welter of seasons, enabling old-timers by boundary fences to dream of resurgent lions and centaur-figures from the past to replenish continually the present.[22]

Manning Clark wrote in similar terms of the religion, of 'An Entire Nation Stricken with a Strange Infirmity', on Grand Final day. He had been struck with this disease for around 60 years, loving it 'to the point of madness' when Carlton was participating. Then it became a day for 'an emotional bath of agony and ecstasy'—with 'magical moments rather like an epiphany' as well as 'all the absurdity of human passions...there in excess'. And the religion could offer fear as well as hope, the prospect of heaven or hell, 'as the game enters the time-on period in the last quarter. Then none of the wisdom of the ages will help'.[23]

In its complexities, Australian Football—in Perth and Hobart and Adelaide, in Albury and Albany, Bendigo and Burnie—offers a range of achievements, struggles and emotions more complex than those of the sporting 'agon' in other games. The interplay of team and individual, of height and speed, strength and subtlety, skill and desire and the often rapidly changing scores run the gamut of human emotions, on and off the field.

For the poets and intellectuals the theme of the corruption of the true religion is omnipresent. Whether they voice the deepest thoughts and emotions of the people, or see the commercialisation of football as a symbol of a larger sense of loss, or worlds we have lost, or whether their cries are an intellectual's lament, like the Russian *narodniki* who sought to identify with the people, are questions easier to raise than to answer. Today, the true believers discern a change, a loss of the grass roots spirituality and community of the game in an era of commercialism, the national league and the wider television congregation. Although not faced with misappropriation of the game by violent youth, as in Britain and Europe, traditionalists still find change threatening. When Ian Turner and Leonie Sandercock's history of the VFL appeared in 1981 its title, *Up Where Cazaly?*, reflected contemporary anxieties.

Manfred Jurgensen, distant now in place, time and culture as an academic at the University of Queensland and the editor of *Outrider*, a journal of multicultural literature, recalled the first great treason of the 1960s—as it then seemed—when Ron Barassi left Melbourne for Carlton. He related it to the contemporary era of commercialism, knowing that 'the game would never be the same'. But despite the 'public adultery', despite Barassi having 'turned Judas', for Jurgensen, the Carlton player, Barassi's practical knowledge, 'his confidence and boyish grin made me forget that he had betrayed the code'.

Jurgensen would find several consolations. As someone who had come to Australia as a twelve-year-old migrant boy in 1961, he found consolation in the new ethnicity of the game as expressed in a roll call of stars including Schimmelbusch, Dipierdomenico, Ditterich, Catoggio, Kourkemelis and a new Silvagni: 'First, second or third generation Australians chasing a ball to score someone else's elusive goal.' For Jurgensen, the player, football had a spiritual and social quality:

> Rovers and followers, back-pocket player, full-forwards and ruckmen wrote plays of loyalty, bravery and deceit. Teams could act as one body. Life was an eternal search for this body. We joined a club, a team to find ourselves again: we depended on others. Their names were adopted as part of our own identity.[24]

It might seem that an appreciation of football is a celebration of male culture and society, that it simply leaves women out. The former is true, the latter is not. At a time when radical academia in the humanities and the social sciences has embraced 'marginalism', celebrating the 'margins', it is not unreasonable to recognise the society and values of several classes and generations who are forgotten by such research. For many Australians who have never thought of themselves as part of the alleged Anglo-Celtic hegemony discerned by the new ideology of multiculturalism (and objectively were never part of the ruling elites), a celebration of their own social and cultural traditions seemed important, even more so in an era of change when some members of the old elites and some multiculturalists share the view that Australia has and/or had no culture.[25]

Neither perspective (or those of the old Establishment elite) appeals to many of those who come from the forgotten margins, the lower orders characterised by class and region rather than by the more fashionable qualities of ethnicity and gender. For males of those classes and generations there is no need to follow American fantasies of tom-tom beating masculinity to discover their roots. In the traditions, tough and tender, physical and aesthetic, of football there are rich lodes to be mined, if ones associated with a sense of local community which is in decline in the contemporary world of mobility, mass media and youth consumer culture.

The perception that the culture and society of football is predominantly male is substantially accurate. It is played mainly, although these days not solely by males; change is reflected in the many girls in the participatory after match 'kick to kick' at League matches and the appearance of women's competitions in recent years. The football hero as idealised role model appeals initially most to boys, young and old. However, the social permeation of football in all Southern states is such that it transcends gender. In its frequent penetration of workplace, locality and family it is simply part of life, impacting more or less on everyone. Anne Summers, in reflecting in 1975 on how 'the disdain many intellectuals feel for the masses does not so often extend to football' referred, ambivalently, to their 'devotion, this mixture of intellectual appreciation of an intricate and skilful game and the sheer cathartic pleasure gained from watching others indulge in purposeful violence, which few women are able either to share or to understand'.[26] The latter assertion is interesting although it might well be qualified by the response of women spectators and supporters to the game. The broadcaster and writer Ramona Koval remembered the necessity of supporting St Kilda at St Kilda Park State School in the 1950s and her disappointment when the red, white and black scarf she asked for materialised in red. Later her fascination was mainly with footballers' thighs on the footy replays.[27]

The sociological analogy of religion used to describe Australian Football's importance in the Southern states involves other elements, particularly the permeation of daily life by football. While the weekly attendances of 150,000 in Melbourne have inevitably receded behind population growth (given the size of the city and ground capacity, despite 80,000–90,000 at some individual roster matches) and the 10 per cent of the population of Hobart attending roster matches in the 1960s has gone,[28] the permeation goes beyond attendances and TV audiences. In the workplace and in daily life football can be pervasive, although often in the form of an agreed reference point, a 'weather' type of subject, a conversation opener, a matter of verbal habit rather than of deeper engagement. In September 1992, as Geelong made its way to the AFL Grand Final, a Geelong scarf draped on the computer monitor in one Deakin office was a visible testament to one woman worker's aspirations. In workplaces one focus of social life is often a tipping competition—from the Canberra parliamentary press gallery to the Victorian Premier's Department to the finance branch and the School of Social Sciences at Deakin University—and football rivalries can be part of Friday and Monday workplace jousting for women as well as men. They can also offer a chance to win a few dollars, although rather fewer dollars than the Saturday lotto. At a July 1992 Melbourne seminar convened by Arts Action Australia to discuss a proposed national cultural policy, the male chair, architect Daryl Jackson, divided the 'game' into 'four quarters' while a female speaker, Janine Gordon, was hopeful that they could 'kick some goals and get the arts agenda into the twenty-first century'.[29] Even on the cultured airwaves of ABC Radio National an announcer dedicated Rossini's 'The Thieving Magpie' to the endeavours of Collingwood on the previous weekend.

While the visual interest of many women is focused on a very particular aesthetic, the tight shorts and tight thighs, it is often social–cultural–political as well as aesthetic–sexual. Oriel Gray, Leftist writer and playwright, learned about football through her three sons. Her support was also for South Melbourne as the 'Theatricals' team', the actors' favourite, appealing because, 'the Bloods were the eternal losers to Fate, as Theatricals were the eternal losers to Management in the days before Actors' Equity and the Australian Writers' Guild'. One of her sons becoming a Fitzroy supporter, she was also aware that Fitzroy had more recently become the team of the stylish, beautiful losers, the team for battlers, actors and disillusioned intellectuals, promising so much against the odds but never quite realising it. For her and many true believers Fitzroy were 'so often the battling underdogs, yet carrying the image of the legendary Haydn Bunton before them like a fragment of the True Cross'.[30]

Beyond the romantic and literary excesses of true believers and fellow travellers is the reality of women's involvement. One quarter to a third of crowds are female[31] (a great contrast with many sports) and women, often in less liberated ways, support clubs, particularly country, suburban and junior teams. Significantly, the defence of Footscray against forced amalgamation with Fitzroy was led by Irene Chatfield and Fight for Football, the grass-roots organisation opposed to the AFL's national/international/mass media view of the world, has a predominance of women amongst its principals.[32]

The theme of Australian Football under challenge from commercial-isation and the commodification of television and big money is a new version of the old Australian tribal lament about the loss of simpler worlds. It is the particularly Australian version of the Edenic lament about the loss of innocence and the romantic lament about the transition from the spiritual *Gemeinschaft* of idealised local community to the material *Gesellschaft* of mass society. Its themes are corruption and exploitation as well as dispossession. Yet the love of football persists, in spite of the reported $300,000 salary package of Ross Oakley as chief AFL commissioner, the disfiguring role of the brewer John Elliott, and the world of business superboxes and the pink helicopter of the now departed medical and Sydney Swans entrepreneur Dr Edelsten.[33]

The great explorer of these themes from a position closer to working class suburban culture is the poet of Preston, the playwright Barry Dickins. His magnificent 1987 play, *Royboys*, takes its title from the 'Royboys' of Fitzroy of whom Dickins writes regularly on the 'Religion' page of the inner suburban newspaper, the *Melbourne Times*.[34] It dramatises the story of the struggling Noble family, a working class family of Fitzroy supporters in outer suburban Aspendale and of their defeats in the game of life by the new capitalists, the 'Masters', who would send their team to Tokyo and rename them 'Fitzaki'. As the play develops the goal umpire standing behind the big sticks raises the two flags for goals for the Nobles or for their opposition, the Masters, while the scoreboard at the back of the stage records the grim totals, quarter by quarter until the final siren, until the final defeat. The academic Graeme Duncan's reflection, 'Through a Glass Sadly', suggests the theme of loss which parallels that of celebration and praise in the collection *The Greatest Game*. Titles such as 'Death of a Hero', 'Loss of a Homespun Legend', 'Never Forget Where You've Come From', 'Sad Memories of Village Footscray', 'Swansong', 'Football the Way It Was' and 'The Perfidy of Ron Barassi' underline the romantic sense of dispossession at a time of change in the traditions of football. Graeme Duncan reflects on the fundamental loyalties which he held despite change in his own life and in football itself:

> I have no doubt that my love for and loyalty to the Roys is a primary one, akin to that felt towards my parents, who retain it even when they stray from the path of virtue or the expected pattern of behaviour. Cry for Fitzroy, curse Fitzroy, but there could never be another team. At worst, if the game continues to change and degenerate, it could be no team at all, and another vital organ would have been cut from my body spiritual.

Looking back from Adelaide, England, Brisbane and England again, Duncan reflects that his:

loyalty to Fitzroy, increasingly touched with doubts though it may be, is not based upon anything as grand as a sociological conception, a class commitment to a proletarian, inner-city, founder member of the League, but upon an early choice the precise origins of which I can only speculate upon.[35]

In comparable terms, Brian Matthews, scion of St Kilda and adopted Croweater (South Australian), laments the decline of traditions (including parochial prejudice) which have been 'cancelled by national league strategists moving teams like chessmen', asking 'What do South Melbourne supporters think of the jazzy, tight-shorted, glad-handing Sydney Swans?'[36] Even while deploring the blood-sucking of the VFL, he recognises that VFL football was 'a miracle seen nowhere else in the country—let alone the world', even if it was not in the blood of those who had not grown up 'kicking footies made of rolled up newspapers or old socks in the smoky back streets of inner suburban or industrial Melbourne'.

'*National* !', a character in his story 'Flying to the Footy' growled with contempt at a Sydney Swans recruiter. 'You chuck one team west and one team east and invent some rabble up north and give them names like American gridiron and that's National!'[37]

Paradoxically, the disillusioned dreamers in the Australian utopian tradition—from social democrats to Maoists—often find populist consolation in the traditions, despite them being under threat from rampant commercialisation, of football.

Ian Turner, who fears that the Australian dream of a better society was fading in the 1960s 'Godzone country' era of suburban materialism, reflects that:

> it has been a long-time lament of Australian socialists that if only the Australian workers transferred the thought they invested in picking winners and the passion they devote to football into politics, we would have had the revolution long ago.[38]

The theme of loss, of worlds we have lost, is part of traditions which go beyond Australia. There are echoes in British folk history, in the nostalgia for an older working-class society which was one of the influences on Richard Hoggart and a more general lament from France to Malaysia to the USA at the relative decline of rural life. In Europe today it has immediate relevance given fears of Eurohomogenisation, from Eurodisney to satellite TV and pasteurised Eurocheese, all part of the freeway of international materialism and mass popular culture. It is a theme of the literature of migration and of some post-colonial writing as well as a theme which helps many writers and academics deal with their own class transitions, of their relationship with the wider society from which they originally came. The parallel theme is in the tradition of romanticism and sociology—

the Fall, seen specifically in the apple of commercialism and the corruption of innocent traditions through Faustian bargains with corporate capital and the mass media.

The question of the relationship between changing organisation of football and 'community' is as complex as it is ever-recurring. Only 'love' and 'nature' exceed 'community' as subjects for rhetoric in the late twentieth century, posing the question of what is meant by the idea of 'loss of community'. Most accurately, this is a loss of the world of a simpler—although not necessarily better—local society in which the locality, or for the churches, the parish, was more important than it is today in the lives of its residents; forty years ago, in the days before the mass mobility of the car and plane, the TV and the telephone, the local world shaped life more than it does today. It was an era of simpler beliefs and prejudices (Protestantism/Catholicism/family/success and pleasure), of fewer serious sports (football/cricket/netball/tennis) and of fewer alternative leisure pursuits. It was a society in which local loyalties (and conflicts) were important: when those who grew up in South Hobart supported Hobart and the scions and daughters of North Hobart tribally supported their own team. It was a world before: before the great migrations—across the suburbs and across the planet—which located Collingwood supporters amongst the *nouveau riche* of Mount Waverley in Melbourne or Sandy Bay in Hobart and found a new generation of working class supporters of European and Asian parentage who had passed through the Collingwood Housing Commission flats or merely identified with the Collingwood traditions of near success or with the 'Magpie army' of frenzied supporters; before the migration to inner city Carlton and Collingwood of 'trendies' and 'Yuppies' who looked with less enthusiasm on the impact of 30,000 football supporters and their cars on their Saturday afternoons; before the migration of clubs to different grounds and cities to play roster matches; before the demands of 80,000 people and technology made it acceptable in 1989 for Geelong to play a 'home' game at the MCG over 85 kilometres from Geelong's Kardinia Park home. In a suburban world the passions are suburban as supporters of different clubs sit in a mixed choir, sharing their hymns of love and hate.

In religion the decline of the parish has brought new forms of mass religion from the fundamentalist halls and edifices of the outer suburbs to TV ministry. In football, similarly, a new world of private televisual spirituality appeals to the deracinated tribal psyche when there is no longer a territory passed on from generation to generation; it appeals also to the ecumenical believer in the game itself ('beauty is truth') and to 'Norm', the great TV sportsman of the lounge-room.

Yet on Friday, 11 October 1991, in the midst of the recession, football was a vehicle for deeper emotions, an outlet for community passion, at the funeral of Darren Millane. The brilliant Collingwood premiership footballer, a son of working-class Noble Park and Dandenong, a nightclubber and a drunk, had written himself off on a freeway in the early hours of the morning while massively under the influence. Up to 5,000 mourners at the funeral and hundreds of death notices over several days in the *Herald–Sun* suggested that the self-inflicted death of a wild young footballer had a deeper social resonance in Victoria than that stemming merely from sporting passion.[39]

In the era of mass media sport and million dollar budgets Melbourne's second competition, the VFA (Victorian Football Association) has sought to define itself and defend its existence as the 'community code', the grass-roots game earthed in the local community in contrast to the *Gesellschaft*-shaped VFL/AFL. Phil Cleary, Coburg coach (and, in 1992, Leftist, populist, independent member for Wills, Bob Hawke's old seat), its strongest and most articulate advocate, puts the case for the VFA in words which suggest a meeting between people and market:

> Despite losing a sizable share of the market and being relegated to the margin, the association survives—albeit with much financial difficulty—because it represents football as we once knew it.[40]

Notwithstanding the dedication of some believers in the Association and/or their club—including players at Springvale and Coburg who accepted severe pay cuts in 1992—in practice the Association has been in decline for several years. Squeezed between the truly local teams and the VFL/AFL it has lost major TV coverage and local sponsorship; thus Geelong West declined and eventually disappeared as sponsorship went either to the local teams in the GFL/GDFL or to a major Geelong FC fund-raising drive or to the new Geelong Supercats national basketball team.[41]

What then of the true religion, of this dreaming, in the last years of the millennium? In the contemporary world of September 1992 three commercial competitions and a number of sporting events suggested the degree of contemporary change. One competition was a 'football game' to win money for TV viewers and ratings for Channel 7, which has the rights to the football. A second competition asked the eaters of Four n' Twenty pies to 'spot the legends', football stars of yesteryear in a company commercial of yesteryear. In the third competition, a Coca-Cola concoction with more debts to Schwarzenegger and to gridiron protective garb than to football focused on an imagined future game, the football of the next century, called 'Futureball' (presumably a similar game was packaged Rugby-League-style for residents of the more barbarous Northern states). Even more important than the commercial fantasies of the competition-makers or the overseas trips which were the prizes for the second and third competition were several events. To the shock of parochial Victorians the AFL had gone national in ways other than expected—the West Coast Eagles defeated Geelong to win the 1992 premiership; the new National Basketball League finals were televised in peak viewing time on a commercial channel, national hockey and basketball leagues were about to begin and there was already a massive adolescent adoption of American sporting clothing. The loss of 'our game' was a double reality despite the true believers of Kensington, as under the impact of commercialism and the Eagles tradition went west. A secular society and new sects were challenging and changing the old religion.

Notes

1. Donald Horne, cited in *The Macquarie Dictionary of Australian Quotations*, Sydney, 1990, p. 367.

2. Richard Stremski, *Kill for Collingwood!*, Sydney, 1986.

3. Ian Turner, 'The Greatest Game: The Barassi Memorial Lecture' in *Room for Manoeuvre*, Melbourne, 1982 p. 318.

4. See Ian Turner and Leonie Sandercock, *Up Where Cazaly?*, Sydney, 1981 and Geoffrey Blainey, *A Game of Our Own: The Origins of Australian Football*, Melbourne, 1990.

5. Oriel Gray, 'Loss of a Homespun Legend' in Ross Fitzgerald and Ken Spillman, eds. *The Greatest Game*, Melbourne, 1988, p. 155.

6. James Bradley, personal communication, September 1992; see also Stephen Alomes, 'The British Press and Australia', *Meanjin*, 46, 2, June, 1987.

7. For the late nineteenth-century debate on 'The Australian Type' see Stephen Alomes and Catherine Jones, eds., *Australian Nationalism: A Documentary History*, Sydney 1991, pp. 46–73, particularly the excerpts from James Hogan's 'The Coming Australian' and the comments of his critics (pp. 50–4).

8. On sport and political rhetoric see Stephen Alomes, 'Politics as Sport: Reality and Metaphor in Australian Politics and Political Coverage' in Stephen Alomes and Dirk den Hartog, eds., *Post-Pop: Popular Culture, Nationalism and Postmodernism*, Footscray, Vic., 1991.

9. *Geelong Advertiser*, 8 June 1991.

10. Hans Mol, *Religion in Australia*, Melbourne, 1971, pp. 5, 122; Hans Mol, *The Faith of Australians*, Sydney, 1985. On conventional religion and Australian culture see Gordon S. Dicker, 'Kerygma and Australian culture; the case of the Aussie Battler' in Victor C. Hayes, ed., *Towards*

Theology in an Australian Context, Bedford Park, S.A., 1979. On football as a religion see also Mark Skulley, 'On the wing without a prayer' in *Eureka Street*, vol. 1, no. 4, June 1991 (a Jesuit public affairs magazine).

11. Mol, *Religion*, p. 122.

12. Keith Hancock, ed., *Australian Society*, Cambridge, 1989.

13. Henry Lawson, 'The New Religion', 1890, in B. Kiernan, ed. *The Portable Henry Lawson*, St. Lucia, 1976, p. 80.

14. Ian Turner, *The Australian Dream*, Melbourne, 1968, pp. x–xi.

15. For a slightly eccentric account of the diversity of 1890s aspirations see John Docker, *The Nervous Nineties*, Melbourne, 1991.

16. See E.J. Hobsbawm and T.O. Ranger, eds., *The Invention of Tradition*, Cambridge, 1983 and J.M. MacKenzie, ed., *Imperialism and Popular Culture*, Manchester, 1984.

17. C.J. Dennis, *The Songs of a Sentimental Bloke*, Sydney, 1915.

18. Geoffrey Serle, 'The Digger Tradition and Australian Nationalism', *Meanjin*, 24, 2, 1965, p. 155. Bill Gammage, *The Broken Years*, Ringwood, 1975, p. 55. On the war cry see Turner and Sandercock, *Up Where Cazaly?*

19. On tourism and religion see David Lodge's novel of Hawaii, *Paradise News*, London, 1991.

20. The relationship between composers and courts, secular and religious, is often complex. Mike Brady, a 1960s rock singer (with the group MPD) is a successful commercial jingle writer with no interest at all in football. The success of the song (as a single it sold over 200,00 copies) derived in part from its working as a video clip, using shots of crowd scenes and football action, in particular high marks.

21. Manfred Jurgensen, 'Highpoint Carlton' in Fitzgerald and Spillman, *The Greatest Game*, pp. 130–2.

22. Bruce Dawe, *Condolences of the Season: Selected Poems*, Melbourne, 1971.

23. Manning Clark, 'An Entire Nation Stricken with a Strange Infirmity', in Fitzgerald and Spillman, *The Greatest Game*, pp. 226–9.

24. Jurgensen, 'Highpoint Carlton'.

25. The social and psychological complexities of these recurrent perceptions are, while outside the brief of this discussion, of singular

importance. Intellectually the perceptions have their roots in and are reinforced by the metropolitan deference inherent in the colonial cultural cringe, particularly in some respectable middle class milieux.

26. Anne Summers, *Damned Whores and God's Police*, Ringwood, 1975, pp. 78–9.

27. Ramona Koval, 'Thighs and Whispers', in Fitzgerald and Spillman, *The Greatest Game*, pp. 90–94.

28. In 1965 when Hobart had a population of 123,000, 235,370 people attended Tasmanian Football League matches on the 20 days (nearly all Saturdays) on which roster matches were played and 57,801 attended the four finals matches, Ken Pinchin, *A Century of Tasmanian Football 1879–1979*, Hobart, n.d. (1979?), p. 109. In 1992 the first four finals of the new statewide TFL, which were played over two rather than four weekends, were attended by only 10,788 people, Hobart *Mercury*, 8 September 1992.

29. *A Cultural Policy for Australia*, transcript of the Sydney and Melbourne Forums (28 and 30 July), Sydney, 1992, pp. 78, 106.

30. Oriel Gray, 'Loss', pp. 155–7. In the spirit of martyrdom, Fitzroy were on the brink of extinction in late 1992, clinging precariously to life for the season of 1993.

31. The size of the oval and the greater space it allows for seated spectators is important. see also Turner and Sandercock, *Up Where Cazaly?*, Appendix II, Mary Brady, 'Miss and Mrs Football, but no Ms Football', pp. 249–56.

32. See Kerrie Gordon and Alan Dalton, *Too Tough to Die: Footscray's Fightback*, Melbourne, 1990 and Fight for Football (Vic.), Inc., *Out of Bounds*, Boronia, Vic., 1991. Fight for Football was founded by Kathy Bisset and Scharlaine Cairns in July 1991.

33. Dr Geoffrey Edelsten was a 1980s doctor cum-medical entrepreneur, with pink helicopter, blonde wife and white baby grand pianos in his clinics, who was the media persona of the private owners of the Sydney Swans. By the 1990s he eventually became debarred from medical practice, divorced and dispossessed of the by then struggling Swans. See *Age* Good Weekend, 21 March 1986, *Age*, 3 December 1992.

34. Barry Dickins, *Royboys*, Currency, Sydney, 1987.

35. Graeme Duncan, 'Through a Glass, Sadly' in Fitzgerald and Spillman, *The Greatest Game*, pp. 139–144.

36. Brian Matthews, 'And the Band Played Something Like "Waltzing Matilda"', in Fitzgerald and Spillman, *The Greatest Game*, p. 35.

37. Brian Matthews, 'Flying to the Footy', in *Oval Dreams: Larrikin Essays on Australian Sport and Low Culture*, McPhee Gribble, Melbourne, 1991, p. 8. One reading of this particular story, in which the narrator flies to Melbourne to kill a feminist reviewer of his book but goes to the football instead, is as a loosely allegorical expression of the feelings of marginalisation of a bearer of an older male culture in an era of new ideological fashions.

38. Ian Turner, 'The Barassi Memorial Lecture', p. 320.

39. Melbourne *Herald–Sun*, 8–11 October 1991. His blood alcohol readingof over 0.3 was not publicised until later.

40. Philip Cleary, 'Beware threat to VFA's identity and tradition', *Sunday Age*, 2 August 1992.

41. Chris Colley, Regionalism and Australia research project, Deakin University, Geelong, 1992.

POPULAR CULTURE AND THE 'MASS' MEDIA

Controlling the Technology of Popular Culture: The Introduction of Television in Australia

JAMES WALTER

I have been exploring the links between political culture and popular culture in the formation of Australian national consciousness between 1945 and 1972. My belief is that this period manifests a cycle in the public culture. The cycle starts with the struggle over a set of values that would be foundational to the 'new' post-war order, the ascendance of a particular complex of values and the attempt to implement them in social policy, and thence to ensure their acceptance in everyday consciousness (to have them 'naturalised'). In time there came to be a recognition of the dysfunctions of certain core assumptions, and with it an unravelling of the agenda of the 1940s, 1950s and 1960s—the early 1970s saw attempts (on both sides of politics) at new directions.

The 1945–72 cycle began with an assumption that people could take control of development and fashion it to their own ends and ended in loss of direction and disillusion. An important part of the story is in analysing the forms taken by and the uses made of the chief agencies of cultural transmission. This is especially so when, as in the case of television, the medium was first introduced within the period of my interest. My concern is less with the concrete detail of what happened than with what various interests argued should happen, how they attempted to sell their ideas to a constituency (and have these ideas 'naturalised'), who won, and with what effects on our understanding. I am, in other words, looking primarily at the public debate, and only secondarily at the archive of who did what to whom (often behind the scenes).[1]

Popular culture is always dependent upon particular technologies of reproduction, representation and dissemination. These technologies do not bring with them their own social imperatives:[2] who has access, how they are deployed, and who benefits are matters of choice and negotiation. That is, the process is the stuff of mainstream politics. The more one looks at the establishment of television as an instance of how popular cultural forms are created, transformed and transmitted by particular technologies, the more quandaries it raises concerning what we actually mean by popular culture. In exploring these quandaries, I have come to the conclusion that postmodern theories are severely circumscribed in helping us to grapple with them.

To foreshadow my argument, if we mean by popular culture something arising from 'the people', then the debate about Australian television suggests to me that there is paradoxically a real question of whether a people's culture can survive within a free market. I refer here to the situation we now face where 'our' market is not local or nationally bounded (as in earlier eras), but part of a world economy. I will concede that the question falls aside if popular culture is an international phenomenon shared by the mass of common people—but if instead you take it to refer to a vernacular culture, resonant with the concerns of specific, local communities, then it retains its force. Further, if you take popular culture to mean something like a statement of consumer preferences, then the question is vitiated, but if you intend by popular culture something more than what a community will 'buy', then the question remains pertinent. Let's turn, then, to the case of Australian television.

The descriptive work on the introduction of television in Australia is now reasonably comprehensive.[3] There were three groups in contention over the manner in which the new medium should be deployed, and its likely cultural impact. First, there were those people who had severe reservations about the introduction of television, and who can be characterised in terms of two subgroups. On the one hand were those who opposed it entirely, either because it could not be afforded (Archbishop Mannix argued succinctly that with public works held up for lack of money, television was an extravagant luxury),[4] or as something whose cultural and social impact might be largely negative:

> The huge costs of television will almost certainly pander to the lower elements in human nature and human society. The perils of low grade television which could steadily contaminate the minds of children and degrade the community are too great to be left to chance. Therefore some form of community control will be necessary (the Archbishop of Sydney, 1952)[5]

On the other hand, some feared that television would provide such a powerful tool for the active manipulation of public opinion by commercial interests that it must be entirely in the control of the state. These latter supported only a non-commercial and regulated national network, and not surprisingly were mainly in the Australian Labor Party (ALP).

Second was a group I designate the culturalists—proponents of Australian television who believed in the efficiency of the new technology as a tool culturally to enlighten the masses, who believed indeed in the possibility of 'making a community'. Most of these believed that the state must play some role in ensuring that the educative value of the medium was achieved. They believed, too, in television enhancing Australian citizenship, being regulated so as to serve nation-building and not fragmentation. They tended to support a national, non-commercial network dedicated to 'higher' values—the 'quality programming' that commercial interests could not be relied on to preserve:

> A real social revolution is taking place...(Television) can become a major, if not the major, single influence on the generations to come...We shall lose something—some warmth, some intimacy some things which are dear to the generation which preceded its appearance. On the other hand it is...an instrument for widening our horizons in an age...when the education of the mass of people is becoming more urgent...The issues of television are so important that every citizen should accept his own share of responsibilty for the manner of its development, for the type of programme exhibited and for its long term effects on the society of which he is a part.[6]

> Television is an instrument with tremendous potentialities, both for information and for entertainment. Its influence will depend on how it is organised and controlled. If its administrators have a definite sense of responsibility to the community, it can be a wonderful educational medium...Its real work will have to be done with the community generally.[7]

> No medium has greater possibilties for helping us spend our leisure intelligently and creatively...We know all about the bad things too...There is a legal fiction of Australian control of the TV stations, but if the strings are pulled abroad, the puppets will dance...The commercial stations must be restrained—it is idle to talk of their being improved. There is no more future for commercial broadcasting than there is for any other form of prostitution.[8]

Third, there were those who were vigorous advocates of a television service, and of private enterprise involvement and initiative as the best means of developing such a service. They took it for granted that the community would get what it wanted, that fears of adverse effects were unwarranted:

> The chief virtue of commercial broadcasting as practised in Australia, is that it is essentially democratic. First and foremost, it tries to please the general public, whose interests it serves...it depends for its very existence upon maintaining the goodwill of the whole body of listeners...The national service is subject to no such checks.[9]

> Commercial TV, with the right to earn revenue, can really serve the purpose of bringing entertainment on a large scale to the family in the home...private enterprise, with programmes sponsored by advertisers, can bring a full TV service to the public at no perceptible cost. The money will come from advertising appropriations, and will not necessarily add anything to the cost of the consumer goods sold by the sponsors.[10]

This is a familiar enough set of protagonists, perhaps, and such oppositions are certainly not unique to Australia. The argument, too, is familiar, boiling down as it does to disagreement over the degree to which the development of a television service should be driven by non-commercial imperatives (core values, neutrality, education, the interests of civil society), and the degree to which it should be driven by the market (the public being best served by competition, programme suppliers being driven by consumer preferences to producing the best outcomes). Yet, if broad principles are familiar, we must not ignore the extent to which each community inflects these arguments in its own way. Nor must we ignore contextual matters particular to specific communities. Some features of the Australian context were especially important. Being relatively late in entering the field, the debate about television in Australia could refer to the experience of other countries, particularly the United States, Canada and Britain—and especially to the BBC as a public broadcasting exemplar. Pragmatic arguments concerning Australian geography, to the effect that broad-casting should serve a public demand and that commercial solutions would always fail to satisfy that demand in remote and scattered communities, and that had already led to the establishment of a dual broadcasting system for radio (a national government-funded service, plus local commercial stations) were inevitably voiced again in the television debate.[11]

The debate in Australia got off to a slow start.[12] The nay-sayers at first could hold sway—the economic demands of post-war reconstruction and the Cold War were higher priorities for both the Chifley (Labor) and the Menzies (conservative) governments until the early 1950s. Then there was dithering between the protagonists concerning the appropriate balance between public and private participation in the service. The ALP government's tentative decision to introduce a national non-commercial service was not implemented before that government fell in 1949. Its successor, Menzies' conservative Liberal–Country Party (L–CP) coalition government, predictably placed more emphasis on commercial arguments and the benefits of competition, but the new entertainment medium remained a low priority. It is said that Menzies was not much interested until the pressures of friendly business interests, and his own perception of the medium's image-making potential, pushed him towards a decision. Even then he opted for a lazy political solution—the appointment of a Royal Commission (in 1953–4) with constraints that ensured that complex issues would not be rethought, but that something like the extant dual broadcasting system would be recommended.[13] Thus the culturalists could be appeased (there would be a national public system), the possibility of a succeeding ALP government being able to dominate television would be precluded (there were also to be commercial networks which could be relied upon to be 'unobtrusively unfair'[14]), and the powerful proprietors of

the press and the electronics industries could be kept on side. Having so
determined, Menzies could leave the detail to others—it was for the Royal
Commission to satisfy all parties (by recommending that the Australian
Broadcasting Commission, ABC, should run a national system and that
private competitors should be selected and regulated by the Australian
Broadcasting Control Board). The forms of regulation eventually
promulgated were inadequate in promoting diversity of ownership (and
hence competition), or diversity of product, in Australian television.
Commercial licences went to existing press and radio interests, allowing a
handful of companies to monopolise Australia's major media. There was
no minimum quota for Australian content initially, allowing television
proprietors to take the cheapest option, which was to import large
quantities of cheap material from overseas.

The scale of capitulation to foreign cultural production is still worth
recalling. One survey in the late 1950s showed that Australian material
comprised only 5 out of 131 half hour shows; another in the early 1960s
that of the 136 evening programmes telecast nationally in the USA, only
12 were not being shown in Australia.[15] A prominent economist
demonstrated that, 'the bulk of programmes, over 60 per cent for most
stations, consist of filmed material that is imported at prices considerably
below overseas cost of production, and is, in fact, a classical case of
dumping'.[16] The specifics of economic concentration are also significant—
by 1958 it could be shown that film interests had bought into television;
some groups had established 'a kind of vertical interest' involving
manufacturing and licence control; newspapers' and radio stations' strong
associations had been extended into television; foreign (especially foreign
press) capital investment was noteworthy. In fact, monopolies ran the
system at key points, preventing even regional programming by country
stations, since these could not afford to produce their own programmes.[17]
The fact that three newspaper proprietors controlled ten television stations
contravened the spirit of the Broadcasting Act's controls, but this only
pointed up how weak regulatory provisions were.

The advent of a television industry with these characteristics had a
tremendous impact on Australian theatre and radio. An obvious, and
frequently noted, impact was on attendance at all forms of live entertainment. Less frequently remarked, however, was the disruption of
employment patterns—actors had survived because of the symbiosis
between radio and theatre. Employment in the radio 'soaps' had always
been a fallback, keeping actors in work in the gaps between theatrical
engagements. The radio soaps virtually disappeared as television took
over that sector of popular entertainment, yet because the television soaps
were predominantly imported, there was little employment in the new
industry for local actors. And at the same time theatrical work all but

disappeared, in the face of the same challenge. The only options for a whole cohort of actors were to give up and seek other employment, or to leave the country—as expatriate Australian actors of that generation will testify.[18] Thus took place a deskilling of the Australian entertainment industry, leaving the country, as it were, without a local 'voice' until the renascence of the 1970s.[19]

What did commentators at the time think of these developments? An article by economic journalist, Kenneth Davidson, reviewing the first ten years of Australian television in 1968, gives us a lead.[20] Davidson analyses the economics of the commercial telecasters, and argues that 'the present structure of commercial television is completely incompatible with "good broadcasting"'.[21] Davidson does not himself define what he means by 'good broadcasting'—his use of that notion is a reference back to the Vincent Report on Australian television (1963)—but he does go on to demonstrate 'that financial considerations, and not "giving the public what it wants," were the major factors underlying the heavy bias towards variety shows and overseas programmes...',[22] and to suggest 'that viewers' tastes in Australia are not being moulded by the local controllers of the television media (sic)...they are controlled vicariously by...American sponsors...'.[23]

Davidson here developed what had already been one of the concerns of the Vincent Report, and it became a sustained line of commentary in subsequent work on Australian television history.[24] Indeed, it was the gradual acceptance of this line of argument that led to new forms of regulation, including the gradual increase in quota requirements for Australian content.[25] One might summarise by saying that, if the commercial advocates more or less had their way in the early years of television, the culturalists gradually gained a foothold for their demand that the local community's interests should be observed at some level. There are also grounds for arguing that only when there were incentives for Australian production, allowing Australian programmes to gain ground, did viewer preferences in favour of local content become clear.[26]

In the 1980s and 1990s, however, alternative interpretations of these events, consonant with new theoretical readings of popular culture, emerged. Ann Curthoys, in her otherwise excellent account of 'The getting of television',[27] hints at what is to come—she rejects the sort of issues Davidson raised to conclude that 'the anti-commercial-TV forces were bound to lose...it is probably just as well, given the immense popularity of commercial television since its introduction, that they did lose'.[28] It is only a short step from this judgment to the assertion that the popularity of the commodity form is to be directly equated with popular culture. And this indeed is the proposition central to John Docker's more recent defence of the commercial patterns of Australian television—a defence predicated upon postmodern theories of popular culture.[29]

Docker claims to argue 'for the market and commodity form' and against 'modernism (with its disdain for mass culture and frequent...desire to regulate it into a desired image)'. He is in favour of 'postmodernism and a pluralist, libertarian aesthetic'.[30] His is a spirited and interesting argument. He is surely right in lambasting the elitist element in the culturalist position, that an enlightened minority could know (and should dictate, through state instrumentalities) what people should see. But that was not the *only* element in their argument: at some level they were also intent on preserving a corner for the community *against* the market, not so much dictating the content of what was produced in that corner, but allowing that there might be a space for production not constrained by market imperatives.[31] Docker ignores this. Putting the opposite case to Docker, Jennifer Craik argues

> The intention of the Australian content regulations has been to encourage diverse Australian production rather than to impose 'higher' forms of culture...It does not seem unreasonable that an independent agency should establish minimum guidelines to encourage local cultural production in order to ensure that national culture remains vibrant and relevant.[32]

Docker concedes that there were almost certainly too many American programmes on Australian television initially, but argues that there was inevitably a drift away in time, a preference for the local product which commercial producers necessarily followed, and hence that regulation was not needed to achieve this. Yet there are grounds for arguing that the preference for Australian material was known, yet ignored for financial reasons[33] until regulation provided commercial television with incentives, and further, that it was as a result of this alerting audiences to the possibilities of local production that demand was fuelled.[34]

Docker is surely right in arguing that audiences are not passive, that they will 'read' programmes in their own way, and for their own purposes. But can he move from this to saying, as he does, that the most popular shows inevitably reflect the tastes and values of ordinary people? Can he argue, what is more, that these people, in the ways they 'read' television, are the inheritors of (and enact) the pre-capitalist carnivalesque tradition of popular culture which subverts the totalising hierarchies of values imposed by elites? To quote from his conclusion:

> to be popular in a majority sense, programs and the overall 'collective drama', the overall tone and feel of commercial stations have to appeal to popular traditions—traditions that at once go back deep into the history of centuries of popular culture and are always open to the new, in technology and form. If stations didn't put on programs that were popular they would financially fail—what could be more obvious?[35]

Now, commercial institutions of course are preoccupied with achieving popularity, mobilising consumer preferences, but can there be an easy elision between what is 'popular' (in the sense that many will buy it), and 'popular' meaning 'of the people' (the sense in which it is usually applied to popular culture)? And what does the pro-market John Docker know about markets? His argument would perhaps apply if there was an infinite choice in the market, if it did offer everything. But is there any market anywhere like this, and what does popularity mean when the choice is constrained, when—as happened in the early years of Australian television—there is simply nothing relating to the vernacular culture on offer?

Would we accept Docker's argument if, say, it applied to the purchase of domestic chairs? Imagine, if you will, that you live in the small town of Gooligulch,[36] a long way from the bright lights (and the furniture stores) of Sydney. You decide one day that you need to buy a lounge chair. There are only two furniture stores in Gooligulch. You visit both. One of these carries a line of plain wooden kitchen chairs. The other stocks an upright but padded chair. Neither carries any sort of lounge chair because, you are told, 'there is no demand'. You opt for the padded chair as being closest to what you want, buy it, and go home feeling frustrated. Unknown to you, there is a small factory on the outskirts of town specialising in lounge furniture, which once supplied both shops. But the local shopkeepers found that they could import upright chairs at substantially lower unit costs from Taiwan, where labour costs of course are cheaper. The local manufacturer, unable to match these prices, could no longer place his product with the local shops and had to aim at another market, the upmarket 'Super Natura' stores in Sydney. There is, the shopkeepers 'know', no upmarket client base in Gooligulch. But they are happy— everybody in town is buying the chairs. Indeed, at the end of the quarter, the proprietor specialising in the padded chair has cause to be especially pleased—the padded version is selling much better than his rival's plain chair. It is clearly the more popular. So the market works. And as for the academics, who have chosen to analyse the lifestyle choices of this small country town, they are intent on explaining the various uses to which the majority of purchasers put their 'popular' padded chairs. Some of the townsfolk, finding the padded vinyl too hot in the outback heat of Gooligulch, tear it off. Others, still searching for the elusive contour of a lounge chair, lean their chairs back against the wall, on two legs. Yet others, who have read Russell Ward, deploy the Australian 'talent' for improvisation, and modify the chairs, sawing off back legs, adding props. Many, in the end, succumb to frustration, and break the chairs up for firewood, or—knowing a thing or two about Russell Drysdale—hang them from a branch of a convenient tree. The observers know exactly what to make of this: the popularity of the commodity is obvious, but the people's refusal to be constrained by the commodity form, their resistances to and novel readings of the chair, their insistence on turning it to their own uses, all these are evident. Would you buy this argument? Is it lampooning Docker too much to say that this is exactly how his argument works?

The point here is that while Docker has elaborate views of the interventionist state and of popular traditions, he has an unsophisticated view of the modern transnational marketplace—indeed, of the commercial nature of high modernity. For him, markets are the best means to serve libertarian ends, since they are most directly responsive to choice. But to believe that choice is, as it were, 'open' is to ignore the fact that control of the technologies and marketing of product for the new popular media simply did not and could not remain within national boundaries. The process inevitably was part of transnational capitalism. As Raymond Williams said of the new visual media, 'many attempts were made to preserve at least domestic corporations, but the paranational scale significantly overbore them. The road to Hollywood was then...inscribed'.[37] Alternatively, to suggest that national bounds are irrelevant to the transnational carnivalesque 'tradition' of popular culture (Docker's other strategy) is to ignore the specificities of local culture, to leave us without any tools to understand the regional vernaculars (and this is leaving aside the question of whether the universality of the carnivalesque mode can be sustained, or even detected in television soaps).[38]

The practical point at issue is that if the political and commercial choices surrounding the introduction of television in Australia led to a very limited set of programme options, dictated by the financial considerations of commercial telecasters (rather than by responses to public choice), and that in consequence audiences were formed within the constraints of those options, then questions remain about whether public preferences could ever be fully expressed. Did what was produced, therefore, have any but the most tenuous links with 'the people'? The theoretical point at issue is this: does the postmodern assumption of 'fragmentation' and abandonment of universals, along with the assertion of plurality and diversity of choice as a means of subverting hegemonic hierarchies of values, provide an adequate response, or even an adequate understanding, of the universalisation of economic structures in modern societies? Against the popularity of postmodernism, Anthony Giddens reminds us that:

> some have...presumed that...fragmentation marks the emergence of a novel phase of social development...a post- modern era. Yet the unifying features of modern institutions are just as central to modernity...processes that established a single 'world' where none existed previously.[39]

The problem is that that 'single world' is not the world of a small country like Australia, hostage to the world economy. Stuart Hall expresses the core of this problem in saying that 'postmodernism is how the world dreams itself to be American'.[40] But the dream is a means of control.

In the single world of the capitalist market, where transnational corporations are uniquely placed to control the capital-intensive technologies of mass communication, how are particular, regional, and local communities to take control? Can popular culture really be sustained by commodity fetishism? Does our 'reading' of television soaps—no matter how 'resistant', how subversive—change anything, or make the formulas on which they rely 'ours'? Terry Eagleton, for one, argues that the playful irony of postmodernism 'is more likely to play into the hands of the ruling powers than to discomfort them'. We may be cynical, knowing, ironic, but we cannot act:

> if political practice takes place only within a context of interpretation, and if that context is notoriously ambiguous and unstable, then action itself is likely to be problematic and unpredictable.[41]

Meanwhile, however, the world market will continue its universalising practices unchecked, decisions will be driven largely by commercial imperatives (limiting, rather than opening up, choices), and the chances of particular communities taking control of the modern technologies that mediate their popular cultures will be lost.

The debate over Australian television shows that at its inception, people did believe that there were choices, and that when policy structures failed to deliver, insistence on government action could achieve change. If, since that time, we seem to have lost the plot, if the emphasis has shifted from political action to audience reaction, is that a measure of how wrong those earlier commentators and activists were, or a measure of how far we have fallen victim to a 'single world' which seems to offer us everything—everything but community, or the means to articulate our popular cultures? Perhaps there is still something to learn from the commitment of the culturalists to preserving a corner where ideas could be pursued free of market constraints.

Notes

1. I have argued the points covered in these opening paragraphs at greater length in J. Walter, 'Necessary Myths', *Journal of Australian Studies*, No. 26, 1990, pp. 26–36.

2. Compare Raymond Williams, 'Culture and Technology', in *The Politics of Modernism*, ed., Tony Pinkney (London, Verso, 1989), pp. 119–39.

3. See Julie James Bailey, 'Australian Television: Why it is the way it is', *Cinema Papers*, No. 23, September–October 1979, pp. 511–15, 584ff.; Ann Curthoys, 'The Getting of Television: Dilemmas in Ownership, Control and Culture, 1941–56', in A. Curthoys and J. Merritt, eds., *Better Dead than Red, Australia's First Cold War: 1945–1959, Vol. 2* (Sydney, Allen & Unwin, 1986), pp. 123–54; Sandra Hall, *Supertoy: 20 Years of Australian Television* (Melbourne, Sun Books, 1976); Cameron Hazlehurst, 'The Advent of Commercial TV', *Australian Cultural History*, No. 2, 1982–3, pp. 104–19; Margot Kerley, 'Commercial Television in Australia: Government Policy and Regulation, 1953 to 1963', PhD thesis, Australian National University, 1992.

4. Cited in Curthoys, 'The Getting of Television', p. 134, and see newspaper reports 15 December, 1952.

5. Quoted in Curthoys, 'The Getting of Television', p. 138.

6. Sir Richard Boyer, 'Television in Perspective', *The Australian Quarterly*, No. 26, September 1957, pp. 15–21.

7. G.S. Browne, 'Television: Friend or Enemy?', *Meanjin*, Vol. 13, No. 2, Winter 1954, p. 179.

8. Gerry Grant, 'T.V. and Us', *Overland*, No. 7, July 1956, pp. 7–8.

9. H.E. Beaver, President, the Australian Federation of Commercial Broadcasting Stations, March 1953, quoted in Curthoys, 'The Getting of Television', p. 143.

10. Hal Lashwood, 'Television and Australia', *Meanjin*, Vol. 13, No. 4, Summer 1954, p. 566.

11. A.F. Davies, 'Mass Communications', in A.F. Davies & S. Encel, eds., *Australian Society: A Sociological Introduction* (Melbourne, Cheshire, 1970).

12. This paragraph follows Geoffrey Bolton's concise summary in *The Oxford History of Australia*, Vol. 5 (Melbourne, Oxford University Press, 1990), pp. 128–30, but see also the works cited in note 3 above.

13. I am following Hazlehurst's argument about Menzies' inclinations and motives here; see his 'The Advent of Commercial TV', pp. 112–14.

14. Hazlehurst, 'The Advent of Commercial TV', p. 114.

15. 'Television' (editorial), *Meanjin*, Vol. 18, No. 4, December 1959, pp. 474–6; Kenneth Davidson, 'Profit—and Loss', in Mungo MacCallum, ed., *Ten Years of Television* (Melbourne, Sun Books, 1968), p. 17.

16. Helen Hughes, *The Impact of Television on the Australian Economy*, The Economic Society of Australia and New Zealand, New South Wales Branch, Economic Monograph No. 222, p. 5.

17. Cecil Holmes, 'Television in Australia: A Survey', *Meanjin*, Vol. 17, No. 1, April 1958, pp. 43–59.

18. This was forcefully brought home to me in a conversation with the distinguished expatriate Australian actor, John Bluthal, in London in December 1990.

19. The enormous popularity in the 1960s of Australian variety show hosts like Graham Kennedy notwithstanding. Programmes like 'In Melbourne Tonight' were based on US formats and formulae, and whatever the success of local adaptation, did not speak to issues of serious concern, and did not interpret the world in a distinctively Australian way.

20. Davidson, 'Profit—and Loss'.

21. Ibid., 'Profit—and Loss', p. 20.

22. Ibid., 'Profit—and Loss', p. 23.

23. Ibid., 'Profit—and Loss', p. 17.

24. See, for instance, Hall, *Supertoy*; Hazlehurst, 'The Advent of Commercial TV'.

25. See Bailey, 'Australian Television: Why it is the Way it is', especially p. 515.

26. See Stuart Cunningham, 'Docker: Criticism, History and Policy', *Media Information Australia*, No. 59, February 1991, pp. 27–30. Docker's thesis is discussed at length below.

27. Curthoys, 'The Getting of Television'.

28. Ibid., p. 154.

29. John Docker, 'Popular Culture versus the State: An Argument against Australian Content Regulations for Television', *Media Information Australia*, No. 59, February 1991, pp. 7–26.

30. Ibid., 'Popular Culture versus the State', p. 7.

31. See, for instance, Leicester Webb, 'The Social Control of Television', *Public Administration* (Sydney), September 1960, pp. 193–214.

32. Jennifer Craik, 'Popular, Commercial and National Imperatives of Australian Broadcasting', *Media Information Australia*, No. 59, February 1991, p. 35.

33. Davidson, 'Profit—and Loss'.

34. Bailey, 'Australian Television: Why it is the Way it is'; Cunningham, 'Docker: Criticism, History and Policy'.

35. Docker, 'Popular Culture versus the State', p. 24.

36. For further insight, see Graeme Base, *My Grandma Lived in Gooligulch* (Melbourne, Thomas Nelson, 1983).

37. Raymond Williams, 'Cinema and Socialism', in *The Politics of Modernism*, p. 110.

38. And for an alternative view of the carnivalesque, see Tony Bennett, 'Political and Theoretical Digressions', *Media Information Australia*, No. 59, February 1991, pp. 37–9.

39. Anthony Giddens, *Modernity and Self-Identity: Self and Society in the Late Modern Age* (Cambridge, Polity Press, 1991), p. 27.

40. S. Elizabeth Bird *et al.*, 'On Postmodernism and Articulation: An Interview with Stuart Hall', *Journal of Communication Enquiry*, No. 10, Summer 1986, p. 46.

41. Terry Eagleton, *Ideology: An Introduction*, (London, Verso, 1991), p. 40.

Crocodile Dundee and the Revival of American Virtue

RUTH BROWN

No popular representation of Australia in the 1980s received broader international circulation than the film *Crocodile Dundee*. In 1986, after a successful six months' run in Australia, it opened simultaneously in 900 cinemas in the US to become the highest grossing foreign film in US history.

It tells the story of Mick Dundee, a crocodile hunter from the Northern Territory, who is invited to New York by an American reporter. The innocence, good humour, resourcefulness and confident masculinity which Mick brings with him from the Australian outback seemed to have a particular appeal for Americans, and amongst the critical comment provoked by the film came the suggestion that it really said more about America than it did about Australia. Peter Ackroyd, for example wrote in *The Spectator*:

> Life in the Bush does in fact resemble that of the Old West...Dundee, wearing his Australian version of the stetson, acts like some representation of the old cowboy and thus reminds the American cinema audience of its more manly, heroic and...good humoured past.

Ruth Abbey and Jo Crawford, writing in *Meanjin*, go even further in claiming for *Crocodile Dundee* that it shows there is nothing seriously wrong with the American present:

> The film could only be an emollient to American audiences. Their society is witnessed through fresh eyes and found not to be wanting, or at least not in ways that a healthy dose of frontier morality can't cure...Blacks are in their place (as servants and attendants), women are in theirs, and even street terrorists are vanquished by a threat of their own medicine.[1]

There are good grounds for these writers' contentions that the 'America' re-affirmed by *Crocodile Dundee* is socially and politically conservative. In the Australian section of the film we learn that Sue, the American reporter, has a boy-friend who has been involved in protests against the political status quo, for instance against nuclear weapons. Mick remarks that such attitudes don't seem to matter very much in the outback, and later, when we meet Sue's boyfriend, we find that he is somewhat effete and foolish. Homosexuality is also ridiculed. By contrast, the world of Big Business is affirmed by Mick's being able to move in it comfortably. Sue is shown to have feminist leanings but when she tries to set out on her own in the outback, without Mick, she soon gets into trouble and her heroic male partner has to rescue her from a crocodile. Similarly in New York she is pleased to have Mick's protection when street terrorists threaten. The way he deals with them is memorable. 'That's not a *knife*' he says to them pityingly. He draws out his larger all-purpose bush knife. '*That's* a knife.' They flee, and an old order is forcefully confirmed.

Recently at a conference in Perth about 'Outside Images of Australia', Professor Albinski, director of the Centre for Australian and New Zealand Studies at Pennsylvania State University, re-affirmed that *Crocodile Dundee* is a film in which Americans can take comfort. Australia should be proud of the image presented, he said, because Mick has a certain lovable clumsiness and innocence with which Americans could identify.[2]

Professor Albinski's comments lead to the main point of my argument, which is that the 'Australia' represented in *Crocodile Dundee* has authority as an image because it meets certain requirements of the United States, Australia's most powerful political ally. Or, as Australian writer Robyn Davidson puts it: 'the power to describe rests with the powerful.'[3] It is not just that Americans are encouraged to see a more laid-back version of themselves in Mick Dundee: the film goes further in that it revives the sense that innocence is accompanied by virtue, ordained by God, and that this virtue justifies the use of superior weaponry, of the big knife.

Despite the humour and the sending up of the tarzan theme in the film, a sense of mystery, of spiritual presence, survives. In the outback, Mick is in contact with eternity, nature, and God, and they are all on his side. This serious proposition is conveyed beneath a level of cheerful mockery of man in communion with nature—Mick checks his watch before telling the time from the sun, but in a more serious moment he tells Sue, who has asked about Aboriginal land rights, that Australia is too vast and eternal for the petty question of present ownership to be at all relevant. (Protesting about nuclear weapons is deemed also to be contrary to the spirit of eternity.) Aborigines are seen not as possible owners of land, but as part of its eternal spirit—to which Mick has additional access via the Aboriginal tribe he says he grew up in. He has read the bible, and associates it with nature as if its message is the same. The apostles were fishermen like him, and God, he feels, would appreciate the Australian outback.

Mick's authority is associated with nature and with God, and what is more significant, it is backed up by a very big knife. The eternal values are armed.

This, I suggest, is the lasting significance of the film. It uses 'Australia' to restore America's sense of manifest destiny and to justify the use of superior weaponry by linking power with innocence and virtue. To say, as Peter Ackroyd does, that Mick is like some old cowboy, reminding the American cinema audience of its more heroic past is to overlook the messianic thrust of American identity. Mick is not just manly, heroic and good humoured enough to cheer up world-weary New Yorkers; he is God's mate, and his knife is bigger than anyone else's. Some of the film's lasting effects can be measured, for example, in increased sales of Foster's lager and in a tourist boom at Kakadu National Park. The unmeasurable, but more significant effect may be that it helped to revive America's sense of virtue following the debacle of Vietnam, and to make possible the righteous confidence with which the Gulf War was fought.

'America remains Christian,' writes Nicholas von Hoffman in the *Independent*, 'and anyone who fails to understand that fails to understand America.'[4] The pledge of allegiance recited daily by American school children confirms that God and country are inter-related, and could well lead to the conclusion that wars are fought and superior power used in a kind of holy crusade against the ungodly. With this background, Americans would be more likely than Australians or Britons to note that Mick has read his bible, and that he thinks God is a part of the outback. In *Crocodile Dundee 2*, Mick has the support of the wild birds, and of Aborigines mysteriously summoned to his aid in his battle against a gang of international drug traffickers: again, right is clearly on his side and the power with which he vanquishes the evil enemy is associated with the forces of nature and eternity.

Because America sees itself as a Christian nation, the impact the film made can appropriately be considered against a background of theology, and I want to draw on Reinhold Niebuhr's explanation of the American state of mind. In his book *The Irony of American History*[5] Niebuhr talks about the American founding fathers' conviction that their country was called out of a wicked and corrupt old world and set apart by Providence to create a new humanity and restore man's lost innocence. The American legend of success and victory fostered and perpetuated what Niebuhr refers to as the illusions of innocence and virtue. He demonstrates that these illusions were preserved well past the nation's infancy and into national adulthood. In the twentieth century, he goes on to argue, America found itself in possession of immense and undreamed-of power, and compelled to use this power in ways that were not innocent and that induced guilt. In clinging to 'infant illusions of innocence' in order to assuage this guilt, America, writes the theologian, is 'involved in ironic perils which compound the experiences of Babylon and Israel'—the perils of over-weening power and overweening virtue.

Directly contrary to Niebuhr's warning, *Crocodile Dundee* re-affirms American innocence and signals that there is no need to feel guilty about the exercise of power. The film irons out the irony implicit in the combination of Babylonian power and Israelite virtue, a resolution which may have encouraged Americans to feel happier about their use of power. At the time of the Gulf War, Alexander Cockburn wrote in the *New*

Statesman[6] that the majority of Americans were violently idealistic and that they believed that a just war was being fought in the Gulf by a principled government. He might have added that the government used its big knife. President Bush had said that this time it would not be like Vietnam, where US troops had to fight with 'one hand tied behind their back'. Later, he re-affirmed America's manifest destiny: 'By the grace of God, America won the Cold War.'

If, as I have argued, *Crocodile Dundee* revives and popularises the conviction that God and America are mates, and sanctions the use of power to force the rest of the world to conform, what can be done to counter-act such a powerful exercise in hegemony? The simple answer is, very little. The most likely model from cultural theory to explain the film's impact is that of the Frankfurt school. According to this school of thought, popular culture is an instrument of domination because it is circulated and produced within a centralised and organised market which has enough money, power, and technology to produce its own version of reality. *Crocodile Dundee* appears to fit this model. Graeme Turner explains that it was distributed by a major American company, supported with an advertising and promotional budget bigger than the original cost of making the film. In twelve days it earned more in the box office in the US than it had taken in the preceding six months in Australia.[7] As a dependent economy, Australia does not have control over its own representations. Turner shows how the 'brutal logic of the market' ensures that Australian films need to demonstrate their commercial viability in the foreign market-place to get financial backing. This could mean that 'Australia' in popular culture will continue to mean whatever its more powerful allies are judged to want it to mean, images of Australia being adapted to suit the requirements of the overseas market just as wool and meat once did. Furthermore, in a trans-oceanic leap, these powerful meanings will be the ones most readily available to Australians at home. Tony Thwaites makes this point about Peter Carey's novel *Illywhacker*.[8] At the end of the novel, 'Australia' is seen as a shop, selling novelties to foreign tourists and to any natives who can afford the entrance money. In other words, the shop's customers have no choice but to see Australia through foreign eyes, as tourists. It is difficult to do other than consent to the image offered by commodified popular entertainment if it is the only product on offer, and according to Professor Albinski, in America at least there is no real alternative to the *Crocodile Dundee* model which he sees as a positive representation of Australia. He explained that chances for Americans to learn about Australia through the media were likely to remain limited, as only one American newspaper employs a resident Australian correspondent. To illustrate the general level of ignorance, Albinski cited a television newsreader who presented a story in front of an upside-down map of Australia.

There are other models of Australia apart from *Crocodile Dundee*, of course, but a film industry dependent on overseas earnings has limited scope to portray them. I don't know enough about Australian cinema to be able to cite many examples, but I can refer to one Australian film which refutes the contention in *Crocodile Dundee* that nuclear weapons, and protesting about them, are irrelevant in the Australian outback. When nuclear testing took place at Maralinga in the 1950s, a film was made about the sufferings of the Warburton Range Aborigines who lived in the affected area. In their book about the 1950s, Lees and Senyard refer to the outrage provoked by the film when it was shown to audiences in South Australia at the time.[9] It is still in the archives, referred to as the Warburton Range film, and it is difficult to imagine that sufficient funding would ever be made available to ensure that it had wider circulation, even though, as Lees and Senyard record, audiences were interested and responded with outrage to what they saw.

What role can universities play in ensuring that there *are* alternatives to the views perpetrated by the mass culture industry? It is possible, as Simon During argues in his article 'Professing the Popular',[10] for the academy to play its part in resisting the hegemonic representations of consumerist popular culture, but the effectiveness of such resistance is limited. As During concedes when talking about the Birmingham school of cultural studies, efforts to increase awareness of the heterogeneity of cultural production are almost always gestural, both because they are not connected to any institutions that might actually change the structures of cultural production, and because the power of the market is so strong. Furthermore, where *Crocodile Dundee* is concerned, it is particularly difficult for anyone to encourage viewers' political sensitivity and a sense of history, which is what During says we should be doing, about a film that is such good fun. To inform people that the film they thought was a good laugh is actually a hegemonic code of representation seducing them into accepting the values of the new right, sounds patronising. Malvolio in *Twelfth Night* is asked whether, just because he is virtuous, there must be no cakes and ale, and it could easily be seen as Malvolio-like self-righteousness to deny that the politically incorrect can ever be funny.

Crocodile Dundee is particularly difficult to resist, not only because it offers the cakes and ale of comedy, but also because it usurps the moral tone more usually associated with 'high' culture with its elitist tradition: if there is to be a distinction between culture and anarchy it is definitely on the side of culture. As Ruth Abbey and Jo Crawford have pointed out, Mick Dundee has elements of Davy Crockett, the outback clown who can out-do the city-slickers for all his apparent simplicity. But on a higher cultural plane he is also related to Fenimore Cooper's fictional hero Leatherstocking, to Daniel Boone (celebrated by Byron in *Don Juan*) whose links with God and eternity were fostered by the Indian tribe which adopted him, and even to Thoreau who also saw himself as a spiritual hunter. Just as Mick cheers up world-weary New Yorkers, Thoreau found that the eternal spirit of nature experienced in the wilderness had the power to revitalise city-dwellers.

> Behold how these cities are refreshed by the mere tradition, or the imperfectly transmuted fragrance and flavour of these wild fruits.[11]

In one episode, *Crocodile Dundee* stresses an alignment with high culture by condemning the popular. Mick's New York hotel room has a television set: he has only ever seen television once before and so he is curious and switches it on. *I Love Lucy* is about to start. Commenting that the same programme was on last time he saw television, he switches it off again. The film and all it represents is thus set on a higher cultural plane than mere television comedy. Mick has read the bible (all of it), he has learnt from nature, which the Romantic poets tell us is a better educator than books, and he doesn't watch television. Nothing could be further from the 'zones of contestation' by which Stuart Hall sees popular culture issuing a challenge to elitist ways of seeing. *Crocodile Dundee* blurs the distinction between high and popular culture, puts God in his heaven and makes all right with the world.

Yet another difficulty in mounting any effective challenge to such a successful hegemonic exercise may lie in a human propensity to hope that despite all the evidence to the contrary this really is the case. God *is* in his heaven: the biggest knives *are* held by the most virtuous: all *is* right with the world. 'The innocent prurience of our tabloid souls,' writes Richard Corliss, 'suggests that a deep part of us craves for people to be good, and for beginnings, at least, to be happy.'[12]

Hence the success of *Crocodile Dundee* . The only optimistic note I can offer about challenging the hegemony of the American Right is that, while flattering versions of America proffered by the Australian film industry are almost bound to be accepted, resistance might come from home-grown American products. In a recent *Time* essay, Richard Brookhiser argues that the ideology of White Anglo-Saxon Protestantism, of Wasp-dom, can be defended on the grounds that it always signified a commitment to hard work and to justice and that, before George Bush at least, it contained the correctives for its own vices. 'The best defence of Waspdom,' he writes, 'is that it always contained people who knew that slavery was wrong, and when it came to a fight, they won the war and the argument.'[13]

George Bush has not totally won the war or the argument about America's right to lead a New World order based on 'our civilised values', despite all the help he has had from *Crocodile Dundee*. In the film *Dances with Wolves*, the hero John Dunbar finds that the American ideal is incompatible with justice: he comes down on the side of the Indians, and nature and God seem to be on that side too. In this film, innocence and virtue are aligned with the opposition: all the white Americans have are the big knives.

In offering America such a re-assuring version of its uncorrected waspish self, *Crocodile Dundee* may have ensured that 'Australia' will remain fixed as a site for American conservatism, while the possibility of resistance is signalled by more liberal models produced by the home market.

Notes

1. Ruth Abbey and Jo Crawford, 'Crocodile Dundee or Davy Crockett?' *Meanjin*, Vol. 46, No. 2, June 1987, pp. 145–52.

2. Professor Albinski's paper is summarised by Michael Casey in 'Hogan's Film Role Positive: US Professor', *West Australian*, 9 July 1992, p. 34.

3. Robyn Davidson, 'The Mythological Crucible', *Australia: Beyond the Dreamtime* (London, 1987), pp. 233–4.

4. Nicholas von Hoffman, 'God's Own Country', *The Independent*, 18 April 1992.

5. Reinhold Niebuhr, *The Irony of American History* (New York, 1952) and commentary by C. Vann Woodward in the Norton Critical Edition of William Faulkner, *The Sound and the Fury* (New York, 1987), p. 197–8.

6. Alexander Cockburn, 'The TV War', *New Statesman and Society*, 8 March 1991, pp. 14–15.

7. Graeme Turner, 'Crocodile Dundee, 10BA, and the Future of the Australian Film Industry', *Australian Studies*, No. 2, 1989, pp. 93–103.

8. Tony Thwaites, 'More Tramps at Home: Seeing Australia First', *Meanjin*, Vol. 46, No. 3, pp. 400–9.

9. Stella Lees and June Senyard, *The 1950s* (Melbourne, 1987), pp. 96–7.

10. Simon During, 'Professing the Popular', *Meanjin*, Vol. 49, No. 3, Spring 1990, pp. 481–91.

11. Thoreau quoted by Richard Slotkin, *Regeneration Through Violence: The Mythology of the American Frontier 1600–1860* (Middletown,

Conn., 1973), p. 525. I have drawn heavily on the ideas in this book, particularly on Chapter One, 'Myth and Literature in a New World'.

12. Richard Corliss, 'Scenes From a Break-up', *Time*, 31 August 1992, p. 42.

13. Richard Brookhiser, 'We Can All Share American Culture', *Time*, 31 August 1992, p. 52.

The Boys from the Bush: Television Co-production in the 1990s

IAN CRAVEN

> Leslie, a rather naive young Englishman in his 20s who has lost his job and whose wife has left him, is on his way to Australia, where he plans to use his redundancy money to explore the countryside and decide if he wants to emigrate. His first stop is to be Melbourne where he is to stay with his father's cousin Reg, Reg's wife Doris and their daughter, Arlene. Reg and Doris emigrated from Shepherd's Bush more than twenty years before and Leslie assumes they will, by now, be totally Australian. Arlene, who was born in Melbourne is Australian...Doris just a little bit so...Reg is as determinedly Shepherd's Bush as the day he left...with not a good word to say for Australia in general and for Melbourne in particular.
>
> Reg, an ex-union man, has recently gone into partnership with Dennis, an Australian in his 40s...fighting desperately to keep his grip on youth and a variety of young women. Together they run 'Melbourne Confidential'...part marriage bureau, part detective agency and part anything that brings in a buck...

The Boys From the Bush is a ten-part television comedy series co-produced in 1990 by the independent British company Cinema Verity, in collaboration with Entertainment Media Australia for transmission by the BBC and the Seven Network. It was broadcast on Friday evenings at 9.25pm in the UK, and achieved reasonable, if not spectacular, ratings of about 5m viewers in an always difficult schedule slot. A second series was commissioned and produced in mid-1991 and was first transmitted in Britain in Spring 1992. The time slot remained 9.25pm and ratings for this series rose to an average of 6.3m viewers (BARB figures).

Critical response to both series was mixed. Previews promised British audiences 'an enjoyable antidote to those Aussie soaps that show only the up side of Down Under' (*The People*, 20 January 1991), but thought it 'too much to hope for a new popular drama just now based on detective work' (*The Daily Telegraph*, 21 January 1991). Reviews were generally more appreciative:

> Like *Minder*, *The Boys From The Bush* combines cynical edge with heartwarming witty optimism, as some sort of happy ending emerges from Reg's clueless ducking and diving. As a bonus it features a visible 'er indoors' in domestic scenes offering some of the most biting satire on working-class mores since the golden years of *Till Death Us Do Part*... (*The Daily Telegraph*, 26 January 1991).

The very few editorial column-inches devoted to the series contented themselves with the standard anecdotal discourse credited to actors by the popular press: under a by-line reading 'Yes, I'm a mug too says Mark', actor Mark Haddigan revealed to readers of *The Daily Mirror* (26 January 1991) that he too, like his screen counterpart Leslie, seems to get 'ripped off a lot':

> I think people must see me coming, because I must have done some of the worst deals you can imagine...I'm probably a bit more outgoing than Leslie, and I hope I'm a little more sensible...He's a big softie, his self-esteem couldn't be much lower. His wife's left him and he's totally shot to bits...But at least I've been a little bit luckier with women...

On the evidence of reception left to the clippings libraries then, the series seems to have created few waves. The 'qualities' grew less impressed by the show as it extended (by episode five *The Independent* (22 February 1991) was describing it as a 'prefabricated and rather depressing commercial comedy drama') whilst the tabloids became mechanically enthusiastic (*The Daily Mirror* (22 February 1991) saw it as 'a smashing low-life comedy thriller'). But commentators on either side found the programme uncontroversial, and with few exceptions offered it neither serious condemnation not outright praise. Rather, reactions were automatic, with little in the show seemingly unsettling the protocols surrounding popular television's insertion into the everyday discourse of both the tabloid and quality newspapers. From the perspective of a concern with Australian popular culture however, *The Boys From The Bush* deserves much closer attention than this, and as a *co-production*, arguably represents a significant departure in recent popular Australian TV drama. One might take this move to be of particular significance in the context of a BASA conference focussed on Australia in 'other' popular cultures, for the series deals precisely with the penetration of 'otherness' into daily life, and with popular culture as a site for the articulation of (or resistance to) ideas of Australian-ness. As one confused, but suggestive review put it (*The Sunday Telegraph*, 17 March 1991) 'the characters look to be involved in a London sitcom transposed to Oz'.

Industry Context

The production of *The Boys From The Bush* needs first to be understood in the context of the highly unstable Australian television industry of the later 1980s. Local independent drama production, often involving collaboration with an overseas partner, had expanded rapidly during the closing years of the decade as Australia's commercial networks (7, 9, 10) found themselves increasingly unable to maintain their traditionally substantial 'in house' support for the drama sector. Always nervous of involvement in this, the most expensive of TV genres, network uncertainty reached new levels in the late 1980s following the protracted media-ownership struggles of 1985 and 1986, which left all three networks with new management teams and their owners facing massive interest repayments on loans secured against other corporate properties (Kitchen, 1989). With 1987's new media ownership laws also forcing station sales, familiar patterns of ownership and control underwent rapid change (Sadlier, 1990). In this context, short-term profitability came to dictate programme policy to an even greater extent than ever. With programme production-costs escalating, the networks gradually severed links with the local 'indies', and the importing of cheap overseas dramas recommended itself early as a strategy for easing liquidity problems. Many well-known British dramas were purchased in the period (*Eastenders*, *Howard's Way*) and became ratings successes throughout Australia.

This shift in turn had predictable consequences. In response to the ever-more conspicuous presence of imported materials in prime-time TV slots, the Australian Broadcasting Tribunal (ABT), the local industry regulating body, began an enquiry in 1987 into the precise levels of Australian 'content' in all genres of production. In this arena, 'content' became a nebulous concept, which could refer to financing, creative control, the nationality of production personnel or crucially, the origin of the script (a key issue in the production of *Boys*). Existing legislation ruled that each station was required to air a little over 100 hours per year of new Australian drama in peak viewing hours, a figure which all the relevant Unions and Trade Associations were campaigning to increase. At the same time (Rodgers, 1987), the ABT's own statistical research was showing that the networks' profitability was dropping rapidly (down by 12 per cent between 1985 and early 1987), echoing the gradual slow-down of the Australian economy in the mid-1980s. This decline was represented most graphically for the networks by their falling income from advertising fees.

Pressure also came from another direction, for as advertising revenues continued to fall steadily in the mid-80s, private funds for investment in drama production also began to disappear. The Division 10BA tax write-off scheme first introduced in 1978 was by 1985 offering much-reduced incentives to possible investors and funds from that source dwindled rapidly. The years 1987 and 1988 saw a six-year low of just $83.5m from 10BA (Spear, 1989, p. 22), and as pre-sales of projects to the networks became rarer, private investment became correspondingly riskier, leaving independent companies created in response to the investment-boom generated by 10BA bereft of pre-production finance as well as a guaranteed outlet for their finished product. As the indies battled to raise revenue for production, the networks struggled to service a growing corporate indebtedness. The downward spiral that resulted culminated in 1989. By that year (Kitchen, 1989) it was estimated that the three major networks owed a little over $2,000m to their financial backers and even the top-rated 9 Network could only record an operating loss of $44m. As part of its licence renewal process the ABT instigated an enquiry into the financial viability of the networks, amidst considerable uncertainty about their ability to continue to trade. Uncertainty was justified when first the 7, and then the 10 network went into receivership in 1990, postponing yet again plans to introduce 'pay' satellite TV to Australia (Atkins, 1991).

Corporate mayhem on this scale forced most local independents to reconsider their production options. Some began to lobby the ABT with a view to getting quotas increased, and thereby enlarging the 'protected' space into which their product might flow. Most indies however remained sceptical about increasing quotas at a time of overall network contraction, and were often not necessarily ideologically disposed to the cultural nationalism long implicit in polemics for increased quotas. Most turned their attention overseas, attracted not only by the possibility of bypassing or supplementing Australian backing, but also by the chances of avoiding foreign quota legislation (Spear, 1989, p. 22). Collaborations with overseas partners, many felt, could both help in securing pre-production finance and maximising opportunities of distribution. As a result, TV producers in Australia increasingly became TV *co-producers*, operating trans-nationally.

Those familiar with the longer-term history of film and television production in Australia might sense a number of wheels turning full-circle at this point. It was after all precisely to combat the supposed cultural effects of a film industry dependent on sporadic international co-production that successive governments from the late 1960s had intervened into the industry, hoping to help foster a more culturally 'exact' cinema and to secure Australian employment within it. It was with these ambitions in mind that the craft unions and trade associations had collaborated so enthusiastically over the same period. Through much of the 1970s and early 1980s the 'protective' rhetorics of the culture industry and those of employee associations had effectively echoed each other, and in so far as these rhetorics held definitional power, had helped sustain a nationally conscious audience which could support 'indigenous' Australian production.

Others contested these positions of course, just as they had around the introduction of commercial TV into Australia which Jim Walter discusses elsewhere in this volume. The more commercially minded had long argued that an obsessive concern for cultural exactitude and employment protection were not in the longer-term interests of the film industry, which should seek to operate on a more international level. The 1980s saw these discourses reinforced by the evidence of worsening economic conditions, and governments committed to reduced public spending. Film producers such as Tony Ginnane and Terry Bourke, who had regularly argued in the 1970s that Australian cinema would remain dependent and parochial so long as it operated within narrow national confines, were joined in the 1980s by a new generation of young independent TV producers such as Phil Gerlach (head of CIC Entertainment) who also maintained (Rodgers, 1987, p. 20) that the protection of local employment continued to limit the overseas sales potentials of a number of TV mini-series:

> For Americans to buy foreign mini-series, the series need some identifiable American faces. A good example is *The Challenge* [a 4-part series dealing with Australia's 1983 America's Cup victory and subsequent defence]. If the producers had been able to use American actors to play the American roles, the series would have been more commercially successful. This series should have had a first-run syndicated market.

By the late 1980s these were persuasive arguments. Even as stringent control of Australian 'content' produced the remarkable spectacle of Australians playing Americans, or Brits, in the eighties' mini-series—a fascinating inversion of traditional mimetic power-relations—most parties did come to recognise in the period that whatever the fascination for semioticians in that phenomenon, too tight a degree of control could certainly limit the overseas potential of much product. This significant change in institutional thinking was indexed by the AFC's decision in 1985 to encourage international co-productions, and to contemplate introducing mechanisms to realise such projects (Court, 1986). This new consensus on co-production between the state- and private-financing agencies marked a dramatic shift in the industry's understanding of questions of Australian 'content' and its subsequent depiction of the Australian environment.

Since 1987, most Australian independent producers have worked increasingly hard to secure overseas co-production deals. Success with early projects has allowed a number of these smaller Australian companies to deficit finance on subsequent programmes against the promise of foreign pre-sales. The most successful (Kennedy-Miller, Roadshow, Coote & Carroll, JNP) have achieved a real continuity of production through the period on this basis and become some of the most respected sources of 'quality' television drama.

Recognition of the importance of international collaboration has forced some modification of more stringent protective measures. It is still necessary to obtain 10BA Certification before assistance from either the Film Finance Corporation (AFFC) (effectively a film bank, set up in 1988) or tax concessions can be considered—an 'eligible' proposal is still defined (AFC, 1991, p. 2) in terms of a project:

made wholly or substantially in Australia and [which] has significant
Australian content as defined in the legislation (this includes consideration
of the subject matter; the place or places where the program is to be made;
the nationalities and places of residence of the creative personnel, the
production and the copyright holders; and the sources of finance).

But AFC treaty legislation clearly acknowledges the importance of international co-productions, and seeks to encourage them on a limited scale.
In this context, rigorously 'purist' definitions of Australian 'content' so
characteristic of 1970s culture-rhetoric, give way to the principle of
reciprocity. An 'official' co-production is now defined as:

> a project made pursuant to a treaty or bi-lateral or multi-lateral arrangement
> between an authority of the federal government and a foreign counterpart
> body...

According to the AFC, treaties, bi-lateral and multi-lateral 'arrangements'
were introduced to encourage producers who wished to produce projects:

- in collaboration with foreign colleagues;
- where the storyline demands foreign creative participation;
- where the budget demands substantial foreign equity.

The legislation also stipulates that there must be a producer from each of
the two countries involved 'and a balance between the Australian financial
equity in the project and the Australian creative components'. At present
this figure is 30 per cent, with 'creative equity' calculated by:

- a points system for key cast and crew;
- an equivalent percentage of other case and crew, and
- an equivalent percentage in the amount of money spent in Australia or
  on Australian elements within the production budget.

Interestingly, it has been the smaller independents which have most
frequently taken advantage of these treaty provisions, and arguably
exploited them to produce innovative Australian drama precisely to meet
the criteria necessary for certification. Developing projects 'where the
storyline demands foreign creative participation' indeed became something
of a sub-industry in the later 1980s (*Call Me Mister*, *The Brides of Christ*)
but one which, in a number of instances, produced some very different
representations of Australia up to an including *The Boys From The Bush*.
Ironically, with such treaty legislation in place it actually became easier
for Australian producers to support measures designed to protect local
employees. Matt Carroll (of Roadshow, Coote & Carroll) illustrates the
shifting register of the debate here very plainly (Rodgers, 1987, p. 21):

There is certainly a case for local protection. It does none of us good to produce mid-Pacific product. This middle-position results in local product losing all identity. Australian stories and series should not be Americanised; hybrids don't work...

Production

In arguing that a consciousness of the need to collaborate internationally has produced some unusual television drama we need to judge individual instances on their particular merits. Co-production has produced some fascinating 'hybrids' that do seem to 'work' over new ground. Not every instance of collaboration is in any sense 'critical' however in the terms that I will claim for *Boys From The Bush*. One need only consider the case of *Families*, a soap opera set *simultaneously* in Britain and Australia, to witness the lengths to which narrative motivation may be strained to exploit the possibilities of the Anglo-Australian audience, conjured up in the minds of producers by treaty legislation and the success of a flood of imported serials (*Neighbours, Richmond Hill, Home and Away*). *Boys* does however exist very much in relation to these programmes and clearly 'took off' from the prominence of Australian dramas on British air-waves from the mid-eighties (e.g. *Prisoner Cell Block H, Richmond Hill, Skyways, Rafferty's Rules* and a stream of mini-series). The argument here is that *Boys'* status as a co-production gives it a rather different edge, a feature of its attempt to manage both British and Australian audiences explicitly, as it works not by erasing their respective positions in relation to some anonymous mid-Pacific fiction, but by dramatising and articulating intensely local pleasures and recognitions in both directions. In *Boys* the comparative element which helps meet the requirements of co-production legislation thus becomes the focus of the fiction itself.

From this perspective, *Boys* instances a much less opportunist impulse within the market I have been describing that might first appear to be the case, with the idea for the series long preceding the creation of the mechanisms that would allow the basic 'concept' to be realised. The project's relatively long gestation period probably accounts in part for its marked difference from other topical co-productions. The impulse to exploit a market opportunity created by the 'Aussie invasion' of British TV clearly came second (perhaps quite a close second) to the desire to produce a drama on Anglo-Australian relations in a popular form. Executive producer Verity Lambert has described this in terms of 'images' and 'deals' (Craven, 1991):

> in this instance...the image came before the production deal. Sometimes in co-productions, the desire to do the co-production and get the finance together energises the idea, so that the idea comes out of the financing,

rather than the finance coming out of the idea. In this instance the idea
came first...

In fact the origins of the series go back to 1979, when Lambert first visited
Australia, and began to think about how a drama which would examine
the contrasting characters of British and Australian culture might be
developed. *Neighbours* however clearly supplied a crucial stimulus, and a
horizon of audience expectations that could be played against:

> I wanted to make a series, that shows people that it's not like *Neighbours*,
> which shows that Australians are quite funny, but also have a lot of
> misconceptions about each other...one of the big misconceptions is that
> they're not a multicultural country...when I started thinking about it I
> decided that it had to be about new Australians and old Australians...

After lengthy discussions on the project, and diversions into other
productions, Lambert's decisive move was to approach writer Douglas
Livingstone, a former collaborator at Thames TV, who agreed to outline
characters and potential storylines following a first trip to Australia in
1989. The BBC was envisaged from the outset as the probable purchaser,
and Lambert's existing 'output deal' with the Corporation helped the series
to find early support from Jonathan Powell (then head of Drama) and
Michael Grade (then head of BBC1). The series was pitched verbally by
Lambert and Livingstone, rather than being offered as a treatment:

> What I tend to do is to go in and pitch something verbally because outlines
> and treatments are so difficult...all drama depends on characters, and
> characters depend on dialogue and scripts...if you have a treatment you fall
> into formulas...and it's very hard to make the characters live...

Changes within the BBC Drama department in 1989 threatened the success
of the project, however, at an early stage. When Powell moved up to head
BBC1 and Michael Grade left for Channel Four, Lambert's output deal was
in fact terminated, but Peter Goodchild, Powell's successor as Head of
Drama was also keen on the idea and commissioned four scripts.
Approaching a potential broadcaster for backing in this way was
undoubtedly risky (the series existed as little more than a sketchy scenario
peopled by shadowy characters) but it certainly helped keep pre-production
costs far lower than would have been possible had Lambert and Livingstone
approached a private investment house of bank for a credit-line.

Even with such high-level support within the BBC, and Lambert's own
proven track record, the assembly of the *Boys* deal went far from smoothly.
With the BBC's guarantee on the table, Lambert approached Channel 7 in
Sydney, who expressed interest in the idea, and agreed to co-develop the
project if the BBC would commit further. Unfortunately the arrival of the
first script in Australia coincided almost exactly with Channel 7 passing

into the hands of the Australian receiver. Amidst network confusion down under, the BBC eventually fully funded the production, with Channel 7 then paying the BBC for Australian transmission rights. Remarkably, despite the sums of money involved in the purchase, Channel 7 has still in fact not aired the programme and has no plans to do so. At the time of writing, the network has also declined offers to buy-back the series and its producers are now in negotiation with the ABC over the screening of Series Two.

With basic funding in place, Lambert approached Entertainment Media Pty as a possible collaborator, a company part-owned by Fred Schepisi, which had overseen the Australian post-production of Lambert's feature film *A Cry In The Dark* (1989). Entertainment Media would become executive producers in Australia and, being based in Melbourne, were conveniently located for the series, which was conceived from the outset (Craven, 1991) as being set in the Victorian capital. On a day-to-day basis the production was overseen by Jane Scott, and the series was crewed entirely by 'Australian-based' technicians:

> I was about to say Australian...but there's such a mixture of people there that almost nobody is Australian...Chris Haywood turned out to be English...we cast Chris, and all the Australians said, 'you know he's English...he just doesn't sound Australian...'

Australian Actors Equity had been approached early, and the ensemble-structure of the casting involved created few union problems, as the series clearly met the 'nett employment benefit' criteria of the appropriate legislative and trade arrangements (AFC, 1991)—only two English actors would need to be imported. Interestingly, the employment of an English writer caused some difficulties, but Lambert was eventually able to persuade the Writer's Guild of the importance of the 'outside' perspective that a foreign writer would bring to Reg Toomer's character:

> although Reg lives there he is still an outsider, and there's the whole energy that comes from this appalling person who has lived in the country, and kind of quite likes it, but actually he doesn't like anywhere really...he isn't going to like Shepherd's Bush when he comes back, it isn't the way it was anymore...

Shooting of the first series took twenty weeks on a ten-day 'turnaround' from June to October 1990. On series one, each director shot two episodes for four weeks. After two months spent arranging music tracks and organising credit sequences, completed episodes were delivered to the BBC by December, and the series featured as a 'flagship show' for the New Year, first airing on Friday 18 January. Overall costs were later estimated at around £2.75m, leaving the series budget slightly below average drama costs at the point of its production.

What emerges clearly from this rapid account is the central importance of the Lambert–Livingstone collaboration. Very few popular series in the 1990s are scripted by a single writer, and undoubtedly this lent a rare integrity to the drama (attempts to share the writer on series two with Australian writers were abandoned after problems over characterisation). Several Livingstone hallmarks are much in evidence: the gradual exploration of characters' obsessions from episode to episode; a subtle playing upon the cumulative knowledge of the audience, which enables characters to transcend the typage which defines their basic comic oppositions; the sub-plotting around minor-characters whose storylines converge with the principle line of narrative; leading from this 'implosion' of narrative, a celebration of coincidence and the illogical that verges on farce; above all, the searching for the eye-catching and the surreal within the commonplace and the everyday. Crucially, one need only view early *Minder* (1979–), *Fox* (1980) or even *Reilly—Ace of Spies* (1983) to recognise how smoothly these preoccupations mesh with those of much of Lambert's definitive work.

In *Boys* these fascinations also synchronise perfectly with the particular form of the drama. Technically, *Boys* is probably best understood not simply as a *series*, but as a *sequential series*, perhaps the most distinctive form of popular television drama in the 1980s. The sequential series fuses the ongoing but episodic narrative of the serial, with the narrative-per-week developing from an unchanging 'base' situation of the series. In *Boys*, potential romance between Arlene and Leslie and the clearly unresolved question of Dennis' relationship with his ex-wife, Corrie, provide a continuous narrative thread across episodes, whilst episode-specific storylines provide alternative pleasures on a more immediate basis. Instalment titles ('The Stuffed Platypus', 'Going Walkabout', 'Multiculture' etc.) mark these discrete progressions, which typically occupy lower and lower profiles as the sequential series extends. This fusion of the 'open' structures most typical of soap opera with the more 'closed' forms of the crime/adventure series or the sitcom has characterised much popular TV drama in the 1980s. In *Boys* the fusion serves the dual roles of (a) allowing a fascinating parody of the soap opera's romance-centred narrative (Arlene's increasingly desperate attempts to corner Leslie), and (b) enabling diversions into fantastic situations—often equally indebted to other television genres—without compromising the basic narrative scenario (episode one has Reg hired by a middle-man to buy a stuffed platypus which he later discovers is stuffed with packets of crushed rhino horn, an illegal and highly-priced aphrodisiac).

It is the tendency towards the surreal, the ludicrous or farcical that clearly appealed to Livingstone about Melbourne. His research visit took him around much of the country but he comments most tellingly in interview on the value of the Victorian capital to the project (Craven, 1992):

> In the end I liked Melbourne best, because it's easier to complain about Melbourne than anywhere else, and the suburbs in Melbourne are a revelation, if you get out to places like Sunshine, it is very depressing, and there's miles and miles of sameness, and it's cold, and it's wet and it's not what you expect in Australia at all, and because I wanted to write comedy this seemed to me the best location for it. I liked a lot of other things too...

Livingstone's writing has always been characterised by a strong sense of place, and the portrayal of lives lived out in connection with very particular environments. Despite his disdain for the 'flatness' of 'TV naturalism', Melbourne clearly appealed at the level of its naturalist surface, offering an abundance of contrasting settings for successive episodes, that would also introduce new images of Australia to British TV viewers and by implication critique other current dramas. At the same time the very 'sameness' of Melbourne would provide a baseline against which increasingly implausible/fantastic plot-structures could be extended.

Boys was certainly promoted and sold in the UK as a show that would give the TV viewer a rather different look at Australia, and was contrasted specifically with the most well-known Australian imports, especially *Neighbours* and *Home and Away*. It was around this comparison that *Boys* was often credited with a greater realism; and the show did seem to proceed through a variety of carefully structured contrasts with these privileged inter-texts; the bleak prospect of working-class Anzac Drive in a remote Melbourne suburb jarred with the cosy affluence of *Neighbours'* Ramsay Street somewhere on the fashionable fringe of an unnamed Australian city; smoky RSL clubs contrasted with *Neighbours'* designer bush-bar at the Lassiters motel; chilly, windswept St Kilda waterfronts were scarcely recognisable as beach-scapes to viewers more familiar with the sun-kissed playground of *Home and Away*; and absolutely nowhere to be seen were the majestic panoramas of outback scenery celebrated week-in week-out in *The Flying Doctors*. Juxtaposed comically against the unremarkability of these settings, one of the series' most telling running gags has Leslie endlessly frustrated in his dreams of visiting the 'real' Australia, which he defines in terms of the outback, exotic flora and fauna, and a catalogue of typed characters from drovers to crocodile-hunters. Only when he returns to London does his sense of connection with Melbourne strike home.

Comedy and Realism

Boys From The Bush can then be understood as a realist drama, whose particular assembly of devices and conventions claims to take us closer to an Australian 'truth' than its better-known competitors for air-space. At the same time, it is inclined towards a certain comic 'excess' which strains against the realist effect that its use of Melbourne's 'sameness' seeks to generate. The comic excess is largely social of course, rather than linguistic, for the commitment to realism ensures an adherence to 'realist' codes rather than any deconstruction of them for the purposes of 'gagging' or special effect. *Boys* is thus close to the traditions of British comedy that John Ellis (1975) has described well in relation to Ealing comedy cinema of the later 1940s:

> Ealing comedy belongs to the type which deals with the disruption of social reality, something that is often defined as the playing out of 'base urges': the enactment of desires that are not socially sanctioned. This applies as much to hatreds and utopian desires as it does to sexuality: comedy is the space in which these motivations can be revealed and played through (p. 113).

This tension between the social reality of 'down to earth' imagery and the increasingly tortuous trajectories of narratives driven by the very 'basest' of urges, establishes an axis around which the meanings of the programme are largely organised. It also indicates shifts from the Ealing model, as the comedy dramatises resentments and senses of guilt which can be identified with senses of national, rather than class resentments, as well as aspirations and utopian desires.

At the centre of the drama stands the comic partnership of Reg Toomer (Tim Healy) and Dennis Tontine (Chris Haywood). Reg is a 'ten quid tourist' who migrated to Australia in the late 1960s but has made little or no attempt to assimilate, hates 'bloody Melbourne' and revels in the display of his utterly unreconstructed affiliation to the mother country via his obsessive support for Queen's Park Rangers football club (he even wears QPR strip to his RSL darts nights). As publicity materials relate (BBC, 1990), Reg's heart and accent:

> are still in his native Shepherd's Bush...a place far different from that of his memories. For nineteen of his Australian years he was a strike-loving union man. He met Dennis in the dole office on the first day of his redundancy...

Dennis, meanwhile, offers a telling contrast to the 'stodgy inertia' of whingeing Reg:

> An ex-country boy who came to the city to make good...has seen the prospect of a future in countless abortive businesses, sees his marriage break up because of his inability to resist other women...and is now trying to pretend that middle age is something that doesn't exist for him. Unfortunately the strain of trying to be Dennis 'No Worries' Tontine and waking every morning with a new scheme for wealth leaves him teetering on the edge of breakdown.

The two come together to run Melbourne Confidential. It is through their business endeavours that comic situations are elaborated and two very different Australian cultures focussed. Locked together in a battle of egos and national loyalties, Reg and Dennis re-express some familiar tensions between Anglophile and Nationalist values still evident in Australian daily life. The ensuing comedy is subtle and full of insight about contemporary Anglo-Australian relations. Their partnership was accidental at the start, and sustained by senses of expediency as much as possibility. Theirs is a love–hate relationship tested to breaking-point by the series of ludicrous situations in which they find themselves, but which both seems unable to relinquish. Both live 'post-' existences (Reg following union notoriety and redundancy, Dennis following a marriage break-up and a succession of temporary liaisons) over-shadowed by definitive former events. The straightened circumstances in which both find themselves—Boys is in a number of senses a 'recessionary' fiction—exacerbate the hostilities between them, and of course provide apparently inexhaustible resources for comedy, though not much in the way of change or resolution. Both improvise their lives around mythical images, marked as removed from their realities: Reg fantasises over a lost sense of connection and community back home ('God's own country, Shepherd's Bush, London W12'); whilst Dennis talks wistfully of returning to his rather different 'bush' when he has finally overcome the unpredictable iniquities of 'factor X', that is, bad luck. Predictably, when each is actually given the opportunity to confront the myths of their own origins and identities they are found comically lacking; Reg returns to London to find it changed almost beyond recognition, whilst Dennis can stand only a couple of days of an uncle's station when he is forced into hiding after yet another disastrous business deal. Both in fact much prefer 'life on the edge' and an existence worked out against the continuous threat of its extinction. If this apocalyptic sensibility does answer a peculiarly Australian consciousness, as is argued by Andrew Milner elsewhere in this volume, Boys also suggests that these are preoccupations that the British have also come to share, and that at least in this sense, the 'old' connections between the two countries remain very real.

This focus on a comic entrepreneurial enterprise with a quasi-detectional element offered immediate reference for audiences seeking to connect with the fiction as consumers, rather than evidence of a 'prematurely post-modern' Australia. Earlier work by the series' creators was repeatedly signposted by reviewers, as offering traditions within which the programme could be understood, and its comedy appreciated. Verity Lambert's previous work was consistently invoked—Minder (1979–) was the most regular point of comparison—although some critics also found continuities with the gentle comedy of feature films such as Restless Natives

(1985) and *Clockwise* (1986). Better-researched commentators found pre-echoes of *Boys* in earlier writing by Douglas Livingstone, notably in a little-known BBC film for actor John Thaw, *We'll Support You Evermore* (1985) and the Thames TV comedy series scripted for Lambert, *Born and Bred* (1978) which is effectively a template for *Boys From The Bush*. Curiously unremarked upon were bridges between *Boys* and the work of the series' Australian co-producer, Jane Scott, and it is this linkage that I want to focus on, since it seems to offer a key of sorts to the comedy of the series.

Scott's *curriculum vitae* is fascinating. After a brief spell in distribution, and then in production at the British Film Institute (BFI), she made short films with Bruce Beresford for BFI and the Arts Council in London. Whilst freelancing, she organised the London production office for *The Adventures of Barry McKenzie* (1973) and helped complete the film in Australia. She then worked for Grundy's in Melbourne and became a resident, after completing *Barry McKenzie Holds His Own* in 1975. Her subsequent associate-producer credits include *In Search of Anna* (1978) and *My Brilliant Career* (1979), and she also worked as line-producer on *Crocodile Dundee* (1986) and co-produced *Crocodile Dundee II* (1988). She now heads the South Australian Film Corporation in Adelaide.

The Adventures of Barry McKenzie and *Crocodile Dundee* in particular offer clear points of contact with *Boys From The Bush*. Generic resemblances abound, indexing the shared aspirations of all three fictions to express national specificities to international audiences. Like its large-screen counterparts, *Boys* is a comedy of displacements. Just as Barry McKenzie comes to London, and Mick Dundee travels to New York, Reg, Doris, and Leslie, are transported to Melbourne. Each tests their 'fish out of water' protagonists (O'Regan, 1989), examining the 'types' they mobilise in alien environments, testing the serviceability of their attitudes and values, both confirming and critiquing typage in that process. So, Barry the ocker confronts decadence in 'swinging' London; Mick Dundee, the 'last' bushman, must survive the quintessential urban jungle in the form of New York City and in *Boys*, Reg Toomer, the ultimate 'whingeing pom' confronts Australian utopianism in the devastating form of Dennis Tontine. As in its cinematic antecedents, the drama of *Boys* proceeds through the activation and the attempted resolution of these contradictions. Once again cynicism gives way to sentimentality as the poles of the drama begin to be merged; Barry is departed from London 'just as he is getting to like the place'; Mick Dundee discovers the 'tribal' in New York City and begins to reform it in his own image; and (after re-visiting London) Reg Toomer has eventually to offer some grudging recognition that Melbourne may have some things to recommend it after all.

Longer-running TV dramas invest less, of course, in the kind of closure and resolution we have learned to expect of mainstream cinema. The pleasures of most sitcoms (and *Boys* is in some sense a 'situation' comedy) are deeply rooted in the largely unchanging structure of relationships they describe. Traces of these trajectories are evident though and characters differentiated by their progress or lack of progress along them. An interesting distinction emerges here between female and male characters. Doris is less and less a 'fish out of water'; she is adaptable, remains realistic but positive about her new country, and her dominant code is one of making-the-best-of-it, looking-on-the bright side, etc. (Series two has her taking up Australian citizenship!) Daughter Arlene is Australian-born and very much on her own turf from the outset, with her calculated pursuit of Leslie Duckett played against his 'English' naivety with a terrifying determination. Her intermittent bouts of sulkiness at his apparent indifference alternate hilariously with frenetic activity around the latest Leslie-catching scheme. The contrast here with Australian popular culture's definitive female teen-icon, Kylie Minogue, is striking in the extreme. In comparison, the central male characters occupy relatively static positions. It is their unchanging nature of course which draws out attention to their typage, and grounds the pleasures of repetition so central to popular culture in general. With his boot-lace tie and dreams of fortune, Dennis is less a larrikin than a cross between a spiv and a cowboy, whilst, in a counter-movement, that supposedly most Australian of all traits, a fanatical attachment to sport, is identified with Reg not Dennis, whose addiction to QPR surely matches anything ever accredited to the most sport-obsessed Australian. Such resolutely unaltered characters mark a stubborn resistance to the merging of 'outside' and 'inside' values which the series celebrates in its portrayal of a growing sense of understanding between Doris and Arlene.

The broad strategy here is regularly one of comic inversion, which Livingstone describes in terms of 'flipping' images:

> I wanted to have Dennis besotted, and chasing women all the time, and not able to get anywhere, and nearly having a heart attack all the time trying to keep himself fit and young for the sake of all these women...and flipping it around and making the Englishman, who is usually regarded as being soft on women, the insensitive one, the chauvinist pig...

This unfixing and exchanging of elements traditionally claimed as unique to one culture or another operates at a number of levels. The deconstruction of Australian vitality begins early and becomes a key source of comedy; in the opening scene of episode one we see an overweight, middle-aged jogger, staggering home through Port Melbourne, close to cardiac arrest. It turns out to be Dennis Tontine. With wonderful understatement we hear stray dialogue from a radio phone-in on his personal hi-fi. A caller wondering 'Where this bloody country is' is answered curtly by an irrascible presenter 'It's north of the south pole and south of Japan. Now stop whingeing!' Australians, apparently, are not all vigorous, and complaining is clearly as highly developed an Australian as well as expatriate-British art form.

This captures the tone and the scale of the comedy very well, as it selects its targets for gentle assault with a remarkable even-handedness. What is unusual about *Boys'* comedy is its ability to move between wry, almost incidental humour of this sort (surely a naturalist impulse?) and intricate comic set-pieces which produce memorable images whose manifest contrivance adds considerably to their appeal. We are left to discover meaning and take pleasure in details of *mise-en-scene* (a verandah decoration sculpted in the form of a swan from a used car tyre outside Reg's Anzac Drive home), or dialogue ('I think he's a couple of sandwiches short of a picnic') or performance (Healy's disgusted curling of his upper lip, Haywood's recurrent expression of amazement as a new scheme dawns on him) and as little apparently ripples the drama's insistently naturalist surface, we are persuaded to accept ever more illogical and implausible situations. Episode two, 'The Poetic Galah' has Leslie, newly arrived from England (BBC, 1990):

> dragooned into escorting a man-eating, volatile, actress-turned-novelist. When Gloria Goodson hits Melbourne, she must be seen in the company of an eligible young man. Melbourne Confidential is given the job of coming up with someone suitable for her visit to an awards ceremony to celebrate the Woman's Day Romantic Poetry Contest...Leslie is completely out of his depth, but Reg and Melbourne Confidential partner Dennis are more worried about heading off Gloria's ex-lover Carlo (infatuated with her since her appearance at the Footscray RSL in the early 1960s). And unknown to Reg, his wife Doris is one of the finalists at the awards ceremony...

In this way the comedy reveals the characters in all their incoherence and contradiction and values them on that basis. Life-on-the-edge can apparently bring out the best in people. Indeed it is Reg's too complete sense of self-sufficiency, certainty and coherence that provide the few points of serious dramatic tension that threaten the euphoric mode cultivated at most levels of the drama. Comparisons of *Boys* with *Till Death Us Do Part* were suggestive (we may recall Alf Garnett's fanatical support for West Ham United); Reg's jokey racism is sometimes held barely in check beneath the surface, his contempt for Melbourne coming within a hair's breadth of threatening to spill over into contempt in particular for its various 'minority' communities. At points this threatens to provoke a reaction that the comedy will not be able to recuperate, even to suggest areas of experience that can not be reconciled with the society depicted in the series.

This note of equivocation marks the distance of *Boys* from its cinematic antecedents. This is not simply a populist fantasy of *ingénue* values resolutely refusing the 'sophistications' of the city, whose cynical representatives ultimately recognise the transportee's ideology and succumb to its attractions. Reg Toomer may remain as resolutely unaltered by his experiences as Mick Dundee, but this marks his isolation rather than his superior capacity; it is symptomatic of an obstacle to be overcome rather than a quality to be cultivated. Dennis Tontine's various failed enterprises represent nothing less than a failure to transpose 'bush skills' to the city, his 'no worries' attitude revealed as a necessary but barely sustainable fiction. Even if this is only dimly apparent to Dennis and Reg, it is made abundantly clear to the audience.

This does mark a critical edge. Rather than celebrating an essential Australian-ness, enshrined in the residual traces of some national ethos that survives within the modern (for a contrast consider Roadshow, Coote & Carroll's *The Paper Man*, 1989), *Boys* constructs Australia as a diverse spectrum of cultures that defy easy separation. Australian 'diversity' of course became something of a cultural *cause célèbre* in the 1980s, but *Boys* draws on the ideology of multiculturalism to unusual ends, for although the series' multicultural credentials are stressed throughout— early episodes reference the Phillipino bride-trade; Greek, Italian and Yugoslavian subcultures—the truly distinctive feature of the show is that it does not focus on any straightforwardly binary opposition between a 'mainstream' and a 'minority', nor does it seek refuge in some postmodern haven of endless relativity in which all cultures are viewed as simply and equally different; rather, *Boys* foregrounds cultural contradictions *within* the supposedly homogeneous 'core' itself.

Conclusions

Revisionist histories of Australian film and television rarely view the strategy of international co-production positively. Rather, the concept has tended to be identified with ideas of media imperialism, and culturally *anonymous* fiction-building. Dominant voices calling for state intervention into the cinema in the sixties and seventies tended to equate co-production with the maintenance of relations of subservience in the cultural sphere, and thus saw co-productions as the very sign of the history that was to be transcended. Whilst the proponents of what Dermody and Jacka (1987 and 1988) term industry-1—the culture lobby, viewing cinema as the definitive national art—held sway, the arguments of the commercialists, traditional advocates of co-production, ended to be marginalised. Elder statesmen such as Ken Hall (1985) often insisted that only TV and co-production could really secure the cinema:

> Co-production for television sale, carefully entered into and just as carefully operated, can quite possibly be the solution for Australia...You cannot build an industry on government handouts. You cannot built an industry with your head in the cultural clouds and your feet off the ground (p. 164).

However, a still self-consciously nationalist cinema remained sceptical about the cultural possibilities of firmer overseas links within the financing, production and distribution of Australian films. Similarly 'traditional' views of its role in cultivating a nationally conscious audience still coloured the ABC's drama policy (Jacka, 1991. p. 11) and hence the programming philosophy of Australia's dominant drama producer. So long as state subsidy to the industry remained reliable, the arguments of Hall and the commercialists could be muted by the guardians of 'official' screen culture.

With the reduction of subsidy to both cinema and TV drama through the eighties that I began by discussing, the 'globalisation' of the Australian image clearly found greater favour both amongst the commercialists of industry-2 and those survivors of industry-1 who had established themselves at the centre of the production sector. In a typically postmodern turn, as these voices grew stronger in the 1980s, they gained ground not by re-stating familiar economic wisdoms about the inability of Australia's population to sustain a self-sufficient industry but by *incorporating* arguments about culture into their polemics. Even a 'coldly' commercial producer of contemporary genre pictures such as Tony Ginnane (Hamilton and Mathews, 1986) started to produce rhetoric involving a fascinating amalgam of commercial and post-nationalist discourse:

> Is there such a difference between Australia and American cultures? The differences exist only here and there, and are the province of sociologists and academics. But on a day-to-day basis, the broad base of Australian culture, from McDonald's to prime-time television and everything in between, is comparable to the American. To some degree, I see a mega-culture embracing Australia, Canada and the US...(p. 95).

Shifting funding structures and the penetration of new ideologies of Australia as a multicultural society into the film and TV production sectors, ensured that the polar options of the 1970s (respectable heritage product or no-nonsense genre flicks) would begin to merge and cross each other. These oppositions between 'Australian' product and product designed for the 'overseas' market also started to break down within the films and programmes themselves, and a number of films/TV dramas began to express their production arrangements in the organisation of their narratives and representation of Australian ways of life. Co-production no longer seemed to mean anonymity, the automatic 'Americanisation' of Australian content, but rather to imply a more comparative space within which processes of cultural interpenetration themselves could be examined.

Whilst Ginnane and others ensured that culturally anonymous production and co-production would persist (could we call this 'concealed' co-production?), what one might term more 'self-reflective' (or 'revealed'?) co-productions, also became a feature of both cinema and TV drama. These 'aware' co-productions envisioned a rather different approach to the question of Australian culture from those described by more purely indigenous fictions. At best, they expressed their collaborative origins in narratives concerned expressly with inter-cultural relations, and the *co-production of culture itself*. As often as not, this comparative element underlined not only areas of difference in the cultures dealt with, but also some starling elements of similarity. This involved not so much a stifling 'Americanisation' but a view of popular culture as a kind of lingua franca, a set of practices to be shared, exchanged and inflected to meet the needs of immediate and everyday circumstances. As just such a series, *The Boys From The Bush* displayed a new confidence in constructing Australia through its largely characteristic elements, and through its wry sense of humour offered a critical re-reading of better-known suburban TV fictions. The show implied that Ginnane, might at least have *part* of a point, as it struggled to re-define Australian nationalism in less chauvinist ways, and to represent Australian culture in more inclusive, and less exclusive terms. Its status as an international co-production gave it a confidence about acknowledging problematical and diverse national origins and finding something explanatory with them. In this shift lies the progressive potential of what is sometimes referred to as a 'turn to the local' in postmodern culture (Dermody and Jacka, 1988), and which defines a new 'suburban' terrain for cultural politics in the 1990s:

> The local doesn't necessarily mean the veristic, in the sense of mirroring or reflecting a society or subculture, because the local can be intensely mediated or mythologised or fantasised or transformed by generic and other operations. However, it probably does mean the authentic, in the sense that what is presented in the local is recognised as applying to a particular and specific set of circumstances and forces that operate at any given time and place, be they signs of place, accent and idiom, or more diffuse but no less vivid ways of hooking into the social unconscious or social 'imagery' of a particular subculture (p, 126).

The Boys From The Bush is such as co-production, making a virtue of its cross-cultural origins, and bearing the device within its fiction of the financing, production and distribution arrangements from which it was born. With its referencing not only of multiculturalism—but also of white-collar and organised crime, legalised prostitution, hard- and soft-drug cultures, the 'Japanisation' of Australian business life, and so on—its revised Australiana of indeterminate landscapes and characters defined in opposition to familiar archetypes, it is no less an Australian fiction than *The Man From Snowy River* (1982). As part of a chain of popular representations of Australian culture in the UK (just as television soap operas in the 1980s displaced more traditional bush images of the Australian context, so a comedy series such as *Boys* takes the now familiar worlds of Erinsbrough and Summer Bay as its pre-texts) it offers a useful and enjoyable critique of more local, but no less mythologised, Australian worlds.

References

Alvarado, Manuel and John Stewart (1985), *Made For Television: Euston Films Ltd*, London: British Film Institute/Thames Methuen

Anon. (1989), untitled report on co-production deals between the Welsh Film Foundation and commercial Australian companies, in *Screen International*, No. 704/5, (13–19 May 1989), p. 40

Anon. (1990), 'Oz Comedy from Spitting Image', *Screen International*, No. 743, (10–16 February 1990), p. 40

Anon. (1990a), 'Drama Series Set To Rescue Australian TV', *Screen International*, No. 747, (10–16 March 1990), p. 6

Anon. (1990b), 'Australian FFC Project Slate Reached 50 Mark', *Screen International*, No. 752, (14–20 April 1990), p. 16

Atkins, William (1991), 'Australian Saga Rolls Last Episode', *Broadcast*, 6 June 1991), p. 12

Australian Broadcasting Tribunal (1987) *Australian Content Enquiry Discussion Paper: Ratings of Australian Drama Series, Mini-Series, Films and Telemovies*, [unpublished]

Australian Film Commission (1991), *Information For Overseas Filmmakers*, Sydney: AFC, February

BBC Enterprises (1990), *The Boys From The Bush* [unpublished promotional materials from the BBC Press Service]

Brown, Charles (1989), 'Fruits of Eden', *Broadcast*, 10 February, p. 37

Brown, Charles (1989a), 'Headliners: Christopher Skase', *Broadcast*, 14 July, p. 10

Collins, Richard (1990), 'After The Gold Rush', *Broadcast*, 20 April, pp. 54–8

Court, David (1987), *Film Assistance: Future Options*, Sydney: Allen & Unwin Australia

Craven, Ian (1991), interview with Verity Lambert, May [unpublished]

Craven, Ian (1992), interview with Douglas Livingstone, April [un–published]

Cunningham, Stuart (1991), 'Cultural Theory and Broadcasting Policy: Some Australian Observations', *Screen*, Vol. 32, No. 1 (Spring), pp. 79–83

Dermody, Susan and Elizabeth Jacka (1987 and 1988), *The Screening of Australia*, (Vols. I and II), Sydney: Currency Press, 1987 and 1988

Ellis, John (1975), 'Made in Ealing', *Screen*, Vol. 16, No. 1 (Spring), pp. 78–127

Goodwin, Peter (1991), 'Educating Auntie', *Broadcast*, 8 February, pp. 28–9

Hall, Ken (1985), 'Strategies for a Industry—Television and Co-production', in Albert Moran and Tom O'Regan (eds.), *An Australian Film Reader*, Sydney: Currency Press, pp. 158–65

Hall, Sandra (1981), *Turning On, Turning Off: Australian Television in The 80s*, North Ryde: Cassell Australia

Hamilton, Peter and Sue Mathews (1986), *American Dreams, Australian Movies*, Sydney: Currency Press

Harbord, Jane (1988), 'Aussie Perestroiaka', *Broadcast*, 15 July, pp. 21–3

Jacka, Elizabeth (1988), 'Overseas Links', in Susan Dermody and Elizabeth Jacka (eds.), *The Imaginary Industry: Australian Film in The Late 1980s*, Sydney: Australian Film Television and Radio School, pp. 50–64

Jacka, Elizabeth (1991), *The ABC of Drama: 1975–1990*, Sydney: Australian Film, Television and Radio School

James-Bailey, Julie (1979), *Australian Television: Historical Overview*, Sydney: Australian Film and Television School

Kitchen, Carl (1989), 'Australia's Red Alert', *Broadcast*, 1 December, p. 8

Lane, John Francis (1992), 'Quid co-production quo', *Screen International*, No. 849, 20–6 March, pp. 18–20

Lee, Harvey (1989), 'Road To Ruin', *Broadcast*, 15 September, p. 21

McMichael, Michael (1990), 'On the Brink', *Screen International*, No. 756, 12–18 May, p. 38

O'Regan, Tom (1989), 'Fair Dinkum Fillums: The *Crocodile Dundee* Phenomenon', in Susan Dermody and Elizabeth Jacka: *The Imaginary Industry: Australian Cinema in the Late 1980s*, Sydney: A.F.T.R.S., pp. 156–163

Roddick, Nick (1985), 'Strewth!: A Beginners Guide to Australian Television', *Sight and Sound*, Vol. 54, No. 4 (Autumn), pp. 250–4

Rodgers, Mary (1987), 'Aussie Indies v. The World', *Broadcast*, 21 August, p. 20

Rowse, Tim (1992), 'Heaven and a Hills Hoist: Australian Critics on Suburbia', in Gillian Whitlock and David Carter (eds.): *Images of Australia: An Introductory Reader in Australian Studies*, St Lucia: University of Queensland Press, pp. 240–50

Sadlier, Kevin (1990), 'Lorimar Sizes Up Warner's New Australian Studies', *Screen International*, No. 771, 25–31 August, p. 2

Sadlier, Kevin (1990a), 'Down, and Going Under', *Screen International*, No. 775, 22–8 September, p. 12

Sadlier, Kevin (1991), 'Australia: Down but Not Under', *Screen International*, Special MIFED Issue (Spring), p. 51

Semmler, Clement (1981), *The ABC: Aunt Sally and Sacred Cow*, Melbourne: Melbourne University Press

Spear, Peta (ed.) (1989), *Get The Picture: Essential Data on Australian Film, Television and Video*, Sydney: AFC, October

Stanley, Raymond (1987), 'Positive Proof That All Is Well Down-Under', *Broadcast*, 21 August, p. 22

Treffry, Sally (1991), 'Up A Gum Tree', *Broadcast*. 8 February, pp. 31–2

Urban, Andrew (1989), 'Anglia TV Buys into Australia', *Screen International*, No. 704/5, 13–19 May, p. 1

Urban, Andrew (1989a), 'Oz Soaps Slip From Grace', *Screen International*, No. 709, 17–23 June, p. 17

Urban, Andrew (1989b), 'Oz Production Plans to Bounce Back', *Screen International*, No. 711, 1–7 July, p. 17

The Vanishing Policeman: Patterns of Control in Australian Crime Fiction

STEPHEN KNIGHT

I

A common characteristic of crime fiction is a structural focus on a central figure who detects the criminal who caused the disorder that is evident at or near the beginning of the story.

But the central detecting figure varies a good deal, and that variation alters the underlying meaning of the story, especially its social meaning. These patterns of change do not only occur across time: remarkable discrepancies also exist between national cultures. In a survey of detection figures made on a basis of 200 authors per country (and including the absence of any detector) the UK figures are: police 38%, private eye 7%, amateur 46%, zero detection 9%. By contrast, the US pattern is: police 13%, private eye 50%, amateur 20%, zero detection 17%.

Those statistics invite speculation about their evident differences, but the purpose of referring to them here is to establish a referential context against which to investigate more fully, and for the first time, the nature and variations of the systems of detection in Australian crime fiction.

The raw figures for the Australian product are: police 31%, private eye 25%, amateur 9%, zero detection 35%. The data indicate differences that deserve exploration and explanation, but there is a good deal more complexity behind the Australian numbers, as striking variations over time are concealed within those statistics. Most of the police in that rather surprising 31% actually appear before 1890; almost all the private eyes are post Second World War. The latter phenomenon is evidently attached to an increasingly trans-pacific tendency in the national culture, but the former requires closer examination, and is a major concern of this paper. Another category in need of scrutiny is zero detection, remarkably high in the case of Australia. These formations are not unrelated: it will be argued here that there is a dynamic relationship between the three special features just mentioned: as the police disappear their place is taken by zero detection until, in recent decades, the private eye becomes a credible figure in Australia, while the amateur has never had much appeal. The processes and intricacies of these patterns need to be traced from the beginning.

II

The first Australian crime writing was vigorously demotic and firmly oriented in favour of the forces of law and order. Both early in date and antique in mode is the figure of George Flower, thief-taker of John George

Lang's *The Forger's Wife*, set in Sydney, serialised in *Frazer's Magazine* and published in book form in Sydney in 1855. Flower was based on the well-known thief-taker Israel Chapman,[1] and continuity with London reality and fiction is clearly indicated when he is called a 'George Street Runner'. The Bow Street Runners had been phased out when the Detective section of the newly formed police was established in 1842 but they were popular in fiction, especially through reprints and imitations of the adventures of 'Richmond', *Scenes in the Life of a Bow Street Runner* (1827), which Lang no doubt had read.

In spite of his street-level realism, however, Flower is still, like most early detectives, a functionary of a hierarchical drama: however humble and self-helping he might be, he is never a force for social criticism or change. Even less so are those who police the pages of more fully squattocratic novels like *The Recollections of Geoffry Hamlyn* (1859). Here there is no effective difference between the police and the army, as the local troopers in the fertile but sometimes convict-ridden lands where Geoffry and his friends prosperously settle are led by Captain Desborough, a cheerful and energetic officer who hunts villains like foxes (and who may take his name from the South East Midlands hunting town Desborough). He is finally, and with the usual concluding improbability of such novels, assumed into the aristocracy, albeit one of its Irish branches. Desborough's amiable relations with the squatters indicate that this class fraction is, in fiction at least, policing society in its own name and interest, a characteristic found in some of the later Sherlock Holmes stories and which will emerge fully in the soldierly and semi-aristocratic detectives of the between-wars mystery, led by Peter Wimsey, but with an Australian equivalent in Colonel Ingram, hero of three stories by Alan Michaelis in *Ingram Intervenes* (1933); the hero is something of a rarity as an Australian-style gentleman police officer produced in this century. The relative paucity of gentry policing may well depend on democratic attitudes in authors and readers after the early colonially conscious days, but it also relates to likelihood: against Kingley's distanced fancies may be set the close-focus realism of *Lucy Cooper* (1846), when the auto-policing efforts of Dr Caveat (the name is an ironic thrust at the Sydney legal aristocracy) are a total failure against genuinely tough escaped convicts, and he is killed in the process.

Apart from the gentry, with their fabled successes and probabilistic failures, there were also less lofty crime detectors in nineteenth-century fiction; in its first years from 1865 on, *The Australian Journal* eagerly pursued the success of policing stories in the new London journals. J.S. Borlase started a series called 'The Adventures of an Australian Mounted Trooper' whose title, and in one instance more than that, was borrowed from W.S. Burrows' *Adventures of a Mounted Trooper in the Australian Constabulary*.[2] The hero of these stories, like that of the very similar 'Memoirs of an

Australian Police Officer' and Mary Fortune's 'The Detective's Album',[3] is a self-reliant, wry character whose success comes from a highly credible mixture of patience, flexibility and good information.

Where, for Borlase, the troopers were the other ranks who faithfully kept order for their aristocratic leaders, in Fortune policing has moved out of Desborough's lordly shadow and we see there a figure not unlike the brave and patient policeman of Charles Martel's English stories in *The Detective's Notebook* (1860) or, indeed, the democratic artisan-class detectors of a century later found in a television series like the BBC's Merseyside 'Z Cars' and an American novel-series about plain policing like that by 'Dell Shannon'. But Australia cannot match the modern florescence of police procedurals, in spite of its early strength, in numbers and quality, in that mode.

The question must arise, what happened to these honourable workaday police in Australian crime fiction? Any answer must base itself on another question—why did they emerge at all in a country which by tradition was so sympathetic towards convicts that police were always under suspicion? The regular and evidently successful occurrence of police stories in *The Australian Journal* clearly indicates there was plenty of faith in positive policing in the goldfields period. The diggers might shout 'Joe' when Borlase's Brooke or Fortune's Sinclair rode past, but the readers themselves evidently thirsted for these fictions of constabulary authority—when Borlase apparently grew tired of the series and was back at his far less interesting historical novels, and when Fortune was at work on mystery romances without formal detection like *Bertha's Legacy*, the editor bought in other detectives, the first being 'The Identification: A Narrative of Facts by an Irish Constabulary Officer' and then in 1866 a New York based police series called 'A Detective's Experiences'. It appears from *The Australian Journal* and other sources like the contemporary newspaper fiction that a solidarity with convicts and bushrangers is by no means shared by the early audience—indeed the villain, as in Fortune's first story 'The Dead Witness', may well be a former convict unsuited to the busy artisan world of the Australian hinterland, and the *Journal* readership. The traditional dislike of the police is not evident in the early crime fiction—but it does soon enough appear.

It would seem that something happened to public attitudes to policing after the 1860s. In Fergus Hume's *The Mystery of a Hansom Cab* (1886) and its near-sequel *Madam Midas* (1888) detection is undertaken by a police detective called Kilsip, who is a capable investigator with a distinctly unpleasant, even bitter, attitude; he is supported, if that is the word, by the unpalatable and almost incompetent short, fat Detective Gorby. Making up for this effective demotion of the police is the increased role given, especially in *Madame Midas*, to a dashing lawyer Carlton, whose name combines an inner Melbourne reference with the suggestion of a noble Dickensian hero: his is the part played by the leading man when these novels have been staged or filmed.

From here on the police tend to be mere supporters, only present to arrest the villains so brilliantly identified by truly independent Aussies like Billy Pagan, the mining engineer detective created by Randolph Bedford; or they are constabulary shadows, emerging from the background to clear up the criminal chaos that is worked out through the hectic plots of outback dramas like Hume Nisbet's *The Swampers* (1897), or the sophisticated tales of upper class malpractice like those by Guy Boothby in the short story collection *Bushigrams* (1897)—before he relocated both himself and his Dr Nikola stories to a devoted, if jingoistic, English audience.

One possible cause of the change in attitudes is that the genre's form changed. Instead of appearing in tight-packed narrow columns on cheap paper, in newspapers as well as the *Journal*, crime fiction moved into the book. But repositioning in terms of market and class do not seem enough to explain the disappearance of the police. After all, the *Bulletin* became a positive sanctuary for demotic fiction, yet it quite lacked stories in admiration of policing practices. Though the *Bulletin* had a strongly working-class audience, *The Australian Journal* was more widely read in class terms and it too moved from admiration of the police to a negative treatment, as in Fortune's essentially ironic mystery of inner Melbourne, 'The Phantom Hearse' from 1890.

Across the range of publishing, from book to inexpensive journal, the official detective disappeared. There must, it would seem, be an ideological point of obstruction against admiration of police which develops in just this late-nineteenth-century period. The context offers clues. As the ideal of the bushman was invented—and the verb has its fullest working out in Richard White's book on the topic[4]—so the notion of an orderly social process of containing crime largely disappeared in the mass market, and so indeed did the idea of crime itself as a problem in the present. When Boldrewood, that important re-organiser of attitudes to both the past and the bush, wrote about murder in 'The Mailman's Yarn'[5] he set it far out in the outback, made it a retrospective narrative, and brought about retribution as the result of natural forces and that wry bush cunning that Lawson was to apotheosise as the only resistance suitable to those who felt marooned by fortune and opposed to all forms of social policing.

Both the radical Lawson and the inherently conservative Paterson—especially in 'Waltzing Matilda'—made enemies out of the troopers who had in the early *Journal* stories been the friends and defenders of the bush workers. Some of the reasons are complicit with an economy and a social structure that in the 1890s appeared to have failed or become oppressive, and the evident corruption and anti-union activities of law-enforcement agencies at the time cannot have hindered the tendencies that drove the police from the pages of crime fiction.

The structure of this change is deeply involved with national self-representations. As the myth of freedom and Australian-ness grew and was focussed on an individual in the bush, other aspects of Australian tradition accreted to the figure, and among them were the convict-bushranger traditions of resistance to law and, if necessary, dying game. The world realised in Borlase and Fortune had well-developed ideals of social coherence and relational establishment among the spreading suburbs of Melbourne and the small towns of the ranges and plains, and in that context police were a crucial ally. But when myth privileged the lone bushman, then the trooper was one of the many Others, including squatter and woman, against which that figure could be delineated: detection and the valued detector changed accordingly.

A different form of police activity has taken much longer to reject, because the threats it bears have not been felt, or not very much, by white Australians. In nineteenth century-crime fiction, Aborigines often appear as a third tier of police, below the troopers who are below the para-aristocratic mounted officers; A.J. Vogan's *The Black Police* (1890) is a good example.

The supportive and quietist role of Aboriginal police is brought to a remarkable head in the highly improbable and, to many people, especially Aborigines, deplorable figure of Napoleon Bonaparte, the detective created in *The Barrakee Mystery* (1929) by Arthur Upfield, to bear both his own interest in native Australians and to be a somewhat mechanical crime detector in exotically set but essentially plodding narratives whose underlying meaning is the resolution not of random outback crimes but the concealment of the racial crimes involved in the founding of the new country.

Bony, readers will hardly forget, is blue-eyed and a graduate of Queensland University, yet is still in touch with his Aboriginality. Gentle, wise and tough, he offers a figure which has for many readers elided the problems of racial conflict in a transcendentally touristic setting. Very recent has been the response of Aboriginal writers themselves. Mudrooroo Narogin has taken up the challenge directly and with characteristic bravura, having now produced three short stories based on the detective exploits of Detective Inspector Watson Holmes Jackamara of the Black Cockatoo Dreaming.

Playful the name may be, but these are serious and engaging stories, especially the powerful first, entitled 'Westralian Lead',[6] in which Jackamara's weighty presence and sombre wit deal firmly, almost pityingly, with some of the criminal confusions introduced by the white invaders. A book of stories may well appear soon and in the future perhaps a novel or two.

An alternative treatment is that offered by Archie Weller in a series of short stories. He writes in terms of his own Western Australian experience; the crimes are in large part against his own people, and the resolutions are elusive, even tragically inoperative, but they derive from the flow of the narrative and the ambient probabilities, not from any authority, white or black. Less formally within the crime genre, Weller's stories of conflict and deviance provide a way of transmuting the white separation of genres into the broader view of a differently located imagination; they offer a good example of the dynamic possibilities of that zero detection which is so common in Australian crime fiction.[7]

III

Resolution without a detector of any kind goes back a long way in the tradition. Mary Fortune herself seems to have been quite happy writing crime-based adventure stories which revealed their mysteries without human intervention, and from her pen detective-free fictions alternate with police stories in the early pages of *The Australian Journal*. By the nineties the police were appearing just to make an arrest or, more often, a mistake, and this tradition continued a long time. After the Second World War, when in the USA and Britain police procedurals were on the rise, the *Journal* maintained the pattern of absent or almost entirely inoperative policing by the official force.

Stories from the 1950s can be taken to represent a whole sub-genre of Australian short crime fiction, now almost completely unread but once, before television, a staple item of monthly consumption in the *Journal*. Writers like Rex Grayson (actually the editor Ron Grayson Campbell), Cole Turnley, B.J. Cronin, Sidney Courtier and Jon Cleary himself all had a similar pattern of policing. In them the constabulary played exactly the same largely off-stage and ideologically marginal role they fulfilled in the English amateur detective sub-genre or the US private eye saga, except that the Australians tended to employ no central detective at all and events themselves would throw up the criminal.

These narratives are the reverse of Lawson's grim ironies about a negative fortune; they suggest that crime will in some way frustrate itself, yet they certainly hand no legislative activity to a functionary of the crown, still less to some random member of the public empowered by class or brains or preferably both, as happened in England. Equally the American tough guy has no credible place. The writers rely on a set of obscurely providential systems through which that mysterious Australian phrase 'she'll be right' would come true.

Such positive irony and hope of accidental order might place some strain on credulity, and this optimistic form appears only, it seems, in the evanescence of the magazines. But while most of the Australian crime novels of the earlier twentieth century did rely for probability on the presence of a human detector, this role was not filled with the easy Anglo-American confidence in human agency to resolve crime, differently validated though it might be by class, cleverness or tough endurance.

J.M. Walsh was one who increased his royalties through exile and he created many confident and flamboyant detectives located in Europe, but when he set stories in Australia, as in *The Lost Valley* (1921), the detecting is largely derived from the plot's self-revelations. This becomes a site of strain in *The League of Missing Men* (1927), one of his best books, where an authoritative detective is created with the imposing name of Bromiley Kay, the apparent weight of an Inspector French and the aura of one of the English learned amateurs, but he actually does very little. The same is true of between-wars stalwarts like Arthur Gask and G.M. Wicking who produced melodramatic mysteries where an initial focus falls on a detective who is steadily elided in the process of the narration: Gask's late twenties hero Gilbert Penrose is markedly more in command of the plotting when he and his author are both transplanted to England by the mid thirties.

This Australian inability—or, perhaps better, refusal—to develop an authoritative and forcefully active detective suggests a distinct tendency in the local writers to shy away from any form of coherently focussed authority: amateur gentlemen and private eyes seem absolutely unacceptable, but police professionals appear little more manageable if they are in control of the narrative development.

Where there are examples that seem to contradict this pattern, they appear to be an imitation of the English patterns in tone and detective methods, and yet themselves have distinct Australian inflections. Two sisters, Margot Goyder and Anne Goyder Joske, wrote as 'Margot Neville'. After some early publication and co-publication in Australia, they came out with the minor London house of Geoffrey Bles, but there were a few Pan reprints in the early sixties to suggest distinct elements of popularity.

For 'Neville', quasi-Englishness rests, in spite of their 'society' tone, on a Scotland Yard archetype—the absence of the amateur detective itself seems an Australian modulation of the clue-puzzle. Other local writers have also made significant variations to the British patterns. Non-professionals are occasionally used throughout the century, but that definition derives from a technical interpretation of the detector's status rather than indicating the story is a paean to the spirit of amateurism. Randolph Bedford's *Billy Pagan: Mining Engineer* (1911) is technically a non-professional inquirer, being a mining engineer who stumbles upon mysteries in the mulga, and Bob Brissenden's journalist Caxton has a similar role in *Poor Boy* (1987) and *Wildcat* (1991), but both have essentially professional and procedurally brisk manners, without the languid self-consciousness of the English amateurs, or indeed many of the American private eye professionals. And though in her twenties' pastiches set in Melbourne, starting with *Cocaine Blues* (1989), Kerry Greenwood does use an adventurous lady who is something like a cross between Wimsey and Lady Ottoline Morrell, her busy and socially engaged manner quite lacks the languid supremacism typical of the English amateurs.

'Neville' is the closest to an English pattern in the way in which Inspector Grogan dominates the story in his timeless way. But this is not the case with the highly interesting police detective created in her first novels by Pat Flower. Born in England and also practising as a script writer, she produced fifteen thrillers, and in the first group of them Inspector Swinton held sway. He is in part a plebeian—perhaps a displaced one: he loves cold Australian meat pies, which smacks of English pastry habits, and also his sentimental eye on Sydney and its people separates him from the native, and compulsive, self-questioning uncertainty.

Those are positive aspects of outsiderism. What alienates Swinton most, though, and diminishes the force of the novels, is the character's apparent failure to appeal strongly to the writer's imagination. Even in the early, Swinton-focussed and fairly derivative *Wax Flowers for Gloria* (1956), an effective department-store murder, it is noticeable that towards the middle of the novel Swinton's control of the action fades, and other characters will dominate the point of view, especially early in a chapter. Flower it seems is not consistently in the mood to privilege her focal figure.

Both playfulness in titles and old-style policing disappeared together, as Flower moved on to a different sub-genre, usually called the psycho-thriller. In the later part of her rather short life she produced a series of zero-policing stories, meticulous fables of derangement and violence that seem in the same category as those produced by Ruth Rendell and P.D. James in England—both of whom, it is not irrelevant to note, also first established police detectives in series form and frequently move away to write different kinds of crime novel where fear, obsession and mutual destruction occur, often without any forms of resolution at all, let alone the process of orderly policing.

IV

It can of course be no accident that women writers seem much more likely to disavow the force of a male police detective, but it was a man, A.E. Martin (who usually used no detector at all, just as he used no setting), who produced a wry piece of proto-feminism in *The Misplaced Corpse* (1944), where Rosie Bosankey is a remarkably active and resilient female private eye, though also framed in a masculinist mould, rather like a Peter Cheyney hero in declassé drag.[8]

That imaginative action from a writer of great but largely overlooked originality has an inner consistency, because when the American writers in the twenties shaped the private eye form, they were not only reacting against English rustic mysteries of high conventionalism and low probability, as Chandler famously remarked in his essay 'The Simple Art of Murder':[9] they were also rejecting the idea of the police as a reliable force in keeping, or rather restoring, any lasting form of peace. Policing itself became part the American individualist dream.

This formation had very little impact in Australia in the past, at least not in specific and locally created terms. In the Second World War, communications and book shipments from England became rare; at the same time large numbers of Americans joined the reading audience, and their tastes had cultural power. American magazines flooded into Australia, particularly Sydney and Brisbane. Presses sprang up in Sydney with names sounding like Coral Sea battleships, Invincible, Currawong, Horwitz, and local writers shelled their audience with tales of cowboys, space heroes and daring urban detectives.

The private eye form was until recently to a remarkable degree restricted to southern California and its uncentred urban areas: the early Sydney imitators, notably 'Carter Brown', set their yarns in an America of adolescent dreams and the trans-pacific translation of the form was not easy. Sydney-based private eyes began as early as the world-roaming hero of 'Mark Corrigan', actually the English pot-boiler expert Norman Lee. Like his other tourist thrillers, *Sydney for Sin* (1955) is a fast moving, fairly witty mixture of masculine poses and physical action, though it does, with curious inconsequentiality, take place mostly in Melbourne.

Lee was a bird of criminographical passage, but some residents attempted to locate a tough guy hero in Sydney. One was Otto Beeby, whose private eye undertook sub-Chandlerian action as in *Blank Cheque for Murder* (1968): six of these little-known titles appeared with an English publisher. Equally muted in impact was Richard Clapperton, whose single novel, *You're a Long Time Dead* (1968), is a fairly clumsy version of the standard form. Better remembered, at least making it into paperback, was Ian Hamilton, whose novels, typified by *The Persecutor* (1965), were technically amateur-based, being focussed on Pete Heyssen, a disc jockey from the febrile world of Sydney radio in the sixties. Journalism had not been an uncommon profession for amateur detectives, especially in Hollywood treatments, and Hamilton's novels belong to that tradition, with some skill and conviction. In keeping with the practice of English crime publishers, these all came first to Australia only in hardback and went mostly into public libraries; though Hamilton had paper reprints, they were not locally produced. The crucial thing is that they had no Australian publicity or reviews to speak of, and so public awareness of them was scarcely any higher on publication than it is today.

This situation quite changed with the novels of Peter Corris, which, like so much Australian fiction through the eighties, were published locally and in paperback, and so both needed and received substantial publicity to generate the sales required to generate profit in a small market. Corris started in hardback with *The Dying Trade* (1980), but he then moved to Pan and since has always appeared initially in paperback. He has become well-known as a result of the marketing and publicity suitable to that mode, and has also been the main agent of establishing the possibility of a genuinely Australian private eye, so much so that he is published in America by Fawcett and not completely unknown in Britain, that most difficult terrain to penetrate for Australian fiction of all kinds.

Corris's skill has been to combine the broad generic structures of the mainstream American private eye—independent-minded, reactively radical, tough and sensitive at the same time—with a traditional Australian male stereotype, ultimately the ironic, laconic, intuitively capable rural hero of many an urban fiction. In an interview Corris has said that Cliff Hardy is in some way modelled on the uncles he recalls from his rural childhood in Stawell, Victoria, men who had come back from the war and had what later generations have learnt to call a laid-back toughness.

Not only has Hardy himself been a force of informal policing in tune with the changing ideas of a credible authority figure, he has given up promiscuous consumption of cigarettes, women and, almost, alcohol. But in negative mode he has stimulated more radical departures from the traditions of detection. Most evidently the figure is reversed in Marele Day's quite sophisticated novels about Claudia Valentine, tall, judicious but also passionate and intellectual, a more flamboyant version of the feminist private eye than most around the world, as in *The Life and Crimes of Harry Lavender* (1988). Earlier women writers did little more than mollify the maleness of their detectors. Christie, Marsh and Allingham sometimes provided a female inquirer, like Miss Marple or Gladys Mitchell's Dame Beatrice Adela Lestrange Bradley; at other times, as with the psychothriller writers, they completely elided the role of detection.

But recently, empowered with the concept of feminism in its sixties form as a set of alternative practices, many women around the world have made the private eye into a woman—of the North Americans, Sara Paretsky is probably the best known, while Marcia Muller is both the most pragmatic and specifically committed to a feminist position, and Sue Grafton offers the most vigorously downmarket version; in England Liza Cody has dealt in detailed realism, Sarah Dunant offers a thoughtful, Paretsky-like analysis and Gillian Slovo and Joan Smith have provided radical amateur detectors with substantial followings.

In Australia Marele Day has had no outstanding imitators, though Jean Bedford has, among her other fiction, published one well-handled novel in this genre, *Worse than Death* (1991) and is producing more. Another suggestion of the limits to this sub-genre is that Day's own interests have spread, producing both subtle mystery stories close to magic realism and also a new amateur investigator, Mrs Levack, a domestic cleaner.[10] Sales of the Claudia Valentine novels have been reasonable but not outstanding; if this figure may have impacted with little authority on the Australian market, that may well derive from the limited size of the audience rather than any inherent weakness in the representation. Other writers have operated in the same areas but without showing the skill or persistence to establish a convincing model of feminist detection, either professional or amateur. The woman who, much like Joan Smith's central figure, detects from within an academic community (in *Unable by Reason of Death*, 1989, by the pseudonymous 'Judith Guerin' and 'Catherine Lewis') is not developed well enough for any authority; nor do formal skills yet sufficiently support the more searching-minded legal inquirer produced in *Too Rich* (1991) by 'Melissa Chan', actually the Melbourne lawyer and feminist Jocelyn Scutt.

More radical positions have provided stronger fictions with greater impact. Claire McNab has modified the positions taken by the ground-breaking US lesbian writer Katherine V. Forrest to create in Carol Ashton a distinctly glamorous detective inspector from one of Sydney's dress circle harbourside suburbs, starting with *Lessons in Murder* (1988 in the US, 1990 in Australia); a less romantic version of a similar structure is offered in the prize-winning *Still Murder* (1990) by Finola Moorhead, where the constraints and complexities of working as a police sergeant in inner Sydney are combined with a lesbian life style as well as a considerable degree of textual radicalism. The novel's success is a timely reminder that there are substantial segments of society—and they are in the habit of reading and buying books—for whom old models of authority, whether male or textual, have many shortcomings. That kind of response can reach even further, as was shown in the *succès d'estime* written by Jan McKemmish, *A Gap in the Records* (1985), where in an espionage context a group of amateur women operate as an elusive and informal policing force—among many other post-modernist intricacies.

If the evidence suggests that what might be called 'normal' police have disappeared since the 1860s, the work of Jon Cleary might seem a contradiction, since he has created successfully a Sydney-based policeman in Scobie Malone, who has reappeared in a range of successful novels from *The High Commissioner* (1966) onwards. Cleary's achievement is nevertheless in some ways itself a proof of the elusive nature of the policeman in modern Australia because of several signs of strain around the formation. Scobie is very conscious of being Irish and his father is highly embarrassed at having a policeman for a son. In addition, he long remained a sergeant: the stigma of English-style officerdom was carefully avoided until recently. More revealingly, there remains an visitor-oriented element about the novels: the first occurs entirely in London, Scobie's wife is an Austrian and remains close to her origins, and a certain sense of an international audience recurs in the emphasis placed upon Sydney settings, from the Opera House and Sydney society context of *Helga's Web* (1970) to a Surry Hills brothel of the recent *Now and Then, Amen* (1988). Cleary's delicate establishment of that rarest thing in a century of Australian crime writing, an honest and successful policeman, is itself a product of both his long-standing skills and international reputation.

Indeed, Cleary's achievement seems the more remarkable against the continuation of an old trend in Australian crime writing, which is a strong form of zero-policing, namely a story told approvingly from the criminal's viewpoint. America has some of these, as in Elmore Leonard's work and the 'Parker' series by 'Richard Stark', and in France they are called existential novels, but Australia is remarkably rich in anti-detective narrative, aspects of which appear in early novels like *His Natural Life* (1874) and ballads like 'Moreton Bay' and more recently in probing novels like Judah Waten's *Shares in Murder* (1957) or Ray Mooney's *A Green Light* (1988).

These authors detect among the detectives themselves, but a reflex form of anti-policing is the story which is restricted entirely to a criminal viewpoint. This is particularly common and popular in Australia, from early ballads and the bushranger cultural industry of the turn of the century (like America's Wild West myth) through to the criminal sagas of modern Sydney, such as Lance Peters' lurid quasi-exposés like *The Dirty Half-Mile* (1979) or the more frank revelling in mischief produced by Robert G. Barrett such as *You Wouldn't Be Dead for Quids* (1985) starring Queensland bonehead turned King's Cross bouncer Les Norton. These sell very well indeed and remind us that one local response is not so much wary of policing as dedicatedly opposed to all its implications.

Across the range of Australian crime fiction, in all but the most anarchic modes of crime fiction, policing does exist but there is no single or simple structure of criminographical defence mechanisms. Rather, a series of overlapping and sometime contradictory types of criminal detection becomes evident in the fiction and equally clearly operating in public attitudes. The faith in professional policing that was lost in the later nineteenth century has never been restored, and the culture has proved, in international terms, both resourceful and original in its construction of dreams of order.

Today, there are emerging developments at once both positive and ironical in that the only acceptable police to be found in contemporary fiction are sexually adventurous, or Aboriginal, or proud of their convict stock. Ashton, Jackamara and Malone imply a discovery of Australian multifariousness as a means of social order; but in the light of this survey it may in fact be no more—and no less—than a *re-discovery*, and is in fact not unlike the intricacies of crime control among the realistically perceived tensions and fragmentations of the early days of gold and crime, where police did the best they could for a self-aware community that placed no value in fantasies of heroism. The startling and enlivening features found in modern Australian crime fiction may indeed suggest that in a period of strong local publishing and increasingly sophisticated ideas about the nature and control of crime, some of the self-conscious fears and anti-social prejudices that made the original policemen disappear are themselves finally vanishing.

Notes

1. Nancy Keesing has written in scholarly detail on Lang's biography and sources in her long introduction to a reprint of the text, *John Lang and 'The Forger's Wife'*, Sydney, 1979.

2. The story 'Pursuing and Pursued' (9th December, 1865) took a lengthy section from Burrows about the troopers' base in Melbourne and re-worked it for more colour and first person drama.

3. Fortune wrote crime stories as 'W.W.', an abbreviation of her usual pseudonym, 'Waif Wander'. She wrote at least some of the later stories in the 'Memoirs' and 'Adventures' series, see the discussion by Lucy Sussex in *The Fortunes of Mary Fortune*, Melbourne, 1989 and her forthcoming edition of *The Detectives' Album*.

4. *Inventing Australia*, Sydney, 1982; of particular relevance is his discussion of 'city dweller's idea of the bush', p. 85 and the way in which 'urban bohemianism contributed to the images of such life', p. 106.

5. Reprinted in *Dead Witness*, ed. Stephen Knight, Melbourne, 1989.

6. In *Crimes for a Summer Christmas*, ed. Stephen Knight, Sydney, 1990; see also 'The Healer' in *More Crimes for a Summer Christmas*, ed. Stephen Knight, Sydney, 1991 and 'Home on the Range' to appear in *Murder at Home*, ed. Stephen Knight, Sydney, 1993.

7. See 'Songs of the Sea' in *Crimes for a Summer Christmas*, 'Dead Roses' in *A Corpse at the Opera House*, ed. Stephen Knight, Sydney, 1992 and 'All the Pretty Little Horses', in *Murder at Home*.

8. The novel was reprinted in 1992 as part of an imaginative series of classic Australian crime novels edited by Michael Tolley and Peter Moss for the Wakefield Press of Adelaide.

9. To be found in the anthology *Pearls Are A Nuisance*, London, 1950, but rather remarkably not appearing in the anthology actually titled *The Simple Art of Murder*, London, 1966, though it had in the American anthology of the same name, Boston, 1950.

10. See the stories in *Crimes for a Summer Christmas*, *More Crimes for a Summer Christmas*, *A Corpse at The Opera House* and *Murder at Home*; the last two involve Mrs Levack, more of which are promised by the author.

National Fictions and The Spycatcher Trial

KEVIN FOSTER

I am concerned here with how reductive representations of Australia, underpinned by eighteenth- and nineteenth-century constructions of *terra australis incognita*, were employed by the British press during the *Spycatcher* trial in an effort to enforce an inequitable system of discursive and cultural relations, limit the case's political fallout and thereby sustain the myth of Britain's political, economic and cultural pre-eminence.

During the nineteenth century, this cultural pre-eminence found expression, according to Martin Green, in the works of Defoe, Scott, Henty, Rider Haggard, Conan Doyle, Stevenson *et al*, in the 'adventure tales that formed the light reading of Englishmen for two hundred years and more after *Robinson Crusoe*'. Cultural expressions of confidence in Britain's manifest destiny, the adventure stories expressed 'the energizing myth of English imperialism. They were, collectively, the story England told itself as it went to sleep at night, and, in the form of its dreams, they charged England's will with the energy to go out into the world and explore, conquer and rule' (p. 3). As the fortunes of the empire waned, however, so too did those of the adventure story. Its place as the ordained, national narrative was gradually lost in the first decades of the twentieth century to the thriller. While the thriller's emergence as a generic and publishing phenomenon partly arose from changes in the publishing industry, the demise of the triple-deck novel, the establishment of circulating libraries and the creation of a popular press, all driven by the developing mass culture of mass literacy, its popularity owed more to its embodiment of broader political and cultural shifts, specifically its sensitivity to what Michael Denning calls 'the crisis in Britain's world hegemony' (p. 5). With their dominant theme of espionage and their emphasis on 'vigilance and protection against invasion', thrillers like Oppenheim's *The Mysterious Mr Sabin* (1898), Childers' *The Riddle of the Sands* (1903) and Le Queux's *The Invasion of 1910* (1906), reified the sense of vulnerability generated by a loss of confidence in the continuing aims and functioning of empire (p. 41). As Denning notes, 'if the adventure tale was the energising myth of English imperialism, the thriller becomes a compensatory myth of the crisis of imperialism' (p. 39). Thrillers like the above blamed the 'crisis' on a combination of foreign malignance and native indifference. As David French points out, 'patriotic writers', in Britain and Germany, alarmed by the other's increasing military power and their government's failures to respond to them, 'urged their governments to make timely preparations to meet these supposed threats. To appeal to the widest possible audience they often couched their warnings in fictional form, and where possible serialised them in the Yellow Press'. One effect of this was to establish an essentially fictional construction of spies, their practices and potential for subversion, as a model for both 'factual', media representations of them and government policy on their detection and interdiction. In 1910, William Le Queux published *Spies for the Kaiser: Plotting the Downfall of England*. David French notes:

> He wrote it with the specific intention of awakening the Government and the public to the inadequacies of the British counter-intelligence system. His constant theme was that the east coast and London were swarming with German spies disguised as waiters, barbers and tourists. They had orders to reconnoitre likely landing beaches, to list the resources of the countryside which might be useful to a hostile army, and to prepare to sabotage telephone, telegraph and railway lines, bridges and water-mains. Almost as soon as the book was published he received a stream of letters telling him of the suspicious behaviour of German waiters, barbers and tourists in the vicinity of telephone, telegraph and railway lines, bridges and water-mains on the east coast and near London. The letters presented an almost exact mirror image of his book. He immediately sent them to [Lieutenant-Colonel James] Edmonds [Director of Military Operations Counter-Intelligence Section MO5], who used them to construct a picture of what he supposed was the German intelligence organisation in Britain (p. 357).

Just as a fictional construction of the spy framed official counter-intelligence policy, so the same construction accounted for its failings: the spy in the thriller, as Denning notes, 'became the figure for the fortunes of Empire in Britain, providing explanations for its decline and betrayal' (p. 14). The utility and popularity of spies partly arises from the protection they have granted to British governments for more than a century from charges of incompetence and presiding over national disaster. Throughout the twentieth century, in moments of social or political crisis, successive governments and the media have invoked the spy as both the symbol and the source of national decline, namely the Zinoviev Letter in 1924, Fuchs and Nunn May in the late 1940s, Burgess and McLean in 1951, George Blake ten years later, Philby in 1963, 'the Fourth Man', Anthony Blunt, in 1979, and the ongoing hunt for 'the Fifth Man'. That 'the Fifth Man' continues to provide British governments with a conveniently invisible other, an alien accountable for decades of continuing decline suggests that the spy is of greater use to the British than he could ever have been to the KGB.

Yet the spy functions as more than a scapegoat atoning for disaster in the narrative of national decline: speculation about the degree of the KGB's penetration of Britain's security services, the import of the intelligence betrayed by Fuchs, Nunn May, McLean and Philby recalls the political and cultural dialectics of the Cold War, when Britain, as a superpower had secrets worth keeping and so worth betraying. The spy, as such, simultaneously signifies both the decline of the present and the glory of the past: in the process of accounting for Britain's demise the spy narrative resists and denies its effects, resiting Britain at the heart of the Cold War struggle and so at the centre of world affairs.

Spycatcher (1987) is Peter Wright's contribution to the debate about 'the Fifth Man'. It exposes the extent to which the British Security services had been compromised, accuses Sir Roger Hollis, a former Director General of MI5 of being 'the Fifth Man' and so brings to a successful—if belated— conclusion Wright's career as a spycatcher. As a fond reminiscence of Britain's place on the front line of the Cold War, the book reconstructs Britain as a political, economic and military superpower, and accordingly it inscribes itself within an appropriately high cultural tradition. Whereas accounts of the 'Cambridge Spy Ring' had inscribed Philby, Burgess and McLean, with their distinguished families and brilliant careers, over a palimpsest of Aristotelian tragedy, as 'people who are better than the average...who enjoy prosperity and a high reputation...whose fall into misery is not due to vice and depravity but rather to some error' (Aristotle, pp. 52, 48), Wright's account of his 'two decades' in the 'top echelons' of the British security services is framed by the forms and structures of epic, combining Le Bossu's insistence on didacticism with the classical imperative of individual and national self-promotion (p. 1).[1] In the tradition of *ubi sunt*, *Spycatcher* recounts an heroic epoch of Cold War warriors bestriding the globe, and its supercession by a meaner bureaucratic age. Writing of the 1970s Wright recalled:

> The Service began to change, and those last four years were an extended farewell...[Hanley, the new Director General of MI5] began to promote his own men. They were young and keen, but they were civil servants: men of safety rather than men of arms. I began to realize that a generation was passing. For all our differences, those of us involved in the great mole hunts, on whichever side, were fast disappearing. The age of heroes was being replaced by the age of mediocrity (p. 357).

In the light of its apology for the decline and betrayal of empire *Spycatcher* also has close affinities with the thriller—more so in its focus on 'the hunt'. Julian Symons has claimed that 'almost all of the best thrillers are concerned, in one form or another, with the theme of the hunted man' (p. 242), and the fabric of *Spycatcher* is woven from the threads of innumerable quests for elusive codes, bugs, sound and radio waves, moles, defectors, spies and lies, all of which rehearse and reinforce the book's central, recurring motif, the hunt for 'the Fifth Man'. The consistent intermingling of the discourses of epic and thriller, however, results in the subversion of Wright's self and national promotion by the parallel imperative to detail—and compensate for—the fruitlessness of his greatest hunt and his failure in any way to arrest the tide of Britain's decline.

Media representations of the *Spycatcher* trial were marked by a similar structure of narrative subversion. The media's attempts to use the trial and its associations with Australia as platforms for self and national promotion were consistently undermined by Australia's traditional place in British literary and media culture. When, in the summer of 1786, Pitt's cabinet designated Botany Bay as the site for a penal colony intended to ease the strain on Britain's overcrowded hulks and jails, it translated Australia in the British popular imagination from a land of botanical and zoological oddities into a synonym for vice, brutality and genetic regression. Its geographical and seasonal inversions were considered an ironically appropriate environment for a society composed of the socially and morally heterodox. Yet, unexpectedly, the colony prospered: by 1850 Australia was producing half of Britain's wool and the demand for labour which this and related industries generated resulted in the migration of over 150,000 free settlers to New South Wales and Van Diemen's Land. In their endeavours to attract further settlers, the colonial authorities were keen to rehabilitate the image of Australia, to assimilate what they had previously anathematised. Once used, according to Richard White, to frighten recalcitrant children and to keep the working classes 'sober, industrious and humble', through the early and mid-nineteenth century Australia was reconstructed as a worker's paradise in the colony's official publications and in pamphlets commissioned by the colonial authorities to encourage emigration (p. 17).[2] Australia's gradual drift from the outer limits of geographical and moral consciousness towards full economic and political integration in the empire was not, however, matched by a corresponding shift towards the centre of British media or literary culture. Coral Lansbury points out that 'the social orbit of the [nineteenth-century British] novel was not enlarged by reference to Australia. Thackeray wrote of life in America, setting it in contrast with conditions in England, and Mrs Gaskell brought a wealthy brother home from India in *Cranford*, as Charlotte Bronte sent St John Rivers there as a missionary in *Jane Eyre*; but Australia was not a fitting place to send anyone unless he had committed a heinous crime' (p. 28). As such, just as Pitt's government had sent its degenerate, recidivist and otherwise unwanted to Australia from the end of the eighteenth century, so through the first half of the nineteenth century it provided a convenient and credible dumping ground for their textual equivalents, peripheral figures, black sheep, socially embarrassing relations, middle-class bankrupts and penitent but fallen women—all characters deserving of but denied happiness or success in England by moral precept or literary convention.

This construction of Australia as a moral and geographical other has shown remarkable resilience and has given rise to an array of reductive, metonymic figures, what Peter Putnis calls a 'prevailing grid of national types' that have flourished most conspicuously in the British media (p. 30). To some extent the survival of these stereotypes (and the framing of new ones) has been a product of British media policy on Australia. In spite of close economic and cultural ties with Britain, Australia has rarely occupied a prominent place in its news. At the time of the *Spycatcher* trial *The Times* and the *Daily Mail* were the only British newspapers with bureaux in Australia. Other than sporting or travel features, the vast majority of information from and about Australia originates with the major wire services. Their compliance with and reinforcement of a construction of newsworthiness that privileges the elite, the negative and the unexpected has ensured Australia's continued, if not increased marginalisation. As a former Reuters bureau chief observed, Australia rarely makes headlines because 'There are no coup d'etats, no mass violence or Governments toppling. It is a pretty stable country which from our point of view means the off-beat story has more chance of being used overseas' (quoted by Alomes, p. 175). 'Off-beat, odd-spot or trivia stories', as Stephen Alomes notes, 'need no elaborate awareness of a country' (p. 175). They justify their inclusion on the basis of their perceived typicality, their advertisement of their particular provenance, hence their functioning within and reinforcement of 'the prevailing grid of national types'. According to Alomes, the favourite Australian stereotypes have been framed around sport and what he calls 'native exotica—flora, fauna and Aborigines' (p. 175). Putnis concurs, identifying 'primitive nature' as the most popular of the 'national types' structuring the British media's representation of Australia (p. 30). British coverage of the Pope's visit to Australia, which coincided with the *Spycatcher* trial, confirms the accuracy of their formulations. The Australian media marked the Pontiff's ten-day visit with a range of earnest debates about the role of religion in an increasingly secular society, the causes of diminishing church attendance among Australian Catholics, the Vatican's stance on birth control, even a possible role for the Pope in the resolution of Aboriginal grievances. *The Times*'s coverage of the visit, however, was restricted to two photographs, one on 26 November 1986 featured the Pope cuddling a koala bear at a Brisbane animal sanctuary: the other, from 1 December, showed him patting 'Melinda, a one year old kangaroo' with whom he 'held a special audience...outside the Adelaide Festival Centre' (1 January 1986, p. 10).

This construction of Australia as, above all else, a site of zoological oddities, 'a land of the physical rather than the intellectual, the simple

rather than the complex', ironically recalls eighteenth-century representations of *terra australis incognita* as a mine of scientific novelties peopled by
a race of primitive savages, a natural other to the centred culture and is,
according to Alomes, 'particularly appealing to a declining imperial power'
(p. 174). This is because it resurrects and reinforces the comforting
hierarchies of a bygone age, rekindling the long dead flame of empire with
the pathetic sparks of denigration—praising Britain by burying Australia.
The resilience of this (discredited) hierarchy and the closed reading of the
Spycatcher case that it sustained owes something to Australian media
constructions of Britain. Their representation of British society as static
and stratified, divided into Royalty, the bowler-hatted nincompoops of the
Establishment and the downtrodden *poilus*, not only travesties and ignores
the kinesis of Britain's complex class structure, it also fails to locate
significant resistance to the existing class hegemony, or to identify the
delight that sections of the British public and media shared in Australian
attacks on the hypocrisy of the Official Secrets Act, and the exposure to
public censure of the Whitehall mandarins protected by it. However,
intended as it was to establish a series of unfavourable comparisons with
Australia's robust, accountable egalitarianism, this media construction
of Britain merely reinforced Australia's 'simplicity' and physicality,
compounding its cultural marginalisation and expediting Britain's
employment of the case as a platform for political and national self-
promotion.

The British Government's case in Sydney and the narrative of national
regeneration which it underpinned rested upon an 'official' construction
of *Spycatcher* as what Wesley Wark calls a 'fantasy of clandestinity'.
Fantasies of clandestinity presume a landscape of binary oppositions
analogous with the political, military and moral dialectics of the Cold
War, and apparently lay bare the secret workings of one or both sides,
offering a privileged, 'inside story' on their most vital forms and functioning.
In Sydney the Government insisted that the publication of Wright's
allegations or their discussion in open court would upset the balance of
these oppositions, exposing vital secrets about the aims, structures and
practices of the intelligence services, thereby jeopardising 'the security of
the western alliance' (*The Times*, 20 November 1986, p. 11). The British
Government and media advocated this 'official' reading of the case by
identifying and isolating the principles purportedly at its heart, organising
them into a framework of moral binaries, freedom vs. restraint, culture vs.
barbarism, good vs. evil, thus constructing the trial as both a mirror image
and an extension of the military and political dialectics of the Cold War.

Australia and its associations threatened to subvert both the symmetry
and the seriousness of this fantasy, and so the stark moral dichotomies
were, as far as was possible, unshackled from their immediate context.

'Incidental revelations' which threatened the narrative's neat dialectics were either found a place within the prevailing structure of binaries or dismissed as insignificant (unsignifying) details, as was the case with Peter Wright's hat (*The Times*, 3 December 1986, p. 17). The hat, an Akubra, which cartoons of the former MI5 man invariably festooned with corks, attracted attention because of its apparent embodiment of an Australian type. On Wright's head, however, this symbol of bush barbarity threatened to confuse the moral and cultural polarities sustained by his construction as the Cold War warrior incarnate. In an effort to defuse its potential for damage *The Times* inscribed it in an innocuous, literally unsignifying place within the narrative:

> A frail, sick old man of 70 who needs a stout stick to support his slow, painful steps and a constant supply of pills to keep him alive, will climb in to the witness box in a New South Wales court today to take on the British Government, the Establishment, Whitehall, and anyone else who stands against him in his personal crusade...
>
> For many, it may be difficult to associate the world of espionage and counter-espionage with a man like Peter Wright. After 10 years of living in the hot and dusty hills of Tasmania [!], he has become accustomed to wearing floppy or wide-brimmed hats to protect his face...
>
> But it is easy to be misled by this picture of an angry, white-haired gentleman who spent much of his working life in a world that very few people understand or care about. For in many ways he typifies, even at the age of 70, the kind of experience-hardened counter-espionage officer who, more than anyone else, understands the threat to Western society posed by the huge intelligence efforts of the Soviet Union and its satellites (8 December 1986, p. 7).

Where Australia was mentioned, its potential for narrative subversion was checked by a closed system of signification which confined it and its representative figures within rigidly circumscribed national types. The theory of national types, which flourished in the early nineteenth century, drew on and enforced a crude social Darwinism that ranked other nations and races on the degree and success of their emulation of the centred Anglo-Saxon ideals of social organisation and physiological structure. It propounded a belief in national and racial physiognomies founded on Pieter Camper's division of higher from lower vertebrate life on the basis of a facial or Camper angle. As Perry Curtis notes, the Camper angle was 'formed by the intersection of two lines one running diagonally or vertically, as the case might be, from the forehead to the foremost point of the front teeth or incisors, and the other running horizontally from the opening of the ear to the nostrils. This relatively, if not alarmingly, simple device permitted Camper to contrive a scale of animal and human evolution or progress from primitive to civilized life, the intervals between each stage being gauged by the size of the facial angle within each category' (p. 7). Convicts and Irishmen shared a lowly place on this scale, somewhere between orang-utans and negroes, and were graphically represented as such, particularly when combined in the form of the militant Fenian (Fig. 1, p. 131). Many cartoons of the *Spycatcher* trial depicted its Australian protagonists as simian, brutish figures, whose obtuse Camper angles, fang-like (or missing) teeth and seeming delight in sadism were strikingly reminiscent of Cruickshank, Tenniel, Leech and Morgan's nineteenth century representations of 'the Fenian Pest' (Fig. 2, p. 132).

The construction and employment of national types in the trial implied that Turnbull's searching cross-examination of Sir Robert Armstrong, and Justice Powell's much publicised displeasure with the British Government's 'serpentine weavings' arose not from the defence of legal principle, but from pathological antagonism, demonstrating not the pursuit of liberty but 'the old inferiority complex that makes the Aussies pretend to hate the poms so much', thus transforming the proceedings into the latest round in 'their favourite sport...Roll up and bash a pom' (*Daily Express*, 18 November 1986, p. 38; 2 December 1986, p. 6–7). The British insistence that events in Sydney said more about antipodean aggression than official British duplicity as such represented a bold attempt politically to decontextualise the case by radically closing the signification of Australia and Australians: whatever was said or happened in the court was inflected, and politically neutered, by Australia's traditional hatred for the poms.

However, the Australians would not signify only what the narrative of national self-promotion dictated; they could be fitted neither comfortably nor usefully within 'the prevailing grid of national types'—though half-hearted attempts were made, most often by the cartoonists. Turnbull, 'the wild colonial boy' with a penchant for pom-bashing, was also a Rhodes Scholar with impeccable Liberal Party connections and an undisguised admiration for Margaret Thatcher: he could hardly be constructed as one of the 'beer-bellied Bruces' hostile to all things English (*Daily Express*, 18 November 1986, p. 38). Justice Powell's refusal to grant the British application for a permanent injunction against Heinemann was, thus, a public, legal confirmation of the government and the media's inability to exercise political, cultural and therefore discursive authority.

To some extent, the media's failure to enforce narrative closure and so promote the Cold War construction of the case arose from the 'heavy' and the popular press's adherence to contrasting constructions of news value and their resultant commitment to differing forms of representation. According to Patricia Holland, 'it is the declared intent of the popular press to entertain'. They do so not only by collapsing the distinctions between 'hard' and 'soft' news but by framing their stories within a formal

Figure 1: 'Two Forces' from *Punch*, 29 October 1881. Anarchy attacks Britannia with a rock.

Figure 2: Griffin's cartoon from the *Daily Mirror*, 11 November 1986.

construction which is both founded on and encourages metaphorical, associative reading:

> striking front pages, double page spreads with dramatic photographs, giant lettering and graphic devices held in a mosaic layout...are the celebratory set pieces at which our mass circulation tabloids excel. These displays are not to be read in a linear fashion but are to be appreciated whole, sampled, a caption here a paragraph there. The mode of appreciation is visual as much as verbal. Laced with jokes and charged with emotion, geared to arouse anger, pity, desire, this vivid and compulsive style is closer to that of cartoon comics than it is to the literary sequences of *The Times* or *The Guardian* (Holland, p. 119).

The tabloids' rejection of narrative linearity in favour of news construction by *bricolage* directly conflicted with the metonymic, syntagmatic structure employed by the heavies, whose indexical, naturalising processes curtailed free association, radically closed meaning and so sustained the Cold War narrative. In accordance with their metaphorical, combinatory construction of the news, tabloid representations of the case were mediated through associated events, most notably contemporary Anglo-Australian sporting contests, the Americas Cup and the Ashes Cricket series, both of which were under way in Australia at the time of the trial. This process extended from the imputation of an implied relationship between the proceedings and sport, to the discursive construction of one entirely in terms of the other.[3] The *Daily Star*, for example, suggested that the Australians were seeking revenge in the courtroom for their defeat in the first test at Brisbane: it counselled the British legal team: 'watch out for those Aussies! Just because they can't beat us at cricket they're trying to have a go at us in the courts' (21 November 1986, p. 8). Evidently, the tabloids had no less faith in British superiority than the rest of Fleet Street: yet their construction of the trial in terms of sport implies that dominance is as uncertain as it is temporary. The British Government and media's failure to legislate the free play of signification, to confine Australia and Australians within 'the prevailing grid of national types' and thereby resume a dominant position in the cultural hierarchy, confirmed that neither the text nor the trial could function as platforms for the acclamation of British hegemony, but served instead as sites for the fixing, unfixing and refixing of competing constructions of national identity.

Notes

1. See Page, Leitch and Knightley (1968), also Andrew Boyle, *The Climate of Treason*.

2. For example David Mackenzie, *The Emigrant's Guide: or Ten Years Practical Experience in Australia*. London 1845.

3. See Wooldridge (1986).

References

Alomes, Stephen (1987), 'The British Press and Australia: Post-Imperial Fantasy and the Contemporary Media', *Meanjin*, Vol. 46, No. 2, (June), pp. 173–83

Aristotle, 'On the Art of Poetry', *Aristotle/Horace/Longinus: Classical Literary Criticism*, Harmondsworth: Penguin, 1988

Boyle, Andrew (1979), *The Climate of Treason: Five who Spied for Russia*, London: Hutchinson

Curtis, Lewis P. (1971), *Apes and Angels: The Irishman in Victorian Caricature*, Newton Abbot: David and Charles

Denning, Michael (1987), *Cover Stories: Narrative and Ideology in the British Spy Thriller*, London: Routledge and Kegan Paul

French, David (1978), 'Edwardian Spy Fever', *The Historical Journal*, Vol. 21, No. 2, pp. 355–70.

Green, Martin (1980), *Dreams of Adventure: Deeds of Empire*, London: Routledge and Kegan Paul.

Holland, Patricia (1982), 'Public Opinion, the Popular Press and the Organisation of Ideas', *Falklands/Malvinas: Whose Crisis?*, London: Latin America Bureau, pp. 119–26

Lansbury, Coral (1970), *Arcady in Australia: The Evocation of Australia in Nineteenth-Century English Literature*, Melbourne: Melbourne University Press

Page, Bruce, David Leitch and Philip Knightley (1968), *Philby: The Spy Who Betrayed A Generation*, London: Andre Deutsch

Putnis, Peter (1985), 'Australia in the British Press', *Media Information Australia*, No. 35, (February/March), pp. 28–35

Symons, Julian (1974), *Bloody Murder*, Harmondsworth: Penguin

Wark, Wesley (ed.) (1992), *Spy Fiction, Spy Films and Real Intelligence*, London: Frank Cass.

White, Richard (1981), *Inventing Australia: Images and Identity 1688–1980*, Sydney: George Allen and Unwin

Wooldridge, Ian (1986), 'MI5 Secrets—it's just not cricket!', *The Sun-Herald*, 30 November

Wright, Peter (1987), *Spycatcher: The Candid Autobiography of a Senior Intelligence Officer*, New York: Viking

Naturalising 'Horror' Stories: Australian Crime News as Popular Culture

CHRISTINE HIGGINS

The question of the relationship between so-called 'reality', itself a linguistic construction, and stories about that reality is a problematic one but one that must be addressed in an attempt to understand how news and other public narratives (such as historical narrative) reflect and represent their culture. I am interested in how news stories function as a component of Australian popular culture, and more specifically, the relationship between news stories and archetypal narratives emanating from our western cultural tradition, and the more recent Australian additions to it.

News-making involves the transformation of events into stories, a term long in use among journalists, but one, paradoxically, that highlights the constructed nature of news narrative rather than the 'transparency' that journalists claim best describes their professional writing.

Many traditional disciplines such as psychology, history and anthropology are now focussing far more on storying as a process of social and personal meaning-making. Whereas personal narratives provide a means of framing and ordering (or distancing) private experience—important in the process of understanding and incorporating it into the consciousness—public narratives, such as news stories, provide wider images of the world and of collective experience. They offer definitions and rationalisations of social practice, highlight certain symbols of power and, in the process, present ideological messages to readers or listeners.

Not many historians would attempt to argue that history is an objective, unmediated record of events, but rather would seek to examine the processes involved in the construction of historical narrative; or to put it another way, their focus would be on the *discourse* of history.

Foucault explains discourse, broadly speaking, as a body of texts—historical political, literary and so on—which make particular statements about our society and its origins. Meanings made by readers from such texts contribute to a larger system of meaning which is constantly evolving and changing, by means of which we apprehend our society and our place in it.

News narratives, I would argue, form one such discursive system; and the various narrative devices used to create such texts far exceed those necessary simply to transmit information clearly and precisely, which is all news journalists claim they are doing.

While news stories appear individually to be fragmentary and unconnected, not to say decontextualised, I believe it can be shown that they are all contributors to a larger symbolic ordering of events, a process in Ricoeur's words of 'constructing meaningful totalities out of scattered events' (1981, p. 278). This 'totality' is culture knowledge.

News is essentially formulaic and ritualistic in its modes of story telling. Tuchmann refers to 'the routinisation of the unexpected' when speaking of news making (1974, p. 110). A journalist may well seem to be creating a new story from an unexpected or novel occurrence, but she/he has to place the event in a context and represent it in a way that will be understood by readers in the light of their previous 'common-sense' experience. So what news-makers ultimately seem to do is to use familiar cultural frames with which to present the story, so that readers can decode it in accordance with pre-existing and pre-known cultural meaning systems.

Such a process is analogous to that of the traditional oral story teller whose ritualistic narration of tales (including news) both drew on and also amplified and potentially transformed an established body of communal knowledge or lore.

While much anthropological work has been done on the mythologies of so-called 'primitive' cultures, the mythological base of contemporary societies is less frequently investigated. Nevertheless, many commentators have noted the myth-making propensities of the mass media (Fiske and Hartley, 1978; Silverstone, 1981; Barthes, 1972) when referring to its ability to articulate and endlessly reiterate the core values and pre-occupations of its culture through its images, icons and ritualistic narratives. The news media in particular functions in ways very similar to that of myth: both news and myth consist of simple formulaic stories that serve to define and legitimate a society's basic structures and processes; both attempt to provide reassuring 'common sense' explanations for that which is unfamiliar or threatening. Frye notes that myth does not necessarily reflect an objective reality, but builds a world of its own (1957); the same point can also be made about news to highlight its constructed nature.

I wish to turn now to one very well known news event to investigate the processes which seemed to be at work in its transformation into a news story, an on-going news story, and especially the mobilisation of mythic archetypes in the construction of a particular kind of horror narrative.

The case I intend to examine is the Azaria Chamberlain case. Readers may well feel a sense of *déjà vu* at the mention the name, but it is especially useful for my purpose as it has perhaps appealed to the popular imagination more than any other Australian case involving the disappearance of a child. It also received wide international coverage, created enormous amounts of speculation, rumour and gossip, polarised the Australian community for almost a decade, and generated a vast volume of official discourse and legal debate arising out of the two inquests, the trial, two appeals and a judicial inquiry. Additionally, it generated a considerable unofficial discourse of jokes, ballads and songs (see Appendix), and other cultural artefacts such as T-shirts and tea towels. The case is said to have positively influenced the tourist industry in the Northern Territory and to have had a negative impact upon the community's faith in the jury system and the reliability of forensic evidence.

The activities of the Chamberlains continue to command considerable media attention both at home and abroad. Even an incident in 1988 involving a dog fight when one of the protagonists was the Chamberlain dog was reported nationally and internationally. The most recent media speculation involves Lindy Chamberlain's future marriage plans. A recent *Sunday Mail* report (2 August 1992) was headlined **Lindy's man a mystery** and subheaded **Veil of secrecy surrounds couple's love affair**. It seems the Chamberlain mystery will not go away!

The original event, the disappearance of baby Azaria on the night of 17 August 1980 at Ayers Rock seems now to act only as a catalyst for what has become a self-generating cultural phenomenon centred on Lindy Chamberlain, as the flow of books (numbering eight at last count), magazine and learned journal articles, further press reports, conference papers, the film *Evil Angels/A Cry in the Dark* and reviews of the books and the film attest. It has been recently reported that the Australian Opera Company is commissioning an opera to be entitled 'Lindy', due for production in 1994.

I want to suggest that the main reason for the extraordinary and continuing prominence of this case and its ready incorporation into Australian popular culture lies in the power of its mythic connotations foregrounded in the news stories, and their ability to impact upon our collective unconscious. The story was positioned within a pre-existing system of meaning, and was then interpreted in the light of that system.

One of the most interesting aspects of the case, I find, on re-reading the news reports, both national and international, is the speed with which the case shifted from being read as a 'lost child' story and then as a 'bereavement' story when no hope was to be had for the child's safe return, to being represented as a bizarre murder story; or as one reporter put it a 'classic horror movie plot'. The reason for the speed and direction of this shift in meaning seems to go far beyond the suspicions of the police or what was seen to be 'peculiar' behaviour on the part of the Chamberlain parents (in that they were not judged to be sufficiently distraught), and to reside rather in the plethora of powerful mythic associations related to the site and the events so that news-makers were predisposed to read fact as if it were fiction and to construct the story as an archetype of 'the strange tale' with Gothic overtones.

There was firstly the Rock, 'an eerie and unsettling place which seemed as if the thing itself had played a part in the events' (*Observer*, 5 September 1982), and its situation in the 'Red Centre' or the 'Dead Heart'; the incident, a child lost in the bush or 'spirited away', as some reports put it. The lost child is a powerful signifier in the Australian bush myth and at least partly derived from the European 'Babes in the Wood' archetype. In the Australian context, however, it is associated with the inimical nature of the land and its active hostility to white settlement, as is the case in Furphy's *Such is Life*, for instance. To others, though, the lost child signified a sacrificial offering.

The dingo is also a part of the bush myth although somewhat ambi-valently so. In this case its mythic force is amplified by associations firstly with the wolf of European legend—traditionally blamed for the dis-appearance of children—and also with the werewolf, a more literary construction. Many spoke of Lindy Chamberlain at the time as the 'two-legged wolf'. Reference was also made to the Kadaitcha Man of Aboriginal legend who acts as executioner before vanishing leaving only the tracks of a wild animal. Lindy Chamberlain was also constructed as Witch, able to change her appearance almost daily:

> On one day, she would look 'like a schoolgirl...light blue dress with a billowing skirt and bobbysocks' and on the next she would look 'like a filmstar with a black dress, red lips, shoes and handbag'
>
> (*Sydney Morning Herald*, 1 November 1982).

One of the legendary attributes of the witch is her ability to change her shape (even assuming that of a beast.) The media were obsessed by Chamberlain's appearance and changing shape. To others she had 'killer eyes', 'a stare that went right through you' or 'bored into you' and was 'witch-like' in its intensity.

I was interested to find that the *Observer* of 5 September 1982 just before the trial, highlights almost all of the mythic associations and archetypes referred to above, in an article entitled **Azaria, the child who died in the wilderness**. This is columnist 'Michael Davie's Notebook' which I assume is a regular feature and does not indicate an agency source which would otherwise account for his familiarity with elements of the Australian bush myth. Part of this article reads thus:

> A very remarkable murder trial is about to open in Darwin, in the Northern Territory of Australia.
>
> It concerns the disappearance of a nine-week-old baby from a tourist campsite, and no case, it is safe to say, has ever laid such a strong grip on the collective Australian imagination, involving as it does the principal natural monument of the outback, Ayers Rock; fundamentalist religion; the dingo—Australia's nearest animal to the wolf; and Aboriginal tribesmen; as well

as—in the person of Professor J.M. Cameron of London—the most complex
and technical skills of modern forensic science.

Almost all of the relevant archetypes are noted in the first paragraph, the
Rock, the dingo and its associations with the wolf, 'fundamentalist religion'
which adds a further dimension of meaning to the evocative title, making
clear connotative links between the biblical wilderness, so often a place of
sacrifice, and the harsh 'alien' landscape of central Australia. By
implication and through its emphasis on mythic archetypes, the text is
able to pose the question as to whether this incident is another such
example of ritual sacrifice, associated with what it later describes as a
'fringe religion'. Associated with this also was the totally unfounded
speculation that the name, Azaria, meant 'sacrifice in the wilderness'.

A nice cultural opposition is foregrounded also in the first paragraph
between 'Aboriginal tribesmen' with connotations of primitive life style
and lore (they acted as trackers in the search for the missing Azaria) and
'Professor Cameron of London' who brings to the wilderness 'the most
complex and technical skills of modern forensic science'—the clash of
ancient and modern cultures.

As the public was polarised concerning the guilt or innocence of Lindy
Chamberlain, the case tended to be read by means of oppositions of the
kind just noted. As the presence of any signifier automatically implicates
its opposite, then in a case where so many cherished Australian institutions
and icons were being interrogated, the use of oppositions provides a
conceptual structure whereby inherent contradictions could surface and
be held up to scrutiny.

Some of the most obvious oppositions to surface in national and
international press coverage are these:

Baby Azaria—sacrificial offering	or	victim of the hostile bush
Lindy Chamberlain—witch and child killer	or	caring, grief-stricken mother
the Dingo—natural predator and extension of the malignant power of the landscape	or	maligned indigenous creature
Michael Chamberlain—sincere man of God; Loving husband and father	or	accessory to infanticide
Religious minority	or	secular majority
The Aborigines—clever trackers one with their environment	or	primitive savages people at incapable of presenting admissible evidence to a court of law

| Eye witness evidence | or | forensic evidence |
| Professor Cameron's truth | or | Lindy Chamberlain's truth |

As a result of reading the case through such oppositions as these, patriarchal, racist and conformist attitudes were privileged, and the Australian community's hostility towards (perhaps fear of) difference (racial, religious and gender) was highlighted. The oppositions pointed up the fact that so far as the media and many members of the public were concerned, the Chamberlains were not like 'us', the majority of Australians. Their life-style was different; they were vegetarians, non-drinking and non-smoking. They were members of a little-known religious sect, and they publicly demonstrated their faith. Lindy, in particular, did not conform to the stereotype of woman and bereaved mother. She was too well (and sexily) dressed in court, as male reporters constantly remarked and she did not express 'normal' maternal feelings of grief; she was too outspoken, and inclined to be aggressive with prosecuting counsel. In other words, she did not behave in the accepted passive, submissive way that a woman should in such circumstances. Once constructed as 'other', it is an easy step to being represented as non-human, monster-like or witch-like; if not normal, then deviant and thus criminal. Overwhelmingly, Lindy Chamberlain had to be the guilty instigator and perpetrator. It would have been possible to construct Lindy Chamberlain as an exemplum of courage, independence, dogged determination and spiritual strength, all prized qualities, and said to form part of the Australian (male) character, according to the bush myth. But Lindy was not male, and thus such characteristics in her were negatively deconstructed. It is noteworthy that Michael Chamberlain was depicted as simply covering up for his wife and thus not especially guilty, and was thus not so punished. One could also suggest that the media found it easy to construct Lindy Chamberlain as witch and 'killer mother', drawing on mythic archetypes, but found it less easy to find a convenient body of myth from which to construct Michael Chamberlain, thus he always appeared less culpable.

The case also valorised the evidence of (forensic) science over eye witness accounts and the evidence of black trackers. This is very evident in the original *Observer* article I mentioned and in another entitled **Azaria: London clues lead to murder charge** (12 September 1982), the sequel, as it were, to the former. This piece deliberately sets the evidence of the Chamberlains and the other witnesses who were camped near the Chamberlains at Ayers Rock at the time against that of a battery of expert scientific witnesses and most notably, Professor Cameron. A pair of photographs which accompany the piece nicely focus the opposition between Lindy Chamberlain's evidence of the dingo attack and Professor Cameron's evidence that indicated that the baby had been murdered. Mother's witness or expert scientist's witness?

That the so-called Australian 'cultural cringe' is not dead is also clear from this report—or to put it another (perhaps better) way, the European sense of superiority over the 'Antipodeans' comes across strongly here. The first paragraph highlights the strange up-side down nature of the Australian seasons where 'carol singing was beginning in the sweltering heat', and also points up our tenacious adherence to European customs and traditions despite the 'new nationalism' of the 1980s. The article, as its headline indicates, goes on to suggest that the mystery cannot be solved in Australia, but will be in London, location of the most advanced scientific expertise. The baby clothes have been secretly sent to London for analysis. Now Professor Cameron, described as 'a confident Scot' comes from London to explain all. We all tend to put our faith in so-called 'specialists' of one kind or another in this technological age, and, I suspect, many Australians have more faith in overseas experts than the local product—as does this English journalist, predictably enough. As we now know, Professor Cameron's evidence and that of some other forensic experts then valorised is now totally discredited, and that of the black trackers and eye witnesses, originally rejected, even derided, is now accepted as that most closely approximating the truth.

In a final summarising article where Michael Davie provides his version of the meaning of the events (*Observer*, 7 November 1982), he makes this comment which refers to the sentence of life imprisonment for Lindy Chamberlain:

> Hard labour, in this context, is not as bad as it sounds. Still, the sentence has shaken a lot of people. Australia does not often get into the world news. Some people feel that the outcome makes them look like a society with a very crude system of rough justice.

This evaluation which reinforces the notion of Australia as still little more than a half-civilised frontier society is redolent of European cultural ideology—which privileges the 'old' world over the new, believing its 'whole way of life' to be more 'civilised', more advanced and more sophisticated than that of that 'other' upside down 'new' world. One may infer generally from Michael Davie's articles that he feels that such a bizarre case could only happen 'down under', and is almost evidence in itself of our peculiar 'otherness'. Lindy Chamberlain herself seems aware of the privileging of things European over things Australian as she once said that:

> whoever drew the world maps had a lot to answer for, because Britain and America were always make to look bigger than they are, while Australia is made to look smaller (*Sunday Times*, 27 January 1991).

The mythic dimension of news derives from its inescapable intertextuality; its relationship with all the other stories that have gone before. As Levi-

Strauss notes 'we define myth as consisting of all its versions' (1972, p. 217), each version feeds into and also from the body of the myth. The Azaria Chamberlain case can be analysed further in terms of both vertical and horizontal intertextuality. I have already made some mention of the vertical dimension of its intertextuality where the representation of the events and the participants can be seen as a rewriting or reconstruction of certain cultural constructs.

It is also possible to examine its horizontal intertextuality—how the primary text—the story of Azaria's disappearance—is related to all the secondary texts it has generated, all of which ultimately refer back to it. I am thinking here of all the subsequent news and magazine articles, works of criticism, the film, *A Cry in the Dark*, book-length accounts, film and book reviews and Lindy Chamberlain's recent autobiography *Through My Eyes*. These are all evidence of the original text's polysemy and its instability of meaning. There is no fixed, stable meaning, of course, in the primary text; as most people would agree, meaning finally rests with the culturally and historically situated reader.

I would now like to examine some more of these secondary texts as textual 'shifters' where new and evolving meanings become evident. For one example I refer to the *Sunday Times* of 7 May 1989, and a review of the film *A Cry in the Dark* entitled **Back from the wilderness**.

> Here she is again, on television this time, with husband Michael, chatting with Meryl Streep. They like each other. You can tell. They smile a lot. They're talking about *A Cry in the Dark*, the film version of Australia's most famous murder trial, the Chamberlain case. And here's Michael on a magazine cover. No, hang on, it's Sam Neill. The story is Sam talking about becoming Michael, and the strange affinity that developed between them. The saga of Lindy and Michael has become the Meryl and Sam show.
>
> When it first became known, two years ago, that Streep and Neill would play Lindy and Michael Chamberlain in a feature film, the reaction in Australia was, in equal parts, awe and incredulity. Wow! From *Out of Africa* to the outback; *Reilly* to the Rock. But could non-Australian actors, no matter how talented, conjure convincing portrayals of a couple who had played lead roles in Australia's real-life legal soap-opera? How could a story spanning eight years be compressed into two hours? But, despite the obvious obstacles, the project went ahead. And along the way a kind of transfiguration took place. The Chamberlains, who co-operated in the film, became interested bystanders. Like everyone else, at the end of it all, they were in the audience: passive observers of a story now much bigger than themselves.

This style of reportage seems to me to promote a reading strategy which plays with or further destabilises the already blurred boundaries between the fictional and the real. I am thinking here particularly of lines such as 'here's Michael on a magazine cover. No, hang on, it's Sam Neill. The story is Sam talking about becoming Michael' and 'the saga of Lindy and Michael has become the Meryl and Sam show'.

This blurring must always take place when actors around whom many popular associations cling play 'real' people and act out a 'true' story, and where the player is identified with the character he or she is made to look like and sound like. We are told Streep 'captured perfectly Chamberlain's nasal whine', for example. It is common for actors to talk about their character parts as if they were real people in soaps and fiction films, 'Sam becoming Michael', but here the position is also reversed—real people are treated like characters—'a couple who played lead roles in Australia's real-life legal soap opera' is the description of the Chamberlains. This is a deliberately engineered blurring of illusion and 'reality' which is magnified by the juxtaposition of photographs of Lindy and Streep playing Lindy. One reason for this kind of construction may lie in the media's tendency to render down all kinds of content into a spectacle, an entertainment. Additionally, the process of becoming a part of popular culture, virtually an icon in Lindy Chamberlain's case, requires that remnants of reality be cast off so as to be replaced by symbolic content.

It is made clear that the Chamberlains have long since lost control of their own story as 'the saga of Lindy and Michael has become the Meryl and Sam show'. The report goes on to mention that the story is now 'much bigger than themselves', is public property, and that their role, now that the media have appropriated their personal tragedy and transformed it into spectacle can only be as 'passive observers' and 'advisers' as the show rolls on.

Paradoxically, the article goes on to discuss the hard work required to reproduce the illusion of the real in the film. It is also obvious that 'hard' textual work is being expended in the reportage to represent the Chamberlains as 'soap stars' in an on-going media spectacular. In commenting on the cultural phenomenon of the star, James Reeves notes that we must:

> conceive of the star performance as dynamically open-ended *discourse*— discourse that can trigger a multiplicity of meanings in the culture. In embracing the complexity of star communication, this interpretive strategy foregrounds the fundamentally *intertextual*, or *dialogic*, nature of media stardom: for as discourse, the star breaks traditional critical boundaries— narrative boundaries, generic boundaries, media boundaries—and weaves through diverse media texts, linking them, inflecting them, and refracting their meaning (1988, pp. 152–3).

Thus reading 'the stars' requires a different set of strategies and competencies than those required for other forms of media discourse. The evolving Chamberlain story now has to be read in conjunction with all the other competing stories of the stars and their exploits.

The *Sunday Times* of 27 January 1991 features an interview by Valarie Grove with Lindy Chamberlain entitled, **Living with the memory of the dingo baby** (also reprinted in the *Montreal Gazette* of 17 February 1991). It continues to concede Lindy star quality—one day 'a housewife next a household word', but the reviewer appears much disappointed that the reality falls short of the (media) constructed image of the celebrity:

> The incongruity of it: this banal person, whose story once absorbed the world. This woman was the talk of two continents. The dingo baby story was a mystery stranger than fiction.

The interviewer also finds it hard to reconcile the person whom she also claims lacks 'intellect and guile' with her story, 'a mystery stranger than fiction'. In a very patronising review, again redolent of European thinking about 'the Antipodes', the interviewer goes on to say:

> There is something touching about this simple soul, a former waitress and shopkeeper, born in New Zealand and raised in the Victorian bible-belt backwoods of Australia, thrust so publicly into a world of which she knows very little.

Lindy Chamberlain is obviously not the stuff of legend to this journalist. She doesn't play the role well. As another commentator put it, 'she is no Hollywood heroine'. Streep clearly does it better.

Originally, Chamberlain was accused of failing to fit the 'bereaved mother' stereotype as she herself says in this interview: 'if I cried I was said to be putting on an act; if I smiled I was heartless.' Now she is accused of not fitting the image of the star, she is too ordinary:

> Last week she was receiving visitors in a pokey room at the Kensington Hilton, courtesy of Heinemann, which is publishing her life story, *Through My Eyes*. It is doing well in Australia but she has not yet learnt the lavish ways of a celebrity author. She sends her son Reagan out of the hotel to buy milk for his breakfast cereal. 'Have you seen the price of room service?' she says.

The Azaria Chamberlain story has been variously framed and either partially or totally transformed from being an account of a child's disappearance, to being a 'mystery story', 'a strange tale', 'a bizarre whodunnit', a 'horror story' and then after the Chamberlains were released and exonerated, 'a poignant tale of suffering', and now a show, the 'Meryl and Sam show', a saga, managed by the media, part of popular culture. Similarly, the Chamberlains have undergone many transformations— from being represented as bereaved parents, suspects, then defendants, committed felons, victims of injustice and now media celebrities, with the spot-light always on Lindy herself.

Journalists seem well aware that the saga appears to be on-going, self-generating, that the story resists closure. Many make such statements as:

> One way or another Lindy Chamberlain and the dingo that she may or may not have seen with her baby in its mouth are going to be a centre of Australian attention for a long time yet (*Observer*, 20 April 1984).

and

> *Cry in the Dark* is not the last word on the case, just the latest...It lacks the words after the final credits...'to be continued' (*Sunday Times*, 7 May 1989).

A factor in all the early reportage of the narrative has been the textual struggle between the mythic and the mimetic. As I have argued above, the myths activated by the 'real' events always tended to overpower them (the real happenings) and to mediate their reception. The myths and archetypes, the lost child, the dingo, the Rock are at least the stuff of the Australian ethos, and derive their strength and meaning from that source.

Recent coverage of the saga no longer activates those same myths. They are no longer relevant because this new coverage relates to the media's own transformations and incorporations of the original narrative—the books, the film, 'Meryl Streep as an accused murderer' heads the *New York Times* film review, 'the book of the film of the Dingo Baby Affair' (as the *Montreal Gazette* put it when referring to *Through My Eyes*), the forthcoming opera, Lindy Chamberlain's 'new man' and so on. The media has created its own new mythic order that manifests itself in the discourse of stardom. As Reeves also suggests:

> Stardom as social phenomenon, then, might best be conceived of as the grand cultural dialogue that arises from the collision of media institutions and their stratified, heterogeneous audience. In this scheme, stardom as media discourse becomes the individualized articulation of relevant, strategic social types that represent culturally significant ways of speaking, of seeing, of being (1988, p. 152).

In conclusion, one might well ask what 'strategic social types' do the Chamberlains represent now that they are stars? One could answer that they have achieved a kind of heroic stature in 'coming through slaughter' as Angela Johnson of the *Guardian* put it in 'triumphing over tragedy'. Speaking particularly of Lindy Chamberlain she says:

> Lindy Chamberlain was hounded by the media, vilified by society and fought bravely to clear her name after being convicted of murdering her baby daughter in the Australian outback.

> Two inquests, a murder trial, three years in jail, two appeals, two bail applications and exoneration by a Royal Commission have left their mark. But she remains remarkably resilient to the enormity of the tragedy that almost destroyed her (31 January 1991).

Now the Chamberlains (and Lindy in particular) exemplify courage in adversity, a kind of spiritual toughness and dogged determination to survive that people find admirable. Perhaps Lindy herself best sums up the popular appeal of her story and the meaning of her stardom:

> Many years ago as a child...I sat on our front veranda steps and read stories of Mary Durand, a 14-year-old who was imprisoned in the Tower of Constance for her faith. For 40 years she was in a dark underground cell with a bare glimpse of the daylight coming through, she scratched deep into the stone one word: RESIST. As a child I could dream of what it really meant to her to resist under those odds. As an adult, when I looked back on the example she set me, I could mentally look at my wall and see RESIST written on it too, and I knew why she did it (*Time*, 22 October 1990).

References

Barthes, R. (1972), *Mythologies*, London: Jonathan Cape

Chamberlain, L. (1990), *Through My Eyes: An Autobiography*, Melbourne: Heinemann

Fiske, J. and Hartley, J. (1978), *Reading Television*, London: Methuen

Frye, N. (1957), *Anatomy of Criticism*, Princeton: Princeton University Press

Foucault, M. (1972), *The Archaeology of Knowledge*, London: Tavistock Publications

Levi-Strauss, C. (1972), *Structural Anthropology*, Harmondsworth: Penguin

Reeves, J. (1988), 'Television Stardom a Ritual of Social Typification and Individualization' in *Media, Myth and Narratives: Television and the Press*, ed. James Carey London: Sage

Ricoeur, P. (1981), 'The narrative function' in J.B. Thompson (ed.), *Paul Ricoeur: Hermeneutics and the human sciences*, New York: Cambridge University Press.

Seal, G. (1987), 'Azaria Chamberlain and the Media Charivari', *Australian Folklore*, March, pp. 68-95

Silverstone, R. (1981), *The Message of Television: Myth and Narrative in Contemporary Culture*, London: Heinemann

Tuchmann, G. (1974), 'Making News by Doing Work: Routinising the Unexpected', *American Journal of Sociology*, Vol. 79, pp. 110-31

Appendix: Jokes

Q.   What were two dingoes arguing about outside a tent?
A.   Eat in or take-away?

Q.   What event could have changed the course of history?
A.   A dingo in Bethlehem

Q.   What's worse than a bull in a china shop?
A.   A dingo in a maternity ward

Q.   Did you hear that they've found Azaria Chamberlain?
A.   In a meat pie in New York!

Q.   What is the definition of anticipation?
A.   The dingo sitting on the steps of Buckingham Palace

Q.   Did you hear the bookmaker's odds on the trial?
A.   1 to 10–Lindy; 1 to 1–Michael; 10 to 1–Kids; 20 to 1–dingo; 100 to 1 –suicide

When the news was revealed that Lindy Chamberlain was pregnant, the folkloric reaction was:
   a rumour has spread through Darwin that Lindy Chamberlain is not really pregnant—she just swallowed the evidence.

'Ode to Azaria'

(Sung to the Tune of Waltzing Matilda)

Once a jolly pastor camped in a caravan
under the shade of a kurrajong tree
and he sang and he prayed as he watched the baby's bottle boil
'You'll be seventh day adventist like me.'

Seventh day adventist, seventh day adventist,
you'll be a seventh day adventist like me
and he sang and he prayed as he watched the baby's bottle boil
'You'll be a seventh day adventist like me.'

Down came a Lindy to snatch up Azaria,
she picked up the scissors and stabbed her with glee
and she smiled as she shoved that baby in the camera bag,
'It's fun being a seventh day adventist like me.

Seventh day adventist, seventh day adventist,
it's fun being a seventh day adventist like me
and she smiled as she shoved that baby in the camera bag
'It's fun being a seventh day adventist like me.

Out came a dingo nosing around the camp fire,
Lindy winked at Michael and said 'it wasn't me...'
what happened to the baby you put into the camera bag,
give it to the dingo and you'll get off scot free.

Give it to the dingo, give it to the dingo,
give it to the dingo and you'll get off scot free.
What happened to the baby you put into the camera bag,
give it to the dingo and you'll get off scot free.

Up jumped the dingo and ran past the camera bag,
you'll never blame her murder on me,
and Azaria's ghost may be heard as you pass by the kurrajong tree
'Mummy was the one who did away with me'.

I am indebted to Graham Seal's 'Azaria Chamberlain and the Media Charivari' for the above.

POPULAR CULTURE AND CRITICAL THEORY

How to be a Singer, Though Married: Domesticity, Leisure and Modern Love

KAY FERRES

In 1904 the *Preston Post* solicited definitions of 'home' from readers of its women's page. Their responses indicated that the notion of separate and sexually differentiated spheres, public and private, was well understood: 'A world of strife shut out, a world of love shut in'.[1] This reader knew that the process of definition has more to do with prescription than with description of an unmediated reality. These sentiments may have expressed a hope of winning the competition more eloquently than they reflected the realities of home life. Marilyn Lake has described the masculine resistance to domesticity and outright hostility to women represented in the *Bulletin* and the *Bull-Ant* in the 1890s; in the women's magazines of the 1900s there is further evidence that strife was very much in the home. The popular culture engaged with debates about the transformation of sexual difference current in the discourses of sexology, feminism, theosophy, socialism and science, and explored the changing meanings of home and domesticity. A series of advertisements for Kitty soap flakes, run in the *Home Journal* in 1905, poke fun at men's domestic incompetence and promote the profession of housework. In the *Australian Woman's Mirror*, Dulcie Deamer recommended that readers discard cross-stitched texts proclaiming 'God Bless our Home' and replace them with a representation of a dancing woman, the embodiment of sensuous vitality and *joie de vivre*. In this paper I want to look particularly at how and where the lines between masculine and feminine, public and private were drawn and redrawn in the figuration of this modern woman and at the ways in which ideas of feminine sexual pleasure were taken up in the popular culture of the 1920s in Australia.

Ideas about home, domestic space and suburbia are not quite so fiercely contested in the intellectual traditions of Australian culture as they were in the popular culture of the 1920s. Anti-suburban sentiment has been a strong current in historical and sociological debates.[2] In *Myths of Oz*, John Fiske, Bob Hodge and Graeme Turner took another look at the suburban house, remarking:

> If 'imaginative' or 'creative' are not words normally associated with a
> description of suburban living in Australia, that is due to the poverty of
> cultural analysis of the society to date and its inability to even hint at the

reasons why most Australians make sense of their lives within that most
maligned of environments, suburbia.[3]

These cultural analysts make a connection between the masculinism of
Australian culture and the maligning of suburbia. Yet their own reading
of a display home indicates that it will take more than a nervous
acknowledgement of masculinism to reframe cultural analysis of domestic
space. These three notice the 'strong signals' which mark out the private
and 'forbidden' territory of the marital couple and pass the bedroom by,
sticking to the safer public spaces, especially to the outdoor living area
and back yard, those liminal spaces between nature and culture where
masculinity comes into its own presiding over the barbecue ritual.

But male cultural analysts are not alone in avoiding the bedroom.
Feminist analysis of domesticity in Australia has concentrated on the issues
surrounding the sexual division of labour and the character of domestic
work, and the problematic identification of women as consumers. The
consideration of women in the home is taken up in terms of a public/
private opposition in which the feminine is associated with reproduction
and the family. Situated in the home, isolated from social relations,
women's activities are measured against other industrial forms of work:
production is contrasted with reproduction and consumption. Domestic
work fits rather uneasily here, both in terms of its practice and its product.
It is also difficult to differentiate women's work from leisure, since it is not
clearly confined within temporal and spatial boundaries. Consumption,
that other feminine domain, is also problematic. The consumer is either
assumed to be passive and subject to manipulation, or the subject of a
fantasy of excess, of endlessly deferred pleasure. These paradigms reproduce
a devaluation of the feminine. The alignment of 'agency' with work and
production in the public sphere affirms a masculine norm.

I want to suggest that the oppositions of production/reproduction and
production/consumption assume an organisation of work which proves
something of a straightjacket for an exploration of the desires which are
organised in the construction of the 'housewife'. Raelene Frances has
recently been critical of the existing, sketchy history of housework in
Australia, which she sees as too dependent on generalisation from overseas
studies of the interventions of experts and scientific technologies on
domestic life. Frances would remedy our ignorance of the impact of the
efficiency experts on the women they targeted with empirical research,
testing claims that such interventions have chained women ever more
firmly to the kitchen sink. While such empirical work would undoubtedly
prove useful, it seems that Frances shares with Raymond Evans and Kay
Saunders an unwarrantedly narrow view of a very rich source of evidence
in the popular culture: women's magazines, radio serials and popular
songs. Frances reads these as evidence only of injunctions and prescriptions

about ideals divorced from lived experience, while Evans and Saunders are even more dismissive:

> A steady parade of saccharine radio serials and songs...relayed directly into the home, provided the necessary romantic pabulum for this optimistic cultural diet.[4]

The 'housewife' is the dupe of advertising campaigns and rampant consumerism, in this view.

The problem with this approach is that it reproduces the conventional representation of passivity which it seeks to displace. The answer is not to detach femininity from its moorings in reproduction and consumption, but to collapse the distinction between active production and passive consumption. Consumption needs to be seen not as a compensation for the active pursuit of desire,[5] but as an activity which 'stands for production, distribution, desiring, obtaining and using, of symbolic goods'.[6] This activity involves complex manipulations of symbols for many purposes:

> On the level of the life-world, it is for the purpose of constructing identity, constructing the self, and constructing relations with others. On the level of society, it is in order to sustain the continuing existence of institutions, of groups, structures and other things like that. And on the systemic level, it is in order to ensure the reproduction of the conditions in which all this is possible.[7]

Consumption then, is another production. It is inventive; it takes already given materials and puts them to countless uses, rather as Michel de Certeau's reader approaches a text:

> [The reader] insinuates into another person's text the ruses of pleasure and appropriation: he poaches on it, is transported into it, pluralises himself in it...A different world (the reader's) slips into the author's place.[8]

My reading of the exchange of views among columnists and readers of the *Australian Woman's Mirror* explores the dynamics of active consumption. This was a purposeful as well as a playful activity: in debates about sexual relations and the arrangement of domestic space women did not merely 'try on' new roles, their exchanges constructed communities across boundaries of class and generation.

The early decades of the twentieth century saw a rapid expansion of consumer culture. Department stores were by then well established, with women on both sides of the counter. Technology was producing labour-saving devices as well as the wireless, gramophone and other instruments of pleasure. Women were caught up in this ambivalence of work and pleasure: on the one hand they argued for the recognition of housework as a professional activity—debating wives' salaries, domestic hygiene and

good housekeeping practice; on the other, they entered into work and social life with a new freedom.

The contradictions—and perhaps confusion—of the identities offered up to them are evident in the Kitty advertisement above: 'How to be Happy Though Married'. The ad draws a clear cut line between the sexes: happiness and marriage are apparently contradictory notions. Kitty offers a clean wash, and more time for leisure, but not domestic bliss. It sells its product by representing the wife's lot as domestic drudgery: housework is work for which she gets little recompense. The ad's comic effect depends on the unsuspecting husband and a feminine reader; but clearly the emasculating wife, poker in hand, is the butt of a much more hostile joke. This joke depends upon the Freudian triangle: a masculine teller, a masculine interlocutor and a feminine object. The stacked soap boxes, and the poster advertising a lecture on marital happiness refer to campaigns to transform marriage and sexuality and perhaps also suggest their failure. What the ad says most forcefully is that women are out of place, and a threatening presence, in public. Kitty's place is in the laundry.

Although the *Medical Journal of Australia*, reviewing *Contraception: Its Theory, History and Practice*, had stipulated that Marie Stopes' work should be perused only by members of the medical profession, it reached a much wider Australian audience. Marian Piddington maintained professional contact with her, and her advice to women was much influenced by Stopes' ideas. Correspondents from such places as Sydney and Stanthorpe also addressed their comments and inquiries directly to Dr Stopes. Her advice on companionate marriage, feminine sexual pleasure and family planning was directed to dispelling the notion of frigidity in women. This was not 'natural', but cultural, a norm which legitimated a lack of control in men. Her advice in *Married Love* and *Enduring Passion* focused on sexual technique and performance, and she insisted that women needed orgasm (perhaps more than once). Stopes recognised that this was a subversive claim, which went to the heart of middle-class domestic arrangements, but she argued that the failure to achieve sexual satisfaction lead to all kinds of neuroses in women, and that men needed early marriage if they were to avoid 'pollution'. Jean Devanny, who worked with Marian Piddington in bringing birth control advice to working-class women, reports Australian women's warm reception of Stopes' ideas, and that these women were eager to have their 'frigidity' explained.[9]

Stopes may have championed women's right to sexual pleasure, but she was no advocate of sexual freedom. She insisted upon *married* love. In the pages of the *Australian Woman's Mirror*, established by the publishers of the *Bulletin* in 1922, the harridan of the 'Kitty' ad is transformed into a sensual woman. She is charming in a pretty frock and silk stockings; a professional in household management, using scientific methods, but not obsessively directing all her energies at dirt. She occupies only a few hours a day in housework, and may well combine marriage (though not usually motherhood) and a career. She is sociable, happy, and keeps her faculties alert. She has her own money and her own friends and likes the cinema, parties and 'jazzing'. Her self-confessed fantasy is escape 'from myself', from the everyday.

The *Mirror* was 'the best and fullest women's paper for Australia yet— democratic and varied' according to Nettie Palmer.[10] She was a frequent contributor, along with Mabel Forrest, Zora Cross and Dulcie Deamer. The *Mirror* also gave its readers a lot of space, in regular 'Between Ourselves' columns, and in longer articles, poems and responses. Before the advent of the *Australian Women's Weekly* in 1933, it had a circulation of 167,000. The magazine regularly featured articles on women's achievements in the professions and sport, as well as reviews of books, films and plays. It also clearly aimed to provoke discussion of controversial topics, particularly topics relating to sexuality and the definition of sexual difference. Masculinity and femininity were problematised and redefined. Men and masculinity were classified and categorised (as 'incompleat kissers', for example) and compared across cultures (the differences between Australian and American men seemed especially interesting to the *Mirror*'s readers). Women were analysed as lovers, wives and mothers and classified as 'modern' or 'advanced'. The category 'feminist' sat rather uneasily, although feminist objectives, such as divorce law reform and political representation, were endorsed. Intelligence was esteemed, but not dulness. It was fine to be daring—shingling your hair, reading Marie Stopes on tramcars—but flappers and good time girls were disparaged.

Readers' views about changing relations between men and women, and the relation of private to social and public life become apparent in debates about marriage and sexuality. The married woman came into her own here, mobilising knowledges which gave her a certain superiority over spinsters and home girls. One correspondent, 'alert and full of interest in the woman-problems of the day', questioned the role spinsters (i.e. the staff of Maternal and Child Welfare clinics) had taken upon themselves in educating mothers. Scientific interventions into child rearing were beneficial, since mothering was not 'instinctive', but spinsters threatened to take over 'the whole *business*':

> When…spinsters talk birth-control, limitation of families, refusal of marriage to any but the fully-fit, and other subjects in which the personal equation bulks largely or wholly, I take leave to suggest that they do not know what they are talking about…Married women understand causes and are competent to discuss remedies, but, when up against the elemental, spinsters can judge only by hearsay and theory—poor premises—and their entry into the discussion can only weaken women's case generally and stiffen reactionaries in their opposition to relief measures.[11]

This comment challenges the clinic's definition of 'expert' advice, which specifically excluded the experience of grandmothers, neighbours and other 'old wives'. It also maps out the terrain of feminist struggles at the times, in which the interests of spinsters and married women came to be sharply distinguished.

The causes and remedies associated with the personal equation were taken up in other spirited exchanges in the *Mirror* in 1925. From April to September controversy raged over the marriage bed. By July 28, 'a deluge of contributions on this apparently absorbing topic' had been received. Supporters claimed that hygiene and decency were served by twin beds. 'Croesus' called double beds 'vulgar accessories to a vulgar custom' (21 April 1925), and a nurse shared her observation of domestic arrangements:

> Sometimes when I have attended professionally one or other of the members of a double-bed household and have noted the condition of the bed, and the state of the member's body, I have marvelled that the partnership has hung together, and with such apparent success, for so long (9 June 1925).

The editors even handedly published letters supporting both views, but the debate was fuelled by Dulcie Deamer, who asked 'What on earth has decency to do with matrimony?':

> Double-bed affection...should improve with age, like violins, whisky and some brands of cheese. Folk who share a double-bed every night should get that way they're as strange away from it as a dog without fleas. Real love isn't any the worse for becoming a habit—the most comfortable habit in the world (23 June 1925).

Real love was valued by the *Mirror* and its readers, and was seen as the key to happy domesticity. New brides were advised that 'it is a mistake to set too high a standard [of cleanliness] in the home' and were cautioned not to isolate themselves, or to 'starve' their intelligence, for fear of becoming 'nervy, petty in outlook, bored' (15 September 1925). This advice cut right across the exhortations of the experts who attached moral value to the opposition of cleanliness (respectability) and slovenliness (promiscuity).

The home, and the wife within it, was not represented in the *Mirror* as isolated from the world of work or from social relations. Women were urged, and urged each other, to keep in touch, to be alert. Leisure and entertainment were important to all women, single and married, if they were to maintain vitality. And vitality was quite explicitly connected with sexuality. Married love may have been the ideal, but love was not exclusive to marriage. The *Mirror* raised the issue of sexuality outside marriage obliquely, in a series of articles on 'jazzing'.

The female craze for jazzing caused a degree of moral panic in Australia, as it had abroad. In 1920, Leila Atherton made her debut during Show Week in Bowen. Leila brought home a Sydney sophistication, and in preparation for the big night, she taught her friends the foxtrot, tango and the two-step:

> She entered the hall in her pretty white dress, and felt very pleased with herself to think she had accomplished the task of teaching her friends to jazz. Imagine how small she felt when the MC told her, while they were doing the two step, that he could not possible allow such an objectionable dance to be performed there.[12]

In May 1925, the *Mirror* reprinted an article from the *Weekly Despatch* which specifies the allure of jazzing for its female victims:

> Sex is at the back of the dance-mad mania, and so I doubt its passing until some vehicle of sex as alluring is found. Women go to dance halls to meet men and to be embraced by men.

This overt and public demonstration of women's 'sex instinct'—evident also in earlier 'crazes' for roller skating and bicycling—was the cause of concern. The threat jazzing posed, according to Jean Devanny, was that it created a sexual excitement which could not be legitimately resolved in the adolescent girls who frequented the dance halls.[13] Her objection is directed at an inappropriate eroticism, and needs to be distinguished from the horror of female sexuality expressed by one of Marie Stopes' critics:

> You have broken up the home; you have let women know about things which only prostitutes ought to know; once you give women a taste for these things, they become vampires, and you have let loose vampires into decent men's homes. When we men want that sort of thing— a woman who knows how to enjoy herself in sex life—we go to prostitutes at our own times when we feel like it. We do not want that sort of thing in our own homes. The wife should be the housekeeper and make the home a place of calm comfort for a man. Instead of that you have made my home a hell: I cannot meet the demands of my wife now she knows. If you create these vampire women, you will rear a race of effeminate men.[14]

The vampire woman had been pathologised in the *Weekly Despatch* article, identified as a neurotic whose conduct had to be curtailed by the law (the article reported the appearance of a 'dance-mad' girl before a magistrate).

The *Mirror's* intervention was not innocent. It followed up with two provocative defences of jazzing. One disingenuously disavowed the 'sex instinct', claiming that 'religious tenets, political legislation, convention and personal repression' had relegated it to a secondary place in modern civilisation. 'Ka-lu-a' argues further that jazzing is regressive, since the best partners are not well adapted to racial progress:

> Speaking from a sex instinct point of view, I adore tall, broad-shouldered, open-air men; speaking from a dancing point of view, I seek short, light ugly men...the man I like best to dance with at one city hall is an extremely ugly little butcher-boy, a person with whom I would not dream of having anything other than dancing to do (30 June 1925).

Dulcie Deamer, who enjoyed a certain notoriety as 'Queen' of Sydney's Bohemia and who wore her experience with an air, took a different tack. She argued that women's sexual nature was not very different from men's: both sexes were not naturally monogamous, but culture provided fewer outlets for women. It is no accident, she declares boldly, that the mutual position of modern dancing simulates 'the immemorial love-grapple':

> We don't jazz merely for the sake of rhythm—and neither do we jazz as a means of deliberately entrapping the Stupid Sex into matrimony, but we *do* jazz in order to experience a mild—very mild—sex adventure, and to allow our repressed polyandrous instinct to get a breath of air (28 June 1925).

The dance hall allowed women, according to Deamer's argument, to give an illegitimate desire symbolic expression.

In a recent discussion of the Victorian barmaid, Peter Bailey has made a similar argument about the redirection of desires which was achieved symbolically and through the spatial organisation of bars and cafes in the late nineteenth century. Bailey identifies 'glamour' as a distinctively modern visual property, embodied in the barmaid. The bar is a barrier, allowing a display of glamour at once alluring and out of reach. Bailey calls this 'parasexuality':

> an inoculation in which a little sexuality is encouraged as an antidote to its subversive properties. Parasexuality...is sexuality that is deployed but contained, carefully channelled rather than fully discharged; in vulgar terms it might be represented as 'everything but'.[15]

But where his account of masculine 'parasexuality' stresses the control and distancing of the gaze, Dulcie Deamer insists upon proximity and contact as central to feminine desire. The glamorous figure of the female jazzer is dangerous because she is uncontained, both spatially and in her daring dress.

Mirror readers, even the 'Sunday school teachers' among them, agreed that jazzing was pleasurable for just these reasons. It stood for more than instant gratification: it was about the exhilaration of improvisation and reinvention. The married woman of the twenties moved confidently into the public domain, probably dressed in a beaded slip she had made from a pattern in the *Australian Woman's Mirror*. Her emergence indicates that the boundaries between public and private were much more permeable than prescription allows. But the construction of the 'married woman' was dependent not only on an opposition or conflict of masculinity and femininity. Her knowledges of 'causes and remedies', her implication in heterosexuality, marked off the married woman from her spinster sister and differentiated their interests. This distinction was a problem for the feminist movement of the day, and is a problem which persists. The work of scholars like Shiela Jeffreys, Lilian Faderman and Carroll Smith Rosenberg has restored the spinster to the historical record and begun to map a feminine culture; but feminism continues to struggle with women's investment in heterosexuality.

Notes

1. Kerreen Reiger, *The Disenchantment of the Home: Modernizing the Australian Family 1880-1940* (Melbourne, Oxford University Press, 1985), p. 38.

2. Alan Gilbert, 'The Roots of Australian Anti-Suburbanism', in *Australian Cultural History*, eds. S.L. Goldberg and F.B. Smith (Melbourne, Cambridge University Press, 1988), p. 33–49.

3. John Fiske, Bob Hodge and Graeme Turner, *Myths of Oz: Reading Australian Popular Culture* (Sydney, Allen and Unwin, 1987), p. 52.

4. Raymond Evans and Kay Saunders, 'No Place Like Home: The Evolution of the Australian Housewife', in *Gender Relations in Australia: Domination and Negotiation* (Sydney, Harcourt, Brace Jovanovich, 1992), p. 191.

5. Lynn Joyrich, 'All that Television Allows: TV Melodrama, Post-modernism and Consumer Culture', in *Private Screenings: Television and the Domestic Consumer*, ed. Lynn Spigel and Denise Mann (Minneapolis, University of Minnesota Press, 1992), p. 227.

6. Zygmunt Bauman, *Intimations of Post-Modernity* (London, Routledge, 1992), p. 223.

7. Ibid.

8. Michel de Certeau, *The Practice of Everyday Life*, trans. Steve Rendall (Berkeley, University of California Press, 1864), p. xxi.

9. Jean Devanny, *Point of Departure: The Autobiography of Jean Devanny*, ed. Carole Ferrier (St Lucia, University of Queensland Press, 1986), p. 156.

10. Letter to Marie Miles O'Reilly, Mitchell Library MSS 231/14.

11. 'Spinster Mothercraft: Can the Unmarried Woman Really Judge?' (23 June 1925).

12. John Atherton Young (ed.)., *Jane Bardsley's Outback Letterbook: Across the Years 1896–1936* (Sydney, Angus and Robertson, 1987), p. 202.

13. Jean Devanny Papers, North Queensland Collection, James Cook University Library, JD MSS 3178.

14. Marie Carmichael Stopes, *Enduring Passion* (London, Putnam, 1928), pp. 5–6.

15. Peter Bailey, 'Parasexuality and Glamour: the Victorian Barmaid as Cultural Prototype', *Gender and History*, Vol. 2, No. 2, Summer 1990, p. 148.

Bibliography

Bailey, Peter (1990), 'Parasexuality and Glamour: The Victorian Barmaid as Cultural Prototype', *Gender and History*, Vol. 2, No. 2, p. 148–72

Bauman, Zygmunt (1992), *Intimations of Post-Modernity*, London: Routledge

Dulcie Deamer Papers, Mitchell Library. ML MSS 3178

de Certeau, Michel (1984), *The Practice of Everyday Life*, trans. Steve Randall, Berkeley: University of California Press

Jean Devanny Papers, North Queensland Collection, James Cook University Library. JD MSS 29/1

Devanny, Jean (1986), *Point of Departure: The Autobiography of Jean Devanny*, ed. Carole Ferrier, St Lucia: University of Queensland Press

Evans, Raymond and Kay Saunders (1992), 'No Place Like Home: The Evolution of the Australian Housewife', *Gender Relations in Australia: Domination and Negotiation*, Sydney: Harcourt, Brace Jovanovich, pp. 175–96

Fiske, John, Bob Hodge and Graeme Turner (1987), *Myths of Oz: Reading Australian Popular Culture*, Sydney: Allen and Unwin

Frances, Raelene (1992), 'Shifting Horizons: Twentieth Century Women's Labour Patterns', in Evans and Saunders, pp. 246–65

Freud, Sigmund (1960), *Jokes and Their Relation to the Unconscious* (1905), trans James Strachey, ed. Angela Richards, Harmondsworth: Penguin

Gilbert, Alan (1988), 'The Roots of Australian Anti-Suburbanism', *Australian Cultural History*, eds. S.L. Goldberg abd F.B. Smith, Melbourne: Cambridge University Press, p. 33–49

Howe, Renata and Shirlee Swain (1992), 'Fertile Grounds for Divorce: Sexuality and Reproductive Imperatives' in Evans and Saunders, pp. 158–74

Joyrich, Lynn (1992), 'All that Television Allows: TV Melodrama, Postmodernism and Consumer Culture', *Private Screenings: Television and the Domestic Consumer*, ed. Lynn Spigel and Denise Mann, Minneapolis: University of Minnesota Press, pp. 227–51

Lake, Marilyn (1986), 'The Politics of Respectability: Identifying the Masculinist Context', *Historical Studies*, Vol. 22, No. 86, pp. 116–31

Leonardi, Susan J. (1989), 'Recipes for Reading: Summer Pasta, Lobster a la Riseholme, and Key Lime Pie', *PMLA*, Vol. 104, No. 3, pp. 340–7

Matthews, Jill Julius (1984), *Good and Mad Women: The Historical Construction of Femininity in Twentieth Century Australia*, Sydney: Allen and Unwin.

Dowell O'Reilly Papers, Mitchell Library. MSS 231/14

Reiger, Kerreen (1985), *The Disenchantment of the Home: Modernizing the Australian Family 1880–1940*, Melbourne: Oxford University Press

Spigel, Lynn (1992), 'Installing the Television Set: Popular Discourses on Television and Domestic Space, 1948–1955', in Spigel and Mann, pp. 3–39

Stopes, Marie Carmichael (1918), *Married Love*, London: Putnam

Stopes, Marie Carmichael (1928), *Enduring Passion*, London: Putnam

Young, John Atherton (ed.) (1987), *Jane Bardsley's Outback Letterbook: Across the Years 1896–1936*, Sydney: Angus and Robertson

The Wild Colonial Boy Rides Again and Again: An Australian Legend Abroad

GRAHAM SEAL

In his classic study of banditry, Eric Hobsbawm pointed out that the pattern of protest and struggle associated with social banditry was 'one of the most universal social phenomena known to history, and one of the most amazingly uniform' (Hobsbawm, 1969, 14). Such phenomena are clearly deserving of some special consideration in the light of the current interest—or is it a revival of interest?—in international connections. The work that I have been pursuing spasmodically for far too many years has to do with the persistence of what I call the outlaw hero tradition in Britain, Australia and America. This is a complex area that has many facets, though the one I wish to focus on is the ability of a particular Australian ballad to lodge itself in the traditions of a number of primarily Anglophone cultures.

A number of outlaws appear to be common to all Anglophone cultures. The figures of Robin Hood, Dick Turpin, William Brennan and The Wild Colonial Boy are known in England, Ireland, USA, Australia, Canada, South Africa and New Zealand. The persistence of songs from British tradition in America, Australia and elsewhere is hardly surprising. But the situation where an Australian text reverses the usual balance of metropolitan centre and colonial periphery is clearly of some interest and this is the case with the Australian ballad of 'The Wild Colonial Boy'. This song is not only well-known in Australia where it appears to have originated in the 1860s, but is also quite widely sung in Ireland, Canada, England and the United States.

What is it about 'The Wild Colonial Boy' that gives the song such apparently pan-Anglophonic appeal and what possible meanings might such a text possess in performance in such diverse places? A number of possible answers immediately suggest themselves. Is this the exoticism, perhaps, of an Australian bushranger abroad? Could it be simply the melodic appeal of the song, its catchiness? Or perhaps there are rather more complex cultural reasons for the wide spread of the song?

Certainly exoticism does not seem to provide much of an answer to the questions posed. In many places the text has been localised in such a way to suggest that those who use it are either unconscious of its Australianness or that this characteristic is of no importance. While Australians may be somewhat incredulous of this, it is clear that attributed, even blatant Australian-ness does not necessarily translate into other cultures.[1]

The 'catchy tune' argument offers no better solution to the problem. The best-known melody for 'The Wild Colonial Boy' is a lugubriously sentimental Victorian waltz which easily misfires in performance, of which fifteen verses and choruses are unlikely to make the song—or the singer—popular!

A more compelling refutation of the 'catchy tune' notion, however, is that 'The Wild Colonial Boy', like all folk songs, is sung to a wide variety of melodies and variants—not only in Australia, but also abroad.[2] So it is clearly not the tune but the text itself that is found to be internationally meaningful.

Perhaps there is some light to be shed on this by examining the origins of 'The Wild Colonial Boy'? Relatively little is known about this, though it is usually suggested (see Meredith, for instance), that it derives from the earlier ballad or ballads about the historical bushranger 'Jack Donohoe' (c. 1830) and that it was composed around the middle of the century. There is some cogency in this argument and some at least circumstantial evidence to support it.[3]

But if we compare the texts of Donohoe ballads and those of 'The Wild Colonial Boy', we find relatively few compelling points of conjunction, apart from the generic and, for colonial New South Wales, mundane similarity of the events described. Of particular significance here, I think, is the celebrated chorus of 'The Wild Colonial Boy', with its splendid defiance of authority and death:

> So come along my hearties, together we will ride
> Together we will plunder and together we will die,
> We'll scour along the mountains and we'll gallop across the plains
> And scorn to live in slavery, bound down with iron chains.

While the earlier Jack Donohoe is certainly defiant, the later Wild Colonial Boy's defiance has always seemed to me to be rather stagey. The give-away, I think, is the dreadful 'come along, my hearties' that begins the chorus. While 'hearties' is a reasonably common terms for workmates in sea shanties it is, as far as I am aware, otherwise unknown in Australian oral tradition. I detect the pen of some obscure literary hack here doing a very creditable job of knocking together a pastiche of folk and popular balladry for some piece of theatrical entertainment. I cannot prove any of this, of course, and anyway it hardly matters as the song has clearly been taken up with enthusiasm by singers throughout the world. Why?

My answer to that question is what I have already introduced as the outlaw hero tradition. This is an Anglophone cultural tradition that can be traced through at least three cultures and numerous centuries. While the outlaw hero exists in non-Anglophone cultures, the English-language manifestation of the tradition has distinctive characteristics that recur and resonate through various periods and circumstances of social, political and economic struggle in three countries. My argument is that 'The Wild

Colonial Boy', formulated in Australia around the mid-nineteenth century, drew upon the traditions associated with Donohoe and other
bushranger heroes, which were themselves derived from existing British
outlaw hero traditions. As the same British-originated tradition also
affected the folklorisation of outlaw heroes in the USA, the ground was
well-prepared for the transmission of 'The Wild Colonial Boy' back into
the matrices of the tradition from which it arose. This seems to me to be a
particularly significant and powerful example of international transmission
and one that has had ongoing consequences. I would like to outline the
outlaw hero tradition now, and try to suggest why 'The Wild Colonial
Boy' has managed to ride from the periphery to the centre.

The outlaw hero is a particular and very well-defined type of folk hero
who frequently inhabits the grey area between criminality and political
protest. His tradition can be traced as a cultural constant that persists
over time and though space and is available to be called into use whenever
circumstances are appropriate. Outlaw heroes, real and fictional, exist in
most of the world's folklores, celebrated particularly in song and narrative,
as well as through other verbal folkloric genres.[4]

Eric Hobsbawm called such outlaw heroes 'social bandits', after
investigating the careers and the legends of a variety of outlaws from a
number of periods, cultures and nationalities. Hobsbawm's thesis has been
reinforced, refined and criticised in various ways but his overall concept of
a *social* bandit—one who has the sympathy and support of his own social
group—has survived as a useful framework for understanding the activities
and origins of historical figures as diverse as the Sicilian Salvatore Giuliano,
the German Schinderhannes, the French Vidocq, as well as more definite
social movements and forces such as Indian Dacoits and Egyptian brigands.

Others have also examined outlaw traditions, if usually in the more
restricted geographical arenas of their own culture. American folklorists,
sociologists and historians in particular have dealt with the figure of the
outlaw or 'badman' in their culture. These include Steckmesser (1966),
Simeone (1958), Meyer (1980) and Roberts (1981). Each of these writers
approaches the topic in a similar manner, even if their emphases differ
somewhat.[5]

Most of these studies proceed by noting the similarities between the
various traditions investigated and in drawing conclusions from these.
While generally recognising the link between outlaw heroes and broadly
similar, recurring sets of socio-historical circumstances of perceived
oppression, relatively little attention is paid to the historical, social,
economic and political environments within which the various outlaws
operated and in which outlaw hero traditions about them circulated.

On the other hand, studies by historians and sociologists, such as White
and to a lesser extent, Hobsbawm, generally pay only limited attention to

the processes of folkloric transmission and stereotyping involved in the creation and—most importantly—the perpetuation—of an outlaw hero. The work that I am currently engaged in seeks to combine both these approaches and, as far as possible, to situate the generation of outlaw heroes and the continuation of their traditions within specific, recurring political and economic circumstances.

Studies of outlaw hero traditions usually begin with and depend upon a deconstruction of the content of the relevant folk articulations—songs, poems, folktales. These are then compared with other like phenomena and a list of similarities is compiled. This list of discrete elements varies in number from commentator to commentator but generally embraces most of the same notions, including that of 'the noble robber', of the hero's boldness and power, and his ultimate betrayal.

My study begins in much the same manner but proceeds to relate the observed elements of the outlaw hero tradition to the concrete circumstances of historical outlaws and to track the continuation of the tradition and the recurrence of similar circumstances over time and space. The result is an attempt to discern the international and the diachronic manifestations of a persistent Anglophone cultural tradition.

Before answering questions about how and why such a tradition persists, the elements that make it up must be identified. Comparison of folkloric expressions related to real and legendary outlaw heroes in Britain, America and Australia reveals a number of common motifs or narrative elements.

The single most important of the elements, indeed the defining motif, is that the outlaw hero 'robs the rich to help the poor'. This formulaic element may be expressed in a number of ways, depending on the circumstances. The 'rich' may be the forces of economic or social oppression, and injustice—the Sheriff of Nottingham's unjust taxes in the Robin Hood legend, the Union in the case of ex-Confederate raider, Jesse James, the 'English' landlords in the case of Irish–Australian Ned Kelly. Similarly the 'poor' are generally those members of the social group that sympathises with and supports the outlaw hero, and from which he has usually arisen, or for whom his activities are appealing. These groups perceive themselves as suffering under various forms of injustice and oppression and see the activities of their outlaw hero as justified revenge against those forces and their representatives.[6]

The perception of deprivation or oppression is a fundamental aspect of the outlaw hero tradition. But while it may be expressed formulaically in the phrase 'he robbed the rich to help the poor' or some variation of that, the simple formula reflects a complex reality of intersecting political and economical factors and group perceptions. Its deployment, in combination with other elements of the tradition, is therefore an indicator of deep and serious social tensions within a community and is not merely a narrative cliché.

The individuals, and the social groups to which they belonged, who told the tales and sang the ballads of outlaw heroes were not simply celebrating criminal activity. What the outlaw's supporters and sympathisers saw in their hero's activities was themselves and the release of their fears and frustrations in the form of an avenging force robbing the rich and powerful, the banks or the railway companies that were often seen as economic oppressors. Outlaw heroes frequently appear among groups who are also deprived of adequate political representation, thus deepening and increasing their sense of oppression and frustration. Such people easily identified themselves as 'the poor' and said so in their songs. All outlaw heroes operate outside and against the official legal system of the state, but remain within the unofficial legal and moral code of those who see them as one of their own. Although the specific circumstances alter in each case, similar patterns of perceived injustice and suffering generate other historical outlaw heroes.

A second important element of the tradition is closely related to the first: it is generally found that the hero is driven to outlawry through no fault of his own. Robin Hood is usually said to have been a Saxon who fled to the forest to escape Norman tyranny; one of Ned Kelly's ballads points out that 'the Governor of Victoria was an enemy of this man'. And even so unlikely a hero as William Bonney, or 'Billy the Kid' was said to have killed first while in his early teens by knifing a man who insulted his mother, traditionally a justifiable form of homicide. Invariably it is the oppression of injustice of others—usually those with authority and power—that compels the hero to take to the forest, bush or other marginal area where the control of the coercive oppressor is weak or non-existent.[7]

This is not to say that *all* constraints and obligations are removed. On the contrary, in order to maintain the respect, sympathy and the active support of his own social group, the outlaw must adhere, or at least be seen to adhere, to a relatively rigid set of guidelines. Some actions are appropriate, even laudable, while others are reprehensible and may not be countenanced if the outlaw is to become a hero. The appropriate moral instructions are coded into the folkloric manifestations of the tradition and are therefore recurring elements within it. Outlaws who disregard these rules are not balladised and, more worryingly for them, are unlikely to have the sympathy and therefore the sustaining support of their own social group or groups.[8]

One of the most important of these moral guidelines is that the outlaw hero never robs or harms in any way the poor, the weak or the otherwise unfortunate. This means in Anglophone tradition at least, the safety of widows, orphans, cripples, fools, and generally, of women, who are not to be molested, even if rich. On the contrary, it is generally considered more than appropriate for the outlaw to treat women with the utmost courtesy. Robin Hood, or course, remains the exemplar in this area, while any highwayman worth his salt must act the gentleman, as does Dick Turpin in his folklore and as most of the badmen and bushrangers are said to do. A number of outlaw heroes have traditions regarding their refusal to let members of their gangs rape or otherwise harm women, often at considerable danger or loss to themselves. True or fictional, the existence of such beliefs indicates the strength of this particular element of the tradition.[9]

In folklore, and in popular literary, filmic and artistic representation, courtesy is usually linked to manliness, an attribute of the outlaw hero expressed as 'bravery', 'boldness', or 'daring'. It is vital for the hero to act heroically, not only in relation to his constituency or support group, but also in relation to his enemies—the police, the Sheriff's men, the troopers. However, despite his physical prowess and the power he accrues from his ability to employ violence, the outlaw hero must not be seen to offer unjustified violence, even to his enemies. The point is often made in outlaw balladry and narratives that the hero has 'never done murder nor killed' (Bold Nevison), or perpetrated any unjustified form of violence (the bushranger Ben Hall). Where the facts of a case make such statements difficult, murders committed by the hero or those around him are presented as acts of justified revenge or self-defence, given humorous treatment or simply ignored. The balladry of Jesse James and Ned Kelly provide ample evidence of this technique.

Related to the masculine notions of manliness and boldness is the requirement that the outlaw hero should 'die game', that is die bravely, preferably with his boots on firing doggedly at the overwhelming police numbers arrayed against him, as do Australia's 'Wild Colonial Boy' and 'Jack Donohoe'. If the outlaw is unable to manage such a glorious finale, his minimal responsibility is to go out at the end of a rope, bravely defiant and preferably uttering some resonant last words. Ned Kelly, for instance, is widely but inaccurately believed to have said before the trap was sprung, 'such is life'. Outlaw heroes were well aware that they were expected to behave in an 'undaunted manner' at their executions and the annals of Tyburn and other trees are full of the elaborate and often witty last speeches and gallows-jests that highwaymen both famous and obscure were said to have delivered at the drop, usually dressed in great and new finery.

The outlaw hero of tradition, and often of fact, is particularly adept at outwitting his captors, pursuers and oppressors and is often a great escaper and disguiser. William Brennan and Jeremiah Grant, among other highwayman figures, were celebrated for their feats of escapology. Billy the Kid and Pretty Boy Floyd also made daring escapes, as did Moondyne Joe in Western Australia.[10]

Connected with the *style* of his death is the *means* by which the outlaw is finally killed or captured. Where history does not allow a gallant and defiant exit by bullet or rope, the outlaw hero is generally betrayed by a trusted friend or accomplice. Outlaw heroes do not give themselves up: they are betrayed while sick, as Robin Hood was poisoned by the Abbess of Kirklees, or, like Jesse James, shot in the back by a member of his own gang.[11]

After death, and in common with some other types of folk hero, the outlaw hero is sometimes rumoured to live on, having escaped the noose or bullet by some trick or chance. Where survival legends do not occur, there may well be after-traces of the hero, such as the birth of his child, usually marked in some way, as in the case of bushranger Ben Hall, or tales of his still undiscovered treasure, as with 'Black Francis' in Ireland and Frank Gardiner in Australia. These after-traces can perhaps best be thought of as metaphorical transpositions of the persistent and widespread folkloric reluctance to accept the death of great heroes—or villains. Relatively recent examples of this tendency might be Adolph Hitler and Elvis Presley, though the claims of both these men to fame or infamy were not related to outlawry.

To summarise the foregoing, it can be said that the outlaw hero tradition consists of nine motifs, or discrete but interacting narrative elements, that can be referred to in shorthand as:

> friend of the poor,
> oppressed,
> forced into outlawry,
> brave,
> generous,
> courteous,
> does not indulge in unjustified violence,
> betrayed,
> lives on after death.

These attributes may be expressed directly as in synonyms for manliness, boldness, bravery, defiance, or they may be implied in the content of the song or narrative concerning an outlaw hero. For instance, while a particular outlaw hero may not be explicitly referred to as a friend of the poor, the victims of his robberies will invariably be the rich or powerful, often both.

These nine essential elements of the tradition constitute a dynamic and interacting group of well-defined motifs that can be used in varying combinations to construct narratives appropriate to a variety of historical events and characters. Not all the elements are present in every expression of a particular outlaw; but enough will be there to indicate to those who listen that an intricately balanced combination of traditional motifs and the values and attitudes embedded within those motifs are being invoked. These elements, in a variety of folkloric forms or genres reflect—and so reinforce—communal attitudes and expectations of those social groupings that support and/or sympathise with particular outlaw heroes.

In short, we are not only dealing with a folk cultural tradition that generates songs, legends and so on from time to time, but also with a set of social, economical and political attitudes and activities that motivate the actions of individuals and groups enmeshed in broadly similar sets of historical events—the deep continuities that condition the attitudes and actions of outlaw heroes and their supporters on three continents and across several centuries.

To return to that Australian legend with which we began, The Wild Colonial Boy, it is clear that all the three countries discussed have perfectly fine indigenous outlaw heroes of their own. Why borrow a mythical Australian bushranger? The answer, I think, lies in the particularly coherent character of the outlaw hero tradition. While the tradition itself—like many other traditions—is quite able to jump cultural and national boundaries to produce local figures to fit it, it is less usual for a text to manage the same international crossing. This is certainly so in terms of the usual one-way flow of cultural dominance. 'The Wild Colonial Boy' is a particularly well-developed articulation of the outlaw hero tradition and, perhaps partly because of its historically ungrounded hero, is therefore capable of adaptation into many other cultures.

In terms of the elements of the outlaw hero tradition described above, 'The Wild Colonial Boy' scores well in various versions of his song:

He is a member of a nationality that is widely represented
        as oppressed.
He is brave and defiant.
He robs the wealth squatters or in some versions, a judge. In an
        American/Irish version he is said to have 'helped the poor'.
He is adept at disguise, eluding pursuers and escaping from tricky
        situations.[12]
He dies game.
While not betrayed in a direct sense, many versions of the song
        have him being deserted by his cowardly companions in the
        ultimate moment of need.

'The Wild Colonial Boy' therefore scores six out of nine, for those who like numbers. But as well as these considerations, it is arguably the very clearly articulated revolt of the Wild Colonial Boy against the powers of authority and law that make the song, in all its variants, so internationally appealing. Given the close connection that I have observed between dissent, protest and the heroisation of certain outlawed individuals, it would seem that the particular permutation of the outlaw hero tradition evinced in the ballad of 'The Wild Colonial Boy' is ideally suited to just about any situation of perceived injustice and oppression.

In the Anglophone context, it is also the Irish element that imparts a distinctive connotation of political dissent. The fact that 'The Wild Colonial Boy' was often sung to the tune of 'The Wearing of the Green', a melodic icon of Irish revolt, is a further indication of the importance of the 'Celtic connection'.[13]

So while the folk traditions of America and Australia usually refer back to British precedents in the case of The Wild Colonial Boy, both British and American cultures (and others) look to an Australian precedent as one important articulation of their own sense of struggle. While the implications of this must wait for another time, I rest my case, and that of the Wild Colonial Boy, with the last few lines of one popular variant of his ballad:, that published by Paterson in his *Old Bush Songs*:

> There were Freincy, Grant, bold Robin Hood, Brennan and O'Hare,
> But with Donohoe this highwayman none of them could compare...

Notes

This paper is based on a longer study, recently completed.

1. A moral tale relevant to this was the appearance in the Irish top twenty some years ago of Eric Bogle's quintessentially Australian song 'And the Band Played Waltzing Matilda'. While the particular rendition of the piece was by an Irish artist, the song which clearly and emotionally describes the Gallipoli campaign and its relevance to that central Australian myth of Anzac, was nevertheless considered to be an Irish song and related to the events, past and present, in Northern Ireland.

2. The noted Australian folklorist John Manifold once observed that ' "The Wild Colonial Boy" has more tunes to it than any other song I have collected', Manifold to Parker, no date (*c.* 1955), in A.L. Lloyd Collection, Goldsmith's College Library, 'Australian Song Notes, Correspondence, etc.'

3. A book published in 1847, for instance, contains a version of 'The Wild Colonial Boy' that is said to refer to Jack Donohoe's fabled activities (Cozens, C., *The Adventures of A Guardsman*; see also Meredith, 1960, pp. 91–2). The historical Jack Donohoe, like the mythical wild

colonial boy, was Irish, was transported, did become a bushranger and was gunned down in a battle with the trooper police, as they were called (technically they were military police). So did a number of other unfortunates who were not celebrated in song, at least as far as we know.

4. Islamic culture, contains a Robin Hood-type hero named Kuroghli, the Son of the Blind Man, who is generous, manly, courageous. the friend of the poor and enemy of the rich and powerful. Russian culture boasts the heroic bandit figures of Van'ka Kain and Sten'ka Razin. The Caucasus has, among others, Arsena of Marabda who operated during the first half of the nineteenth century, was a friend of the poor, a great escaper and disguiser. Welsh tradition supports the figure of Thomas Jones, a sixteenth-century landowner, better known as *Twm Sion Cati*, a highway robber adept at disguise and escapes. Scots tradition celebrates William Wallace, briefly Guardian of Scotland, in outlaw hero terms. And the English traditions of Hereward the Wake who fought against William the Conqueror are well-known. Mexican-American tradition has, among others, the figure of Joaquin Murieta ('The Robin Hood of California') and Gregorio Cortez, whose life, times and legend were impressively documented and analysed by Amerigo Paredes.

5. Simeone was concerned to compare and contrast the American outlaw hero with the legendary Robin Hood and convincingly established the continuation of the Robin Hood image in American tradition. Steckmesser looked at a number of outlaws, noting both the similarities in their individual traditions and their historical contexts, an approach which he extended in his book-length study. Meyer identified twelve essential elements in the image of the American outlaw, most of which had been noted by previous commentators. Roberts applied these twelve elements to a discussion of the 'Railroad Bill' ballad(s) and their accompanying narrative complex, apparently without knowledge of the earlier work of Steckmesser and Simeone, or for that matter of Paredes' cognate work on the Mexican-American outlaw, Gregorio Cortez.

6. In the case of Robin Hood the poor are indeed the archetypal peasants or serfs. One of the earliest Robin Hood ballads tells us that the outlaw 'did poore men much gode'. According to his ballad, Jesse James 'stole from the rich and he gave to the poor', in this case primarily the farmers of the Kansas–Missouri border, many of whom believed themselves to be dispossessed and discriminated against in the aftermath of the Civil War. In Australia the 'poor' are the small selectors, trying to scratch a living on inferior land after the New

South Wales and Victorian free selection acts of the 1860s. Bush-rangers such as Ben Hall, who 'never robbed a needy man', or the bushranger of northern New South Wales known as 'Thunderbolt' or 'Captain Thunderbolt' (Frederick Ward), whose persona speaks in some of the few remaining lines of his ballad:

> My name is Frederick Ward,
> I am a native of this isle;
> I rob the rich to feed the poor
> And make the children smile.

7. Not only is this peripheral or liminal space important from a logistic and tactical viewpoint, it is also a symbolic indication of the hero's change of social status. Before it, he is generally a reasonably law-abiding, occasionally model, citizen, acting within the bounds of his community's values and mores, if now always in accordance with the official legal system. After he becomes an outlaw, usually through some act of justifiable violence or vengeance against one or more representatives of the oppressors, the hero moves out of the everyday set of routine rights and obligations and passes to a different space *outside* the boundaries of the everyday. He is no longer controlled by the same laws and values but is outside them, literally an outlaw.

8. There are a number of British ballads about highway robbers who act in a manner that does not accord with tradition. They are shown to suffer the consequences of their failure to adhere to the appropriate moral guidelines.

9. The courteous 'gentleman robber' is a notion that has been pumped up in romantic fiction treatments of outlaw heroes to the point where it has the status of a defining generic feature. While it can be readily seen in the examples provided that courtesy is a fundamental element of outlaw hero folklore, it must be seen as one of an inter-related set of characteristics that function together to form the folklore of the outlaw. As will be seen, this folklore is not a closed system but also intersects with more formal effusions about outlaw heroes, such as those presented in literature and the mass media. It is the intersection of the folkloric and the popular that creates—and continues—the outlaw hero tradition.

10. As in so many other areas, the outlaw in Lincoln green is the archetype here and there is clearly some affinity with another important form of folk hero, the trickster, who bamboozles and so ridicules the forces of authority and respectability. The ride from London to York in just one day, allegedly carried out by Dick Turpin, is another example of this

172   GRAHAME SEAL

outwitting motif, as is the use of disguise by Jesse James in the American tradition. In Australia, the Kelly gang was believed to possess unusually good bush skills that allowed them to elude the considerable police numbers that tracked them for eighteen months between 1878 and 1880.

11.   That dirty little coward that shot Mr Howard
          Has laid poor Jesse in his grave...

A further instance—one of many—is provided in the legendry of the bushranger Ben Hall, shot by police while sleeping, they having been led to the scene by a once-trusted friend:

> Savagely they murdered him,
> Those cowardly blue-coat imps
> Who were laid on to where he slept
> By informing peelers' pimps.

12. See Cozens, *The Journal of Captain Henry Thomas Fox*, 1852, quoted in Meredith, p. 95)

13. Explicit connections between political dissent and outlawry are made in one version collected by Bill Scott from Mr H. Beatty, Brisbane where the boy 'turned out as a Tory boy, as I'd often done before' (Meredith, 1960, p. 52). On this see Seal, 1980 and Seal, 1988, and also H. Anderson, *The Story of Australian Folklore*, 1970 (third edn, p. 125).

References

Hobsbawm, E. (1969), *Bandits*, London

Meredith, J. (1960), *The Wild Colonial Boy: The Life and Times of Jack Donohoe, 1808–1830*, Sydney

Meyer, R. (1980, 'The Outlaw: A Distinctive American Folktype', *Journal of the Foklore Institute*, No. 17

Roberts, J.W. (1981), '"Railroad Bill" and the American Outlaw Tradition', *Folklore*, No. 40

Simeone, W.E. (1958), 'Robin Hood and some Other American Outlaws', *Journal of American Folklore*, No. 71

Steckmesser, K.L. (1966), 'Robin Hood and the American Outlaw' *Journal of American Folklore*, No. 79

Shaping the 'Plain Australian' from War into Prosperity: Social Analysis in the 1940s and 1950s

NICHOLAS BROWN

'Popular culture' was not a concept used by those who sought to comprehend and influence social change in Australia in the 1940s and 1950s, but it was latent in their work. Those commentators—whether intellectuals, educators, critics or administrators—would have been precocious had it been explicit, for what was 'said to be popular culture' was only gradually becoming a field of analysis, initially in Britain, at that time.[1] The concept was forming in association with the imperatives of directing wartime mobilisation, with aspirations for post-war reform and democratisation, and with a more general awareness that 'the people' were being drawn into the economy and the government of society in unprecedented ways: through centralisation, consumerism, the penetration of the mass media, and so on. 'The popular' became a question begged rather than an object defined in searching for ways to secure the interests attributed to 'the people' and to manage their demands. Such a task was envisaged with enthusiasm by Kenneth Henderson, for example, Editor of Special Talks with the ABC and a member of the Australian Institute of Sociology—an association primarily of 'social scientist academics and clergy'[2] based in the Anthropology Department at the University of Sydney, and founded to help maintain the wartime morale of a population still disillusioned by the Great Depression. In 1943 Henderson counselled that 'to change the plain man in his condition we must know and respect him'. In facing this challenge, 'the scholar should not despair of the techniques of the press, the radio and other networks of popular persuasion'.[3] So in seeking an engagement with 'the plain man', social analysts of the period turned to those technical, institutional and even conceptual resources ready to hand. It is in this respect that there is a particular interest in following the Australian process of defining and negotiating 'the popular', since the resources then available to commentators shaped understandings of 'popular culture' in Australia in distinctive ways.

This article, then, does not study an aspect of Australian popular culture as such, but seeks to add to a recent, growing literature in that field a complementary sense of how the 'popular' was defined in a formative context. There is not space for a resolved discussion of this process, and there is a danger that this kind of genealogical exercise creates what it cannot find. But if popular cultures are identified by others rather than by 'the people' themselves,[4] then the context of that process as well as the

content of the subject might repay examination. What follows is at best a
suggestive outline, tracing some of the intersecting interests identifying
the 'popular' and shaping its characteristics in social analysis.

'The people' had, of course, been addressed in various ways prior to
the Second World War. Like most nations, Australians had gone through
phases of 'inventing' themselves, or of being invented, in images and
stereotypes.[5] These images, reflecting Australia's modernity, were
constructed more around ideals of the nation-to-be-made than around
the claims of heritage or folklore. But the complexities of the wartime and
post-war period, which might be summarised in terms of an appeal to 'the
people' conflicting with a perception of the challenge of 'the mass', gave
an awareness of 'the popular' an especially wide range of resonances.
Evocations of the old left stalwart of 'the bush', with its motifs of collectivism
and egalitarianism, made little headway against competing images of a
suburban society.[6] There were instead injuctions such as that by Lloyd
Ross, Publicity Officer of the Department of Post-War Reconstruction, who
spoke of opportunities for social advancement through 'science camoufl-
aged to suit the prejudices of Everyman';[7] or there were the uncertainties
expressed by the private-enterprise-based Institute of Public Affairs, not so
much about the spread of socialism but about 'the growth of the mass
mentality'.[8] In either formulation, 'the people' were attributed with a
resilience of 'prejudice' or of 'the mass'—variants, perhaps, of what Hoggart
termed the 'dense and concrete life'[9] of the British working class—which
eluded appeals to a common rationality or trust in social evolution, and
needed to be addressed in other ways. What is striking in the Australian
case is a relative weakness in the role that might expected of 'the popular'
in comparison with the part it played, in different ways, in Britain or the
United States during that same period: the role of mediating between
evocations of a collective integrity on the one hand and fears of an
amorphous, selfish mob on the other. For reasons that reflected their own
institutional and cultural placement, Australian social analysts seem to
have been ill-equipped to conceptualise 'the popular' in ways suited to
advance the reformism many concurrently held.

Something of these complexities can be traced in the concept of 'the
plain Australian' as it was articulated in the small book published by
C.E.W. Bean in 1943, *War Aims of a Plain Australian*. Without suggesting
that Bean was directly influential, or that the concept was highly
formalised, Bean's use of it was symptomatic of an emerging emphasis.
Even in its informality, the concept defined both a basic model in
understanding society—the normal, the average within an implied scale
of social adjustment and deviation—and also suggested an attributed self-
image among the audience addressed. Both these senses—the analytical

and the rhetorical—are important in inquiring into the formulation of 'the popular' as a post-war medium.

In *War Aims* Bean partly returned to the task he had set himself as official war historian in a similar booklet of 1919: to encourage Australians to make a better post-war world. That earlier book, *In Your Hands, Australians*, was written for 'soldiers and school-children': those responsible for upholding the national character Bean had seen proven on the fields of war. Then social progress had seemed to be a matter of deploying the 'brains and character' of a generic figure: the 'Australian'.[10] Looking back in 1943 it seemed to Bean that in that promise 'we failed absolutely', although the reasons—exhaustion and economic crisis—lay outside Australia's control.[11] In 1943 it was also clear that such collapse need not happen again. Public policy could now regulate the economy, and Bean indicated a range of what he termed 'tertiary industries' which would offer support for cultural and social reconstruction: 'government offices, schools, hospitals, national theatres, halls, community centres, art galleries, museums, libraries'—his list went on.[12] And in addition to the provision of such public services, it was also significant that in 1943 Bean was not addressing the future custodians of a national type but the whole of a present society, mobilised for war: the ranks of the 'plain Australians'.

His use of this term was not a mere choice of words; nor were the contrasts with the book of 1919 matters of style alone. At the end of the First World War the problem had been that the people had returned to the patterns of the past and had forsaken their potential. In 1943 Bean's fear was that they would seek the perpetuation into the future of that concession of individual rights to centralised authority which had been propelled by 'war necessities'. Quoting J.E. Davis's 'wise book', *Mission to Moscow*, Bean saw the crucial test to be in 'restoring individualism' not to a generic type but to an average citizen.[13] Yet it was also true that by 1943 Bean had difficulty in keeping concepts of 'community', once defined through what he saw as a characteristically Australian voluntarism, from sliding into the provision of services by the state through those same 'tertiary industries'. The citizen had become vulnerable to selfishness and apathy. To counter this tendency, the 'plain Australian' exemplified moderate needs and capacities. Bean's image was of 'the co-operator': 'a man who by internal law, apart from any external one, gives to every other man his due and trusts that others will treat him in the same manner'. So the 'national character' of 1919 became the 'internal law' of 1943; the 'brains' of 1919 prone to becoming 'the half-developed minds' of 1943, needing both 'negative and positive incentives' lest the welfare state render them weak—for there may be, Bean confided, 'a limit beyond which work cannot be reduced without moral damage to us all'.[14]

In this shift of concepts—as an inherent national type becomes the individually accountable average—there are aspects of the lack of a middle ground in social analysis which often marked attempts by Australian commentators to engage with what seemed a new strength of popular aspirations. In searching for a form of appeal to this changing population, Bean's declension from the generic is striking in short-circuiting a sense of intermediary loyalties, experiences, values or needs between the individual and society. His citizens stand in an individual relation to other citizens, and in an equivocal relation to the state and the rather disembodied provision of public services, agencies which must in turn serve community interests without advancing self-interestedness. While there is no reason to look to Bean, given his experience, his politics, and his intentions, for any equivalent of Raymond Williams's refrain of the 1950s, that 'culture is ordinary'—in the sense of being based in 'common meanings' which nevertheless allowed for 'growth', 'debate' and 'amendment'[15]—Bean's 'plain Australian' did not participate in the *making* of popular culture, but was at best its litmus, and at least was insulated from its demands.

It was certainly true that a sense of the 'average' had been heightened by the war in a number of ways. When, by 1943, 90 per cent of men and 30 per cent of women were directly involved in the war effort, and in civilian industries more so than at 'the front', then the heroic digger became a less effective image than the loyal citizen. Maximum efficiency in 'total war' required that individual competencies and skills were precisely identified and deployed through interventions such as aptitude and vocational testing. Even *Pix* magazine was aware of the need to adjust, for in 1945 it allowed that while pin-up girls may have been a feature of the First World War in a furtive kind of way, by the Second World War they had become a 'weapon for morale', and the magazine contributed to the celebration of victory by drawing together 'the quintessense of all the pin-ups of the war': a kind of collage or identikit of features from the years' models: the averaging of a popular, necessary form; private desire as public role.[16] At the other extreme, and in accordance with the emerging concept that 'wars begin in the minds of man', as the 'awful secrets' of Nazi concentration camps were revealed in 1945, Australian editorials spoke of the 'terrible indictment' of a 'whole nation', demanding that even the 'average' German civilian face, in tours of the camps and in streetside posters, the horrors or the actions they, in individual conscience and collective action, had 'heedlessly' allowed. More immediately, and putting Bean into a more appropriate context, it seems that in other ways Australian political culture had difficulty in adjusting both its rhetoric and its underlying concepts to the world of mobilisation and reconstruction. Evatt, as Attorney-General and Minister for External Affairs, may have allowed in 1943 that private interests and public regulation would be reconciled in wartime in the interests of 'the great middle groups',[17] but as Hasluck later indicated in his official history of the war at home, the government was incapable of subtlety in dealing with such a new sense of 'the people'. 'The political leaders,' he observed, 'complained frequently during this period of extravagance and spending and they no longer made the complaints, as they formally had done, about some small privileged group, but about the general populace, including the average wage-earner.' There seemed to be little confidence in 'the response of the people, and their own interest in helping to win the war'.[18] As class was eased aside in favour of the average, and society came to be known through individual morale and efficiency, the 'culture' of the 'plain Australian' became of great concern.

So what was it that shaped this concept of 'the plain Australian'? How, at a time in which there was such an imperative to comprehend the interests and aspirations of the people, was a nascent concept of 'the popular' understood? Perhaps the clearest example of this process is provided by the operation of the Australian Army Education Service (AAES), established in 1941, and in many ways marking out in application the transition Bean had signalled. For those who had been involved in providing adult education in the inter-war years, the AAES offered the first opportunity, with 'a reasonable budget and reasonable staff', to achieve something of earlier aspirations to offer rational and improving instruction.[19] Yet the AAES was also conscious, through the very scale of its operations, of inheriting something of that 'deadness' which Bean had depicted falling over Australia since the First World War. More particularly, there came early to AAES officers a disturbing realisation of a widespread lack among the Australian population of what seemed to be the 'fundamental' and 'simplest' atttributes of general knowledge, literacy and comprehension. Soldiers might be 'highly intelligent', as R.B. Madgwick, Director of the AAES, observed, but their distance from the 'ordinary techniques' of education meant that they required the demonstration methods of kindergarten teaching rather than a continuation of the university models of instruction which had been assumed to be appropriate in the education of adults before the war.[20] It was not sufficient to provide information and the opportunity to demonstrate latent intelligence; instruction would need to be appeal to a more subjective interest: to 'the plain man in his condition'.

There were up to 500 AAES officers by the end of the war, offering an education 'for victory, 'welfare' and 'citizenship'. Not only were they to 'boldly attack...the causes of moral weakness and disaffection among the men', but their objective was to prepare soldiers to return to the community 'as good and useful citizens'. Vocational training was central to these goals, for some soldiers, casualties of the Depression, had no skills. Yet there was emphasis, too, on 'fostering and broadening the troops' sense of social responsibility, keeping them in touch with their civic interests, and encouraging them to think intelligently about the problems of reconstruction which will face the community'.[21] 'Citizenship', then, emerged as a central theme, defined not only through participation in society but through individual attitude and morale.

That the AAES attempted to reach beyond 'training' to the more subjective bases of social conduct was indicated by the inclusion of aesthetic education among its programmes. Together with lectures, discussion groups and sessions developing manual skills in art and craft work, there was an emphasis on literary and music appreciation. Here the aim was both 'entertainment' and a commitment 'to raise and extend the troops cultural interests', giving them higher standards of taste and making them 'more receptive to new ideas'.[22] Assisted by whatever technical aids were available, from film to talks and the distribution of the Service's *Current Affairs Bulletin*, the AAES officer was to instil in soldiers a critical awareness of 'what they're fighting for'. The cultivation of personal independence was seen to be a crucial objective, drawing on the observation that 'in Europe at the end of the last war...many of the demobilised soldiers were spiritually lost...That frame of mind contributed to the breakdown of democracy'.[23] That 'frame of mind', then, was to become the basis of reformist strategies, developing from a concept of the average similar to Bean's 'plain Australian' into a more intimate interest in personality itself.

So the AAES officer had to be adept at balancing a commitment to encouraging independent thought with collective goals; to addressing their subjects *within* their culture but also of seeking to draw them beyond it. The Service's weekly newspaper, *Salt*—as in 'pass the ...'—encouraged discussion among soldiers, inviting contributions and correspondence. As with similar programmes in Britain, 'participatory citizenship' existed here in the ironic context of military discipline.[24] *Salt* took up the role of encouraging soldiers to extend into peace-time the 'special skills and aptitudes' they had acquired during the war, while also cautioning them that the world of rapid obsolescence to which they would be returning could guarantee them no continuity. Individual adaptability might have to be weighed against older expectations and loyalties. And *Salt* also carried articles from soldiers expressing a widening cultural interest—for example, an enthusiasm for jazz, new to many since their enlistment and the subject of quite learned disputes on, for instance, the nature of 'negro influence'. But when one letter enquired why a series of gramophone recitals of jazz by an AAES Sergeant had been cancelled on instruction from above,[25] the editor referred the correspondent to an earlier article which had argued, half-seriously, that any Council for the Development of Culture which was rumoured to be forming within the Department of Post-War

Reconstruction, should include a section for the Control of Jazz. There was concern that those who 'eat, play and work to the strains of that cataleptic cantata, "Pistol Packin' Momma" ' would otherwise never rise above such 'vulgar music' (this particular example hardly did justice to the sophistication of jazz enthusiasts' interests).[26] Similarly, one issue carried a letter calling for more Australian literature; the next number featured a 'Guest Author' section, that week filled by Leo Tolstoy.[27] In brief, to look through *Salt* is to gain a privileged view onto the range of popular discussion within the compass of reconstruction, to be struck by its vitality and by the interests vested in that forum.[28] Even that forum, however, had its boundaries. There was, for example, perhaps the first article by a 23-year-old Sergeant Robin Boyd, VX138171, later a prominent architectural critic of 'the Australian ugliness', suggesting plans for service-men's post-war housing. Here were Boyd's enduring concerns: 'simple, direct, livable' housing, providing 'greater freedom' because uncluttered by trimmings: a neutral environment in which a balance between utility and personal 'idiosyncracy' might be observed—for individual taste, paradoxically, could easily slide into the merely popular and overwhelm houses which were designed to give that same individual 'freedom'.[29]

Towards the end of the war many educators hoped that the AAES would be continued on an equivalent scale but in a form more appropriate to a civilian society. Anticipating this form, Madgwick argued in 1944 that a lower standard of teaching must be adopted to meet the abilities of students, premised not on the topicality of issues but on an immediately accessible approach 'adapted to their own experience, problems and aptitudes'.[30] Here again is something of a precursor to Hoggart's call to understand 'the local and concrete world' of 'the people'[31] which marked early explicit formulations of 'popular culture' in Britain in the 1950s. But where Hoggart and others saw possibilities for some adaptability and resistance based on communal spirit and enduring class interests, the Australian commentary shifted steadily towards a focus on the adaptability of the individual as a discrete unit to a society. The experience of, and participation in mobilisation of many intellectuals and commentators in Australia seems to have reoriented an earlier culture evoking a latent national type to one which sought the allegiance of a self-regulating citizen. Neither of these formulations was particularly atuned to the actual context of 'the people's' lives. Coupled to this conceptual legacy were political struggles over 'planning'. Aspirations for maintaining the AAES were dissipated at the end of the war in a series of unresolved inquiries at State and Commonwealth levels,[32] indicating the equivocal position of the Service on issues of the systematic direction of instruction by governments against the task of restoring initiative to 'the community' and 'individual-ism' to a new citizenry. This tension can be seen in the strongest inheritor of the AAES's initiatives, the Council for Adult Education (CAE), established in Victoria in 1946.

C.R. Badger was appointed the first Director of the CAE. He came to that position already disillusioned with the 'secular ministry' of inter-war adult education, and with a commitment instead to a provision which might correspond more to the needs and interests of the people: education almost as a tertiary industry in Bean's sense, 'along with broadcasting, the cinema and the travel industry'.[33] Badger had been involved with the AAES in writing discussion pamphlets, giving lectures and contributing to *Salt*, and he admired the Service's work. He also saw that the world was changing, making new demands on the population and conceding to them more of an almost inarticulate power. In his pre-war and wartime correspondence with W.K. Hancock, then in London, the issues of propaganda, popular escapism and the battle for morale had been canvassed, often with concern at the 'breakdown of intellectual self-control' in the late 1930s, and at the tendency of the war effort to level down the population, producing 'the kind of standardisation which squashes personality'.[34] As a remedy, it seems, Badger defined his task with the CAE in terms of 'providing an opportunity for civilised living' to 'the masses'. 'Economic advance', he argued, 'is already creating the possibility of greater leisure and of greater income' for the majority—a leisure which, as Bean had feared, could be abused in political or economic demands, or which might weaken character. What was needed was access and inducements to appropriate forms of recreation which would, as Badger phrased it, encourage 'self-training' for the duties of citizenship.[35]

Given post-war affluence—however initially unstable—the imperative to reformism through vocational rehabilitation seemed to be passing, yet themes of popular management in social analysis remained. Prominent economists, such as D.B. Copland and F.R.E. Mauldon, expressed concern that unrestrained consumer spending in the 'milk bar economy' threatened the prospects for balanced, planned economic development. For them, the 'consumer' was associated with 'a psychological tendency for individuals to make their own interpretations of the degree to which the productive system can be made to yield more real income through leisure and to require less labour'.[36] Here was another pressure of 'the popular', an area in which the CAE equipped itself to intervene. Already, in 1941, Badger had steered the Melbourne University Extension Board away from the 'severely economic and political courses...offered as especially relevant to working class education' and welcomed instead 'new topics—folk dancing, practical painting, music and drama, the natural sciences, etc. —[which] began to figure prominently in the syllabus'.[37] What was being offered was not so much opportunities for people to express *themselves*, but structures in which the self might be subsumed in a collective tradition, or in 'art', or in a methodical knowledge of the world around them. The CAE sought to create 'opportunities for co-operative social action' which were to emerge through communities determining their own activities in a field which, Badger noted in 1951, 'is rather unhappily being called "cultural entertainment" '. There was, it seemed, an implicit distinction to be drawn between the merely popular, which might slide into the selfishness of the mass, and the refined popular of the self-improving community which might, according the first editorial of CAE's journal in 1956, provide 'the essential equipment for a full and thoroughly enjoyable life'.[38]

The activities of the CAE in both metropolitan and country areas included the provision of classes in subjects ranging from gymnastics to logic, the encouragement of discussion groupings, and the organisation of exhibitions, performances and documentary film screenings. Its ostensible model was the British Arts Council, which emphasised the subsidisation of touring professional companies and exhibitions to increase access to the arts outside major centres. Yet, while the CAE also sponsored touring companies, its services were geared more to civic voluntarism and encouraging, as Badger put it, 'a sense of responsibility for self-discipline'.[39] In seeking to identify a role for the individual amid social change, concepts of 'civic education' were given priority over more extensive access to diverse and perhaps challenging forms of cultural consumption, either of arts professionally produced and effectively disseminated (Badger opposed the emphasis of the Elizabethan Theatre Trust on establishing professional companies and favoured assistance for local, primarily amateur groupings),[40] or in activities in which individuals were seen to be lost in the merely popular. By the late 1950s, for example, the CAE—representing a self-proclaimed 'positive and constructive citizenry' now devoted to 'mental and spiritual health'—was casting a critical eye over Melbourne's Moomba Festival, which seemed to have descended, in their terms, to the level of a 'tawdry' 'popular carnival', with commercial floats, American symbolism and the 'kitsch use of Aboriginal artefacts and motifs'.[41] It had foresaken any aspiration to offer an educative programme 'at the highest cultural levels'.

The point here is not to suggest some conspiracy of wowsers, but to indicate something of the overlapping institutional and cultural contexts in which post-war change was comprehended. Many examples could be given of comparable strategies which were not necessarily 'influential' but indicate instead the pervasiveness of these themes of individual accountability against 'the popular'. The period abounded in attempts to enter into 'the networks of popular persuasion', to 'know' the 'plain man in his condition', but scarcely to trust him or her in it. The ABC, for instance, recognised that a civilian population 'disciplined' by the war, and 'sophisticated' by participation in the responsibilities of the home front, was now keen to shake off 'restriction-mindedness'. They demanded new forms of programming once radio, as the Commission's Chairman, Richard Boyer put it, 'entered the field of discussion of controversial topics, of political, social and ethical debate'.[42] When the ABC released a journal, *Talk*, to publish some of the material broadcast in this more intimate 'talk' form, it did so explicitly to serve a society now identified as keen to make up its own mind, but implicitly out of a concern to balance a more individual, private engagement with the written word against what Boyer, in another context, identified as radio's inherent tendency to propaganda, the easy appeal of the spoken word to an undifferentiated mass.[43] Words of wise counsel from 'many of our distinguished men and women' would appeal directly to the conscience of the individual listener. Broadcast debates, or the more vernacular appeal to the audience sought by the BBC at the time, were avoided. 'Discussion groups', to be assembled around their radios with materials supplied by the ABC to help guide them through the issues presented over the radio, were another attempt to negotiate between the message, the popular medium and an individualised audience.

In the late 1940s Cheshire publishers released a series of booklets in the *Quest* series, similarly designed to guide the reader 'carefully through the maze of social and cultural subjects' that suddenly confronted them. One essay on the role of the media, for example, directed its readers to questions which would assist them to identify their personal convictions against mere popular opinion: 'Have you ever tried to estimate the part the training you had at school has had on your mental development? How often, when you express an opinion, do you take time off to wonder whether it is your own or merely a restatement of something you read in the paper or heard on the radio?' [44] What might be left of the 'self' once these extraneous influences, the intrusions of the popular, were filleted out? Innate gifts?—the talent of women for housework was given as one example of an aptitude that stood beyond manufactured opinion. And this example also indicates that on those rare occasions when 'the plain Australian' was explicitly gendered, the average weighed particularly heavily on women as a conservative vision of their contribution to social stability via a kind of 'internal law'—as Bean would have termed it. And in turn, this more intimate awareness of the average personality opened up new avenues for assessing a relationship between individual sexuality in particular and the lure of the popular.

It is as if Australian social analysis, so accustomed to defining its subject in terms of a national developmentalism and the kind of evolutionary social holism implied by Bean's generic Australian, had little purchase on a society which had been mobilised into what appeared to be a mass of individuals who in turn were attributed with no intermediary loyalties.

All that lay to hand was the residue of that holism, the average or 'plain' Australian: no longer a type but, in a key word of the period, a personality.

Australian commentators were not alone in the general themes of such a perception, however distinctive they may have been in the application of them. In America David Reisman's influential 1950 study, *The Lonely Crowd*, had identified a contemporary transition from 'the widely variegated *social* character types of an ununified world' to 'the even more divergent *individual* character of a unified but less oppressive world'. Reisman was prepared to trust this 'new "plastic" man' to the interplay of 'technology and organisation', 'peer group and school',[45] just as the participants in a 1952 *Partisan Review* symposium testified to a conviction among intellectuals that, 'in their chastened mood, American democracy looks like the real thing'.[46] The challenge to them was to reconcile themselves to working through popular forms as expressive fields in themselves. In Britain, on the other hand, the consolidation of the Welfare State and the related heightening of issues of class, offered a similar if less pluralistic field of engagement for intellectuals.[47] As Williams saw it, for example, the paradoxes present in the work of George Orwell—'the scepticism and contempt for slogans, [the] praise of common sense and decency'[48] -constituted a major inheritance in understanding popular culture as 'an arena of consent and resistance'.[49] In Australia, however, social analysis tended to adapt its characteristically more intrumentalist approach to a more limited sense of the nature of 'the people' and their 'culture'. Even the most systematic studies of the condition of 'the people', such as those co-ordinated from the Department of Psychology at the University of Melbourne by Oeser, Hammond and Emery of 'social structure and personality' in Australian rural and urban communities, worked within a very limited frame of reference, primarily dealing with the home, childhood, family and school. These assessments of individual 'adjustment' were built around the assumption that 'personal independence' was the central feature of dominant Australian 'personality structures', an emphasis which rendered other more socially, culturally, economically or politically integrative spheres of only secondary importance, if any at all.[50]

This was poor soil for the identification of 'popular culture', but the plant struggled to survive, its runners searching for better nourishment. Some hoped to make the most of new innovations in communication: film, for example, and especially documentary. It was a medium which, in America in the 1930s had been deployed in an attempt to create an 'authentic' national culture, a conscience recognising the hardships of the Depression. In Britain, through the work of the GPO Film Unit, there had been a comparable interest in depicting the patterns of community surrounding local industries. It was, as the leading British Director, John Grierson, expressed it, a form which 'would crystallise sentiments in a muddled world', replacing 'the sloppy romanticism of the person in private' with 'an aesthetic of the person in public'.[51] The AAES and the CAE, as already noted, were keen advocates of this message, which Grierson brought personally to Australia in 1941.[52] Yet while the Commonwealth government established a Film Unit, and while New South Wales had its own Documentary Film Commission, their story is one of frustration with an official emphasis on 'promotional' film.[53] Critics of this state instrumentalism sometimes displayed their own versions of this same characteristic. A.K. Stout, Professor of Philosophy at Sydney, was one such critic, envisaging the role of documentary in these terms: 'our various institutions, social, political and industrial, are the means whereby we resolve the contradictions between man and man...there is a rich field for documentary in showing us to ourselves, showing how these institutions work'. Stout's insistence that 'public services render themselves especially to this treatment'[54] indicated another dimension of such an instrument-alism: here is a society to be understood downwards from its 'tertiary industries', albeit with a critical edge; it is not one to be evoked through its cultures of labour, region, class, family and home.

Film and then television appeared to be the ultimate 'popular media' in terms of access and impact. Again, it appears that those interested in more participatory concepts of 'popular culture' in Britain or America came gradually to concede these media a place in developing a faculty of discrimination, a sense of resistance and engagement among popular audiences, who would not necessarily leave other values and loyalties at the door. The individualised popular audience in Australia, however, was initially accorded less flexibility: evaluations of the 'message' of film, for example, allowed for little cultural mediation between technique and the receiving personality. Turning his attention to popular film, Stout argued in 1951 that concern should not be directed at depictions of sexuality but at the portrayal of crime and 'the repetition and glorification of false patterns of life'—especially materialism and images of 'the ideal life as one of luxury' which would break down those patterns of work and duty necessary for the citizen.[55] From a comparable perspective, a reviewer in the *Age* questioned whether gangster films should receive unqualified disapprobation. While in many cases censorship was warranted to protect teenage audiences from 'the exposition of crookedness [which]...is generally closely related to sex', it was also suggested that there were instances in which explicit violence might be of valuable effect in pointing 'memorials to police officers who have lost their lives in the cause of civil justice and discipline'.[56] These films were be accorded the status of being 'semi-documentary' in their 'authenticity'. Yet they were not seen to encourage critical evaluation from their audience, and these commentators neglected as insignificant the extent to which such films engaged with areas of experience—areas such as sexuality or personal violence—which were not accorded by them a direct connection with 'good citizenship'. In dealing with a popular audience, it seems, there was no room for subtlety in assessing the impact of film. Perhaps the last word can be given to Lady Paton, President of the Australian Council for Children's Film, who gave evidence to the Vincent Committee in 1963 to the effect that she was prepared to accept the access of children to 'sex films' and even 'free-for-all' violence, so long as the selection offered 'a more extensive and authentic representation of the Australian way of life'.[57]

It is easy to anthologise points such as these, and to draw contrasts between Australian commentators and those elsewhere when shades of emphasis, or allowances for mitigating circumstances, might be more appropriate. Clearly, there is a need for a more complete development of these suggestions before they can be assessed in a balanced way. But there is also a remarkable consistency running through these evaluations of how the new demands of 'the popular' were addressed in the 1940s and 1950s. The 'plain Australian' ushered in a peculiarly normative approach to 'the popular', as if Australian social analysis, so accustomed to visions of the 'coming man', had no basis on which to deal with the phenonemon once it actually arrived. Other features might seem to be connected with this distinctive comprehension of 'the popular', features with some influence on subsequent social analysis. Citizenship, for example, was often referred to as a potential moderator of the 'popular', and there might be a residue of the narrow frame of reference identified in this paper in recent citizenship campaigns in Australia which seem largely to ignore the concept of *social* citizenship. In these campaigns the primary focus has been on reports of political illiteracy among school children, as if not knowing how parliament works was a cause and not a symptom of an underdeveloped sense of social participation. Even in 1989 a Senate Committee, advising on 'active citizenship', spoke of the 'apathy' arising from 'political ignorance' as 'opening the way for a victory of self-centredness over a sense of community responsibility'.[58] Is there no other way, more immediate to experience, that the task of democratising Australian society can be broached? No alternative has been handed down from the period under discussion. It is not co-incidental that Barry Humphries created the revealingly named Edna Everage in the 1950s, a character—in its first incarnation—shrewdly seen by Rowse as 'innocent' of her averageness, and providing the intellectuals who lauded her 'truth' with an opportunity 'to savour an authentic Australianness without making an emotional commitment to it'.[59] However ironically, those seeking to understand and influence 'the land of the long weekend' through the post-war years of consolidation were not all that good at comprehending and accepting a concept of 'the popular' as a field that might have some integrity, warranting more than 'management'.

Notes

1. See Raymond Williams, *Culture and Society 1780–1950* (Harmondsworth, Penguin, 1958), p. 295. For a valuable outline of the emergence of the concept of popular culture, see Jim McGuigan, *Cultural Populism* (London, Routledge, 1992), Part One.

2. Tim Rowse, *Australian Liberalism and National Character* (Malmsbury, Vic., Kibble Books, 1978), p. 166.

3. K. Henderson, 'The Scholar in Reconstruction', *Social Horizons*, No. 1, 1943, pp. 82–3.

4. See Raymond Williams, *Keywords: A Vocabulary of Culture and Society* (New York, Oxford University Press, 1976), p. 199.

5. The classic text here is, of course, Richard White, *Inventing Australia: Images and Identity 1688–1980* (Sydney, Allen and Unwin, 1981).

6. See David Carter, 'Coming Home After the Party: *Overland*'s First Decade', *Meanjin*, Vol. 44, No. 4, 1985, pp. 462–76.

7. Lloyd Ross, 'A New Social Order' in D.A.S. Campbell (ed.), *Post-War Reconstruction in Australia* (Sydney, Angus and Robertson, 1944), p. 221.

8. 'The Threat to the Individual', *IPA Review*, Vol. 3, No. 1, 1949, p. 175.

9. Richard Hoggart, *The Uses of Literacy* (Harmondsworth, Penguin, 1958), p. 104.

10. C.E.W. Bean, *In Your Hands, Australians* (London, Cassell, 1919).

11. C.E.W. Bean, *War Aims of a Plain Australian* (Sydney, Angus and Robertson, 1943), Ch. 1.

12. Ibid., p. 16.

13. Ibid., p. vi.

14. Ibid., pp. 51, 69–70, 91, 21.

15. Raymond Williams, 'Culture is Ordinary', first published in 1958, repr. in Raymond Williams, *Resources of Hope: Culture, Democracy, Socialism* (London, Verso, 1989), pp. 3–18, esp. p. 4.

16. 'Pix Creates Perfect Pin-Up Girl', *Pix*, 15 September 1945, p. 16.

17. See W.J. Waters, 'Labor, Socialism and World War II', *Labour History*, No. 16, 1969, pp. 14–19.

18. Paul Hasluck, *The Government and the People 1942–1945* (Canberra, Australian War Memorial, 1970), pp. 223, 247.

19. R.B. Madgwick, 'Adult Education as a Commonwealth Movement' in W.G.K. Duncan (ed.), *The Future of Adult Education in Australia* (Sydney, Angus and Robertson, 1944), p. 24.

20. Ibid., pp. 24–7.

21. AAES, *Handbook for Education Officers*, n.d, p. 7.

22. Ibid., p. 9.

23. Ibid., pp. 18, 20.

24. See Neil Grant, 'Citizen Soldiers: Army Education in World War II', *Formations of Nation and People*, Vol. 1, 1984, pp. 171–87.

25. Letter from C.R. Shaw, *Salt*, Vol. 10, No. 1, 1945, p. 51.

26. B. Jones, 'Moonlight Sinatra', *Salt*, Vol. 9, No. 13, 1945, pp. 22–3.

27. See Vol. 10, No. 2, 1945, pp. 59–64.

28. As Ian Turner recalled, the AAES had provided 'an obvious point of communist concentration': Ian Turner, 'My Long March' in *Room for Manoeuvre* (Melbourne, Drummond, 1982), p. 117.

29. Robin P. Boyd, 'Houses in the Air', *Salt*, Vol. 7, No. 2, 1943, pp. 32–5.

30. Madgwick, 'Adult Education', pp. 24–7.

31. Hoggart, *Uses of Literacy*, p. 104.

32. See D.M. Waddington, W.C. Radford, J.A. Keats, *Review of Education in Australia 1940–1948* (Melbourne, ACER, 1950), pp. 167–73; also Derek Whitelock, 'A Brief History of Adult Education in Australia and an Outline of Current Provision' in Whitelock (ed.), *Adult Education in Australia* (Sydney, Pergamon, 1970), pp. 16–27.

33. See Colin R. Badger, *Who Was Badger?* (Melbourne, CAE, 1984), p. 45.

34. See the correspondence from Hancock to Badger and others in the Hancock Papers, ANU Archives of Business and Labour, P96/23 (Q4).

35. C.R. Badger, *Adult Education in Post-War Australia* (Melbourne, ACER, 1944), pp. 6, 16.

36. See for example F.R.E. Mauldon, 'The Consumer in a Planned Economy', *Economic Record*, Vol. 25, No. 1, 1949, pp. 14–15.

37. Badger, *Who Was Badger?*, p. 73.

38. C.R. Badger, 'Adult Education in Victoria', *Australian Quarterly*, Vol. 23, No. 3, 1951, p. 32; Editorial, *Adult Education*, Vol. 1, No. 1, 1956, p. 5.

39. Badger, *Adult Education in Post-War Australia*, p. 6.

40. See Badger, *Who Was Badger?*, pp. 151–5.

41. Editorial, *Adult Education*, Vol. 2, No. 1, 1958, p. 5; R.A. Gardner, 'The Moomba Festival', *Adult Education*, Vol. 2, No. 4, 1958, pp. 6–11; Stephen Alomes, 'Parades of Meaning: The Moomba Festival and Contemporary Culture', *Journal of Australian Studies*, No. 17, 1985, pp. 3–17.

42. R.J.F. Boyer, 'Why We Publish *Talk*', *Talk*, Vol. 1, No. 1, 1946, pp. 7–8.

43. R.J.F. Boyer, 'Radio in Education Conference', *Australian Quarterly*, Vol. 28, No. 1, 1946, p. 97.

44. Lewis Wilcher, *Education, Press, Radio* (Melbourne, Cheshire, 1948), pp. 5–6.

45. David Reisman, *The Lonely Crowd: A Study of the Changing American Character* (New Haven, Conn., Yale University Press, 1950), p. xxv.

46. Quote from Philip Rahv's essay in the 'Our Country and Our Culture' symposium, *Partisan Review*, Vol. 19, No. 3, 1952, p. 304. See generally Andrew Ross, 'Containing Culture in the Cold War', *Cultural Studies*, Vol. 1, No. 3, 1987, pp. 328–48.

47. See Alistair Davies and Peter Saunders, 'Literature, Politics and Society' in Alan Sinfield (ed.), *Society and Literature 1945–1970* (New York, Holmes and Meier, 1973), pp. 24–39.

48. Williams, *Culture and Society*, ch.6.

49. Stuart Hall, quoted in McGuigan, *Cultural Populism*, p. 16.

50. See S.B. Hammond, 'Class Strata and Politics' in O.A. Oeser and S.B. Hammond (eds.), *Social Structure and Personality in an Urban Community*

(London, Routledge, 1954), p. 312; also O.A. Oeser and F.E. Emery, *Social Structure and Personality in a Rural Community* (London, Routledge, 1954).

51. Quoted in Forsyth Hardy (ed.), *Grierson on Documentary* (London, Faber, 1966), p. 18.

52. Grierson actually gave Badger a projector and prints of *Drifters* and *Night Mail to Edinburgh*, which Badger showed to classes and in lectures until the Army requisitioned the projector. See Badger, *Who is Badger?*, p. 71.

53. See Tom Politis, '1940s—Australia' in Ross Lansell and Peter Beilby (eds.), *The Documentary Film in Australia* (Melbourne, Nelson, 1982), p. 39; A.K. Stout, 'Films in Australia: My 35 Years Saga', *Media Information Australia*, Vol. 2, No. 6, 1977, pp. 14–5.

54. Typescript for a talk on documentary, undated but circa 1944, in A.K. Stout papers, National Library of Australia, Ms.5712, Box 2.

55. A.K. Stout, 'Danger of Film Is Its False View Of Life', *Argus*, 16 December 1951, p. 7.

56. 'Youth and Crime', *Age*, 27 January 1951, p. 12.

57. Minutes, *Report of the Select Committee on the Encouragement of Australian Productions for Television* (Canberra, AGPS, 1963), pp. 76–9.

58. Senate Standing Committee on Employment, Education and Training, *Education for Active Citizenship in Australian Schools and Youth Organisations* (Canberra, AGPS, 1989), p. 7.

59. Rowse, *Australian Liberalism*, pp. 205–6.

On the Beach: Apocalyptic Hedonism and the Origins of Postmodernism

ANDREW MILNER

During 1990 and 1991 Mandarin Paperbacks released a new edition of the novels of Nevil Shute. Among the first lot of six titles was *On the Beach* (Shute, 1990), the front cover of which proudly proclaimed it 'The Great Australian Novel of Our Time'. This is a judgement which finds very little echo in university English Literature departments, whether in Australia or in England. And yet there is an important sense in which it asserts little more than a commonplace: when judged by the criteria of the marketplace, *On the Beach* is indeed precisely *the* great Australian novel of our time. It was first published in 1957, by Heinemann simultaneously in Melbourne, London and Toronto (Shute, 1957), and by Morrow in New York. The novel had two printings in 1957, a third in 1958 and a fourth in 1959. Subsequently reprintings followed regularly, the title remaining more or less continuously in print thereafter. The Mandarin edition was itself reprinted in 1992. In 1984 there had even been a large print edition (Shute, 1984). In 1978, the UNESCO *Statistical Yearbook* would show Shute as the 133rd most translated author in the world: there had been 96 translations of his work during the period 1961–1965 and 22 in 1973 alone (UNESCO, 1978: 915). The vast majority of these must have been of either *A Town Like Alice* (Shute, 1950) or *On the Beach*. Certainly, the first full-length study of Shute's work, written with the active cooperation of his family, records that *On the Beach* 'quickly became his greatest financial and critical success' (Smith, 1976: 133). The United Artists film version, a 'solid prestige job' (Walker, 1991: 815), appeared in 1959. Directed by Stanley Kramer, it ran for over two hours (134 minutes!) and starred Gregory Peck as Dwight Towers, the commander of the American submarine, the *USS Scorpion*, and Ava Gardner and Fred Astaire somewhat improbably as the main Australian characters, Moira Davidson and John Osborne. Filming actually began near Shute's home at Langwarrin, about thirty miles south of Melbourne, and continued in or near Melbourne during the spring of 1958. At a time when the Australian cinema industry had itself fallen into near-complete decrepitude, 'the presence of a major motion picture company spending millions of dollars was a sensation generating...massive public curiosity' (Smith, 1976: 138). The film was widely perceived as the most important thing to happen to Melbourne since the Olympic Games, and some might add that it still appears thus. In short, *On the Beach* became a major local and international cultural event, what we might today term a 'blockbuster'.

Set largely in and around Melbourne during the second year after a full-scale nuclear war, the novel's subject matter was nothing less than the slow extinction of the last affluent remains of the human race. When Shute had first broached with Heinemann the matter of a cover design, he had suggested 'a scene of the main four or five characters standing together quite cheerfully highlighted on a shadowy beach of a shadowy river—the Styx' (Smith, 1976: 129). Sophisticated critical theory has long since given up on idle speculation about authorial intentions. But were we so to indulge, we might well find in this juxtaposition between light and shade, cheerfulness and death, a concise and economical representation of what Shute himself had apparently intended as a central organising principle of the novel: *On the Beach* derives much of its power from what I will term its 'apocalyptic hedonism', that is, from the peculiar *frisson* of a textual erotics deriving from the simultaneous juxtaposition of the terrors of imminent extinction and the delights of hedonistic affluence. The novel opens with a young Australian naval officer, Peter Holmes, still sore from a day spent partly on the beach and partly sailing, drowsily recalling the Christmas barbecue of two days earlier (Shute, 1990: 7). The 'short, bewildering war...of which no history...ever would be written' (ibid.: 9–10) is introduced into this almost quintessentially Australian idyll at exactly the moment when Holmes and his wife, Mary, are planning to meet at their club and to go on for a swim. It closes with Towers and Davidson, he aboard the *Scorpion* heading south from the Heads, she ashore near Port Lonsdale, and an analogous, though now much darker juxtaposition, that between the bottle of brandy and the government-issue suicide tablets (ibid.: 316), between the 'big car' with 'plenty of petrol in the tank' (ibid.: 314) and the nuclear submarine. Similar motifs recur throughout: Osborne's new red Ferrari, for example, 'washed and polished with loving care' (ibid.: 151), and his enthusiastic pursuit of what must be the very last Australian Grand Prix; his Uncle Douglas's sturdy determination to work through the Pastoral Club's wine cellar—'we've got over three thousand bottles of vintage port left in the cellars...and only about six months left to go, if what you scientists say is right' (ibid.: 102); or the fishing trip on the Jamieson River (ibid.: 273–83) made possible by a Government decision to bring forward the trout season 'for this year only' (ibid.: 232)

Asked her opinion of Melbourne, Ava Gardner is reputed to have judged it unusually well suited to a movie about the end of the world. Apocryphal or not, the remark has provoked much subsequent amusement in Sydney and equivalent umbrage in Melbourne. And yet Garner was absolutely right: both Australia and Melbourne were indeed ideal locations for a film or a book about the end of the world. Which takes me elliptically from one blockbuster to another, to what Meaghan Morris describes as contemp-

orary cultural theory's 'own version of cinema's blockbuster: the state-of-
the-globe, state-of-the-arts, Big Speculation' (Morris, 1988: 242), that is,
to postmodernism. *On the Beach* was, of course, a determinedly 'popular'
work, neither modernist nor postmodernist in form (though its intertextual
effects continue to be played out in such declaredly postmodernist work as
Robert Wilson and Philip Glass's 'opera' *Einstein on the Beach*). But in its
apocalyptic hedonism, at least, Shute's novel importantly prefigures much
of what has become characteristic of contemporary postmodern sensibility.
Like all blockbusters, postmodernist cultural theory derives its success in
part from a capacity to appeal to as wide an audience as possible, high
philosophy in the art house cinemas of the academy and middlebrow multi-
screen literary criticism as much as local fleapit sociology. If not exactly
meaning all things to all people, the term very obviously signifies differently
within different discourses: in short, it is as polysemic a sign as they come.
An apparently enduring postmodern trope, however, is that of 'being after'.
'*Post*modernism,' writes Ferenc Fehér, 'like many of its conceptual
brethren...understands themselves not in terms of what they are but in
terms of what they come after' (Fehér, 1990: 87). But after what? After
modernism certainly, after modernity perhaps, and crucially also after
'the War'. For the generations that would eventually attempt to theorise
these many and varied postmodern conditions had grown up in a world
that considered itself quite decisively 'post-War'. Here, surely, is the trope
in initio: to quote Meaghan Morris yet again, 'the postmodern era could be
said to begin in 1945, at Hiroshima and Nagasaki' (Morris, 1988: 186).
The Second World War, however, unlike the First, had never been a war
to end war: the defeat of the Axis had merely announced the beginnings of
the Cold War, itself all too readily imaginable as the prelude to the war
that would indeed finally end war, and with it all human life. Postmodernity
was thus haunted from its inception by an imminent apprehension of the
last days and of the end of things. And yet this was also and simultaneously
a prodigiously consumerist economy of affluence, originally confined to
the United States, Canada and Australia, later dispersed throughout the
West. This was a culture predisposed, then, towards a much more general
apocalyptic hedonism than that exhibited in Shute's novel.

Such early datings of the beginnings of 'postmodernity' as Morris's are
by no means uncontroversial: the more typical focus in recent cultural
theory has fallen on the supposedly more radical transformations of the
late 1950s and the early 1960s, as in Fredric Jameson's *Postmodernism, or
The Cultural Logic of Late Capitalism* (Jameson, 1991: 1), or even those of
the 1970s and 1980s, as in the analyses of 'New Times' developed by the
now defunct British journal *Marxism Today* (*Marxism Today*, 1988). These
later datings often call attention to quite significant changes within post-
war society and culture, for example the rise of the 'new social movements'

or the development of new 'post-industrial' technologies. But the more fundamental shift is that registered by Morris, that to a distinctively post-war world, the more general characteristics of which continue to structure our contemporary reality. That shift is peculiarly visible in precisely the 'high cultural' social sub-sector from which the 'postmodernist' debate derives much of its vocabulary. Both modernist high culture in general and the cultural avant-garde in particular were the creations of the great cities of continental Europe—Berlin and Vienna, Moscow and St Petersburg, above all Paris (Bradbury, 1976)—and as such, they were fated to become direct casualties of the twin totalitarianisms of Nazism and Stalinism. What survived into post-war New York was an increasingly commodified imitation of avant-garde style, increasingly bereft of avant-garde social purpose. This is post-modernism in the most obvious of senses, that of the 'high' culture that survived after modernism, and it is a culture which clearly dates from the 1940s. This is a 'post-modernism' grudgingly acknowledged by even those most hostile to the notion itself: Alex Callinicos, for example, agrees that the 'postwar stabilization of capitalism left the few still committed to avant-garde objectives beached' (Callinicos, 1989: 60); Perry Anderson that 'the Second World War...cut off the vitality of modernism' (Anderson, 1988: 326). And, as Jameson nicely observes of the latter, 'whatever Perry Anderson...thinks of the utility of the period term—postmodernism—his paper demonstrates that...the conditions of existence of modernism were no longer present. So we are in something else' (Jameson, 1988: 359). This something else is postmodernism. Postmodernism is thus neither a specific type of art not a specific type of cultural theory nor even a specific type of politics. It is, rather, a particular cultural space available for analysis to many different kinds of contemporary cultural theory and for intervention to many different kinds of contemporary artistic and political practice. The term is best understood, then, as denoting a 'cultural dominant', in Jameson's phrase (Jameson, 1991: 4), or even, in Williams's terms, a 'structure of feeling' (Williams, 1965: 64–5). In this sense, Habermas's sustained polemic against the implied neo-conservatism of French post-structuralism (Habermas, 1985; Habermas, 1987) can be read as an intervention within postmodernism as much as an argument against it.

Celebratory postmodernism as a major academic event dates from the 1970s, from the first publication of Lyotard's The Postmodern Condition, a specifically Canadian text originally prepared for the Conseil des Universitiés of the Government of Quebec (Lyotard, 1979). For Lyotard, modernism and modernity had been characterised above all by the co-presence of science and of a series of universalising and legitimating metanarratives which ultimately derived from the Enlightenment. These metanarrative paradigms had run aground, he argued, in the period since the Second World War: 'in contemporary society and culture—post-industrial society, postmodern culture—the...grand narrative has lost its credibility, regardless of what mode of unification it uses, regardless of whether it is a speculative narrative or a narrative of emancipation' (Lyotard, 1984: 37). The postmodern conditions's 'incredulity towards metanarratives', whether in aesthetics or science or politics, is for Lyotard in part a consequence of the internal logic of the metanarratives themselves, which proceed from scepticism to pluralism, in part also a correlate of postindustrialism, in which knowledge itself becomes a principal form of production, thereby shifting emphasis 'from the ends of action to its means' (ibid.). Lyotard's slightly later 'What is Postmodernism?', first published in 1982, recapitulates much of the earlier analysis, despite its, in my view very unhelpful, retreat from the initial attempt at cultural periodisation (Lyotard, 1984a: 79). Here, the postmodern continues to be understood as that which 'denies itself the solace of good forms, the consensus of a taste which would make it possible to share collectively the nostalgia for the unattainable: that which searches for new representations...in order to impart a strong sense of the unpresentable' (ibid.: 81). The postmodern, Lyotard tells us, will 'wage a war on totality', that 'transcendental illusion' of the nineteenth century, the full price of which has proven to be 'terror' (ibid.: 81–2).

The term 'postmodern' was by no means an original coinage, however. To the contrary, Lyotard's initial argument is quite deliberately inserted into an already existing North American discourse: as he explained, 'the word *postmodern*...is in current use on the American continent among sociologists and critics' (Lyotard, 1984: xxiii). One of Lyotard's North American sources was Daniel Bell, whose *The Coming of Post-Industrial Society* (Bell, 1973) figures in the text's very first footnote. Curiously, Lyotard makes no reference to Bell's more specific attempts at a cultural sociology of postmodernism *per se*, especially *The Cultural Contradictions of Capitalism* (Bell, 1976), which had been published only three years previously, and the even more recent essay, 'Beyond Modernism, Beyond Self' (Bell, 1977). For Bell, following Lionel Trilling (Trilling, 1967), modernism represented a radically 'adversary culture', opposed not merely to this society but to any and all conceivable societies. As the capitalist economic system had developed, he argued, it had rendered the older Puritan values progressively obsolescent, thereby unleashing an increasingly unrestrained modernism, the simultaneous product of Hobbesian individualism on the one hand, corporate capitalism on the other (Bell, 1976: 80–1, 84). The 'postmodernism' of the 1960s—and this is the term Bell actually uses—finally subverts all restraints: 'It is a programme to erase all boundaries, to obliterate any distinction between the self and the external world, between man and woman, subject and object, mind and body' (Bell, 1977: 243). 'In doctrine and cultural life-style,' he concludes, 'the anti-bourgeois has won...The difficulty in the West...is that bourgeois society—which in its emphasis on individuality and the self gave rise to modernism—is itself culturally exhausted' (ibid.: 250–2).

By and large, Australian cultural criticism has found Lyotard's celebration of the postmodern much more interesting than Bell's indictment. But note their common origins in a specifically North American, rather than European, perception of the postmodern as at once uniquely contemporary and uniquely transgressive. Where Lyotard cries liberty and Bell finds licence, both mean transgression, in the sense of the continuous disturbance and subversion of pre-existing cultural norms. Which lead us to the proposition, firstly, that postmodernism is above all a culture of transgression; and secondly that, whatever the current fashion for French theory, this is a culture which remains particularly visible from a New World, extra-European vantage point. Lyotard's various accounts of the postmodern are stories told by a Frenchman it is true, but they are told in the first place to Canadians nonetheless. They are also, no doubt, in themselves grand narratives of dissolution, which bespeak a political and cultural history at once much richer and much more fraught than any endured to date by the European colonies of settlement in North America or Australasia. For Lyotard, modernity is quite specifically European, its transcendental illusion explicitly that of Hegel and Marx, its terror that of Stalin and Hitler. Doubtless, the settler colonies have had their own philosophers and their own terrors: yet theirs has been a different experience from the European, provincial in origin rather than metropol-itan, often suburban rather than urban, civilising rather than cultured, terrorising rather than terrorised. This too is a postmodern condition, perhaps the paradigmatically postmodern condition which provides both Bell and Lyotard with their original empirical datum, a condition often named as 'postcolonialism' (Ashcroft et al., 1989; During, 1990; Adam and Tiffin, 1991), but better understood, surely, as 'post-imperialism'.

Discounting Lyotard's later conceit that postmodernism is 'modern-ism...in the nascent state' (Lyotard, 1984a: 79), we need to define postmodernism in terms of its own difference from a modernism to which it is, if not chronologically then at least logically, subsequent. High modernism can, in turn, best be characterised substantially in terms of its own antithetical relationship not only to bourgeois realism, the predecessor culture, but also to contemporary 'mass', that is, popular culture. It is only in the late nineteenth century that we can observe the more or less simultaneous emergence both of a new modernist high culture and of a new mass popular culture. The new modernism is characterised above all by its aesthetic self-consciousness, by a formalist experimentalism that recurs in painting and drama, poetry and music, the novel and sculpture; the new mass culture by the rapid development of a whole range of technically novel cultural forms each of which is in principle near universally available. Whenever we date the beginnings of modernism, whether from 1890, as does one standard academic text (Bradbury and McFarlane, 1976), or from December 1910, as rather more interestingly did Virginia Woolf (Woolf, 1966: 321), there can be no doubt that high modernism and mass culture are indeed contemporaneous. However we may characterise the cultural avant-garde, whether as integral to high modernism, as do Bradbury and McFarlane (Bradbury and McFarlane, 1976: 29), or as internally opposed to it, as does Peter Bürger, 1984: 22), there can be no doubt that both stand in essentially adversarial relation not only to bourgeois realism but also to mass culture.

Bürger himself argues that bourgeois art consists in a celebration in form of the liberation of art from religion, from the court, and eventually even from the bourgeoisie (ibid.: 46–9). Modernist art thus emerges as an autonomous social 'institution', the preserve and prerogative of an increasingly autonomous intellectual class, and thereby necessarily counterposed to other non-autonomous arts. In short, both high modernism and the historical avant-garde ascribe some real redemptive function to high art. And as the historical memory of bourgeois realism recedes, it is hostility to contemporary popular culture in particular which develops into perhaps the most characteristic topos of early to mid twentieth-century intellectual life. Which returns us to postmodernism. For, however else we might care to characterise the postmodern, there can be little doubt that postmodernist art typically attempts, or at least results from, the collapse precisely of this antithesis between high and low, elite and popular. It is this boundary, as much as any other, that is transgressed in postmodern culture. Almost all the available theorisations of postmodernism, whether celebratory or condemnatory, whether or not themselves postmodernist, agree on the centrality of this progressive deconstruction and dissolution of what was once, in Bourdieu's phrase, 'distinction' (Bourdieu, 1984). Huyssen goes so far as to locate postmodernism quite specifically 'after the great divide' between modernism and mass culture (Huyssen, 1988). But even for Bell, postmodernism was a kind of 'porno-pop' which 'overflows the vessels of art...tears down the boundaries and insists that *acting out*, rather than making distinctions, is the way to gain knowledge' (Bell, 1976: 51–2). For Lyotard, the postmodern incredulity towards metanarratives applies not only to the metanarratives of science and politics, but also to that of art as enlightenment. For Baudrillard, postmodernity is characterised by 'the disappearance of aesthetics and higher values in kitsch and hyperreality...the disappearance of history and the real in the televisual'

(Baudrillard, 1988: 101). For Bürger, postmodernism is initiated essentially by the failure of the historical avant-garde to subvert from within the cultural institutions of high modernism, a failure which results nonetheless in the final loss of criteria for determining the paradigmatic work of art (Bürger, 1984: 63) and, hence, in a loss of criteria for distinguishing between art and non-art. For Jameson, postmodernism is above all a kind of aesthetic populism, in which pastiche eclipses parody, constituted within a 'field of stylistic and discursive heterogeneity without a norm', a culture 'fascinated by this whole "degraded" landscape of schlock and kitsch, of TV series and Readers' Digest culture, or advertising and motels, of the late show and the grade-B Hollywood film, of so-called paraliterature' (Jameson, 1991: 17, 2). For Lash, postmodernist 'de-differentiation' is present in the transgression 'between literature and theory, between high and popular culture, between what is properly cultural and properly social' (Lash, 1990: 173–4).

Whichever account we adopt, we should note that what is being charted here is primarily an endogenous transformation, internal to elite culture itself, rather to any wider, mass or popular culture. Postmodernism proper is neither a popular culture, not, in any sense that Leavis or even Williams might have understood, a common culture: it is post-modernist, but not necessarily post-popular. What postmodernism provides us with, then, is an index of the range and extent of the Western intelligentsia's own internal crisis, that is, its collective crisis of faith in its own previously proclaimed adversarial and redemptive functions. Let us be clear what is at stake here. Any society will possess some institutional arrangements for the regulation of symbolic artefacts and practices. These institutions have very often been 'cultural', in the properly 'culturalist' sense of a set of specialist, pseudo-consensual institutions for the generation of authoritative, but not in fact politically coercive, judgements of value. Such institutions are typically staffed by what Gramsci termed 'traditional' intellectuals (Gramsci, 1971: 7): obvious instances include the church and the academy. But their pretensions to cultural authority can also be replicated by counter-cultural intelligentsias associated with either the literary and artistic avant-garde or the revolutionary political party. It is the collapse of all such pretensions, whether traditional, avant-garde or vanguardist, which most clearly marks the moment of postmodernism.

Certain aspect of this collective crisis of faith are no doubt very specific: to the European intellectual confronted by America; to the literary intellectual confronted by the mass media; to the male intellectual confronted by the female. But their sum adds up to a Jamesonian cultural dominant, rather than to any particular literary or artistic style. Indeed, much effort to define a distinctively postmodernist style serves only so as to remind us of the latter's deeply derivative relation to high modernism.

It is the general crisis of faith, rather than any particular set of cultural techniques, which is truly defining. Here Zygmunt Bauman's distinction between the role of the intellectual as legislator and that as interpreter, as also his account of the ways in which the latter function progressively displaces the former, becomes instructive (Bauman, 1992: 1–24). As Bauman concludes: 'The postmodernity/modernity opposition focuses on the waning of certainty and transition to a situation characterized by a coexistence or armistice between values...which makes the questions of objective standards impracticable and hence theoretically futile' (ibid.: 24). The central social functions of the post-war, postmodern Western intelligentsia have, then, become primarily interpretive rather than legislative. The novelty of this situation is registered in Foucault's distinction between the 'universal' intellectual, called upon to act as 'the consciousness/conscience of us all', and the 'specific' intellectual, working 'at the precise points where their own conditions of life or work situate them' (Foucault, 1980: 126). It is registered also in the only limited applicability of the Gramscian distinction between 'traditional' and 'organic' intellectuals to the cultural sociology of the post-war West. No doubt, there are still Gramscian traditional intellectuals, representative of a certain 'historical continuity' (Gramsci, 1971: 7), at work within the clergy or the judiciary, perhaps even within academia. No doubt, there are still Gramscian organic intellectuals, integral either to the bourgeois class or to the working class, serving so as give 'their' class a certain 'homogeneity and an awareness of its own function' (ibid.: 5): the bourgeoisie have their economists, engineers and accountants; the proletariat its trade union officials and socialist politicians. Gramsci, however, clearly envisaged both kinds of intellectual as performing an essential legislative or universal function, whereas in fact the dominant role of each has now become primarily interpretive and specific.

Postmodernism, Jameson argues, represents the final and full commodification of art: 'What has happened is that aesthetic production today has become integrated into commodity production generally: the frantic economic urgency of producing fresh waves of ever more novel-seeming goods...at even greater rates of turnover, now assigns an increasingly essential structural function and position to aesthetic innovation and experimentation' (Jameson, 1991: 4–5). Thus understood, postmodernism is a commodity culture in a double sense: both as a set of commodified artefacts actually available for sale in the culture market, and as a set of texts the very textuality of which often affirms their own commodity status. As Jameson insists, 'the various postmodernisms...all at least share a resonant affirmation, when not an outright celebration, of the market as such' (ibid.: 305). Here, it seems to me, Jameson captures much of what it is that is truly distinctive about our contemporary culture.

The more commodified that culture has become, the less plausible the intelligentsia's erstwhile pretensions to legislative cultural authority have appeared, both to themselves and to their prospective audiences. Nineteenth- and early twentieth-century conceptions of culture, whether literary-critical, anthropological or sociological, had almost invariably envisaged culture, not simply as distinct from economy and polity, but also as itself the central source of social cohesion: human society as such appeared inconceivable without culture. But it is so *now*: postmodern capitalism is held together, not by culture, understood as a normative value system, but by the market. As Jameson writes: 'ideologies in the sense of codes and discursive systems are no longer particularly determinant...ideology...has ceased to be functional in perpetuating and reproducing the system' (ibid.: 398).

In short, postmodern intellectual culture is at once both peculiarly normless and peculiarly hedonistic. The hedonism arises very directly from out of the commodity cultures of affluence, as they impinge both on the wider society and on the intelligentsia in particular. The normlessness, however, may well have its origins elsewhere: on the one hand, in the radically internationalising nature of post-war society and culture, which progressively detached erstwhile national intelligentsias from the national cultural 'canons' of which they had hitherto been the custodians; and on the other, in a recurring apocalyptic motif within post-war culture, which must surely bear some more or less direct relation to the threat of nuclear extinction. Let me say a little more about the apocalypse. If postmodernism is indeed the cultural dominant of late capitalism, then late capitalism itself has been not only consumerist, computerised and televisual, but also, as Jameson appears to forget, hyper-militarised. Postmodernism, we must insist, has been underwritten throughout by the arms economy, the visual symbol of which—the mushroom cloud, not the missile—has become so universally culturally available as to have in effect displaced the phallus as the ultimate signifier. As such, it has signified the ultimate hurt, the ultimate refusal of desire. No matter how much it is able to consume, a civilisation permanently confronted by the prospect of its own extinction, such as ours has been, is understandably tempted by the notion that history might come to an end. That global environmental catastrophe comes increasingly to substitute for large-scale nuclear warfare in no way diminishes the power of the trope. The postmodernist effacement of history by 'the random cannibalization of...the past, the...increasing primacy of the "neo"', which Jameson also records (ibid.: 18), thus runs in counterpoint to the powerfully apocalyptic element in the post-war culture of the West.

To summarise: postmodernist intellectual culture is in its form uniquely commodified and in its content characterisable by a quite distinctive 'apocalyptic hedonism'; both form and content announce the end of the cultural authority of both traditional and counter-cultural intelligentsias. At this point, I wish to register the extent to which Australia in particular can come to exemplify the postmodern in general. For, however we may choose to define the latter, it is surely not difficult to recognise in Australian society and culture its peculiarly adequate instance. Indeed, we might well venture the hypothesis that Australian postmodernity has been the specific outcome of a history in which neither cultural nor social modernity were ever anything more than approximately realised. Thus Australia has been catapulted towards post-industrialism at a speed possible only in a society that had never fully industrialised; towards consumerism in a fashion barely imaginable in historically less affluent societies; towards an aesthetic populism unresisted by any indigenous experience of a seriously adversarial high culture; towards an integration into multi-national late capitalism easily facilitated by longstanding, pre-existing patterns of economic dependence; towards a sense of 'being after', and of being post-European, entirely apposite to a colony of European settlement suddenly set adrift, in intellectually and imaginatively uncharted Asian waters, by the precipitous decline of a distant empire; towards a hyper-militarism long anticipated in the legend of ANZAC and in an unrivalled record of enthusiastic participation in brutish, imperial wars. Post-imperialism, we have said, is Australia's own distinctively postmodern condition. What intellectual reflex could be more readily understandable than to announce, as do both postmodernism and poststructuralism, the end of history to a culture which has never known that it had begun?

Let me stress in particular the ways in which the relative absence of an adversarial high culture became peculiarly overdetermining in the specifically Australian case. The post-Second World War expansion of the Australian culture industries (publishing, recording, film and TV, academia, advertising) occurred on the basis of an extraordinarily underdeveloped set of pre-existent cultural foundations: within the pre-war moral and aesthetic economy of Australia, the Greater British Imperial culture remained near-absolutely hegemonic, both normatively and institutionally, at both elite and popular levels, though especially at the former. The tragi-comic failure in the 1940s of Harris and Reed's avant-gardist *Angry Penguins* remains deeply suggestive of the radically circumscribed options actually available to any indigenously Australian high modernism. And McAuley and Stewart's exposure of Ern Malley's 'the Darkening Ecliptic'—in the Sydney *Sun* of all places—can surely be seen as in itself a wonderfully anticipatory 'postmodern' gesture. Deliberately anti-modernist in intent, the Ern Malley hoax proved all too successful. As *The Oxford Companion to Australian Literature* would later conclude: 'More important than the hoax itself was the effect that it had on the development of Australian poetry. The...movement for modernism in Australian writing...received a severe setback' (Wilde *et al.*, 1985: 238). Reversing the presumed causality but endorsing the substantive judgement nonetheless, *The Oxford History of Australian Literature* deduces that in so far as 'the hoax killed genuine experimentalism in Australia...then it is a comment on the thinness of Australian poetic culture, and the lack of nerve in the poets themselves' (Smith, 1981: 371). The cultural resources on hand to fuel the post-war, and especially the post-sixties, expansion were thus comparatively slight, and so much so as to demand a kind of cultural hyper-efficiency that could scarcely afford the necessary waste entailed in any rigorous policing of the elite/popular boundary.

Certain aspects of post-imperial postmodernity are as characteristic of the settler states of North America as they are of Australia: in Canada and even in the United States, intellectual high culture remained seriously dependent on Europe until well into this century; in Canada and in the United States, a relative absence of traditional status hierarchies made for a much more rapid commodification of cultural life than occurred in Europe; in Canada and in the United States, the novelty of postmodernity became peculiarly visible, the attractions of post-structuralism peculiarly telling. But neither in Canada nor in the United States are the deep historical roots of what we have been calling 'apocalyptic hedonism' so firmly entrenched as in Australia. White Australia has had a longstanding and historically by no means unrealistic sense of itself as an unusually affluent and hedonistic society: in 1950 only the United States and Canada enjoyed a higher per capita GNP. But, unlike the North American settler colonies, it has suffered from an almost equally longstanding, and perhaps less realistic, sense of itself as unusually exposed to the threat of invasion and extinction. Such threats were conceived as emanating invariably from the Asiatic north rather from the indigenous peoples of Australia.

As early as 1851, only three years after the first Chinese immigrants had arrived in Moreton Bay (Brisbane), Sydney and Port Phillip (Melbourne), the *Moreton Bay Courier* had declared that: 'There cannot be a shadow of doubt that the worst conjectures on this horrible subject are substantially founded. The blood thrills at the contemplation of this beautiful country being colonized by...beings so grossly debased and wicked' (quoted in Evans, 1988: 178). White blood would continue to thrill at the fear of counter-colonisation for much of the next century. A 1907 tract, *The Peril of Melbourne*, published by the Immigration League of Australia, envisaged White Australia permanently threatened by the teeming millions of Asia (Markus, 1988: 88). In 1909 C.H. Kirmess's bestselling novel, *The Australian Crisis*, depicted the gallant resistance of a fictional Australian 'White Guard' to a successful Japanese invasion of the Northern Territory (Kirmess, 1909). Billy Hughes's 1920 diaries were haunted by 'fitful dreams of Japanese invasion' (Evans, 1988: 172) and in retirement during the 1930s he would warn Australia, in a phrase that inspired much of post-war immigration policy, that the country must 'populate or perish', so as 'to avert national extinction' (Fitzhardinge, 1979: 630). The point to note here is not so much that Australian culture was deeply racist, which was at least as true of the United States, but that this racism evolved within a very particular context—that of a relatively small colony located both at the extremes of distance from the mother country and in relative proximity to comparatively 'advanced' and populous non-European societies—which became peculiarly conductive to the genesis of dystopian collective fantasies of racial extinction. Such fantasies would find a wider audience beyond Australia only after Hiroshima. For in the coincidence of a nuclear arms race and a general economy of affluence, the whole of the West finally had Australianness thrust upon it. And it fell to Nevil Shute, bestselling popular author, British immigrant and avid enthusiast for the Australian dream, to effect the translation from a specifically Australian to a more generally Western eschatology.

References

Adam, I. and Tiffin, H. (eds.) (1991), *Past the Last Post: Theorizing Post-Colonialism and Post-Modernism*, London: Harvester Wheatsheaf

Anderson, P. (1988), 'Modernity and Revolution' in C. Nelson and L. Grossberg (eds.), *Marxism and the Interpretation of Culture*, London: Macmillan

Ashcroft, B. et al. (1989), *The Empire Writes Back: Theory and Practice in Post-Colonial Literatures*, London: Routledge

Baudrillard, J. (1988), *America*, trans. C. Turner, London: Verso

Bauman, Z. (1992), *Intimations of Postmodernity*, London: Routledge

Bell, D. (1973), *The Coming of Post-Industrial Society*, New York: Basic Books

Bell, D. (1976), *The Cultural Contradictions of Capitalism*, London: Heinemann

Bell, D. (1977), 'Beyond Modernism, Beyond Self' in Q. Anderson, S. Donadio and S. Marcus (ed.), *Art, Politics and Will: Essays in Honor of Lionel Trilling*, New York: Basic Books

Bourdieu, P. (1984), *Distinction: A Social Critique of the Judgement of Taste*, trans. R. Nice, London: Routledge and Kegan Paul

Bradbury, M. (1976), 'The Cities of Modernism' in M. Bradbury and J. McFarlane (eds), *Modernism 1890–1930*, Harmondsworth: Penguin

Bradbury, M. and McFarlane, J. (eds.) (1976), *Modernism 1890–1930*, Harmondsworth: Penguin

Bürger, P. (1984), *Theory of the Avant-Garde*, trans. M. Shaw, Minneapolis: University of Minnesota Press

Callinicos, A. (1989), *Against Postmodernism: A Marxist Critique*, Oxford: Polity Press

During, S. (1990), 'Postmodernism or Post-Colonialism Today?' in A. Milner et al. (eds.), *Postmodern Conditions*, Oxford: Berg

Evans, R. (1988), 'Keeping Australia Clean White' in V. Burgmann and J. Lee (eds.), *A Most Valuable Acquisition*, Melbourne: Penguin

Fehér, F. (1990), 'The Pyrrhic Victory of Art in its War of Liberation: Remarks on the Postmodernist Intermezzo' in A. Milner et al. (eds.), *Postmodern Conditions*, Oxford: Berg

Fitzhardinge, L.F. (1979), *The Little Digger 1914–1952*, Sydney: Angus and Robertson

Foucault, M. (1980), *Power/Knowledge: Selected Interviews and Other Writings, 1972–1977*, ed. C. Gordon, Brighton: Harvester

Gramsci, A. (1971), *Selections from Prison Notebooks*, trans. Q. Hoare and G. Nowell Smith, London: Lawrence and Wishart

Habermas, J. (1985), 'Modernity—An Incomplete Project' in H. Foster (ed.), *Postmodern Culture*, London: Pluto Press

Habermas, J. (1987), *The Philosophical Discourse of Modernity*, trans. F. Lawrence, Cambridge: Polity Press

Huyssen, A. (1988), *After the Great Divide: Modernism, Mass Culture and Postmodernism*, London: Macmillan

Jameson, F. (1988), 'Discussion' in C. Nelson and L. Grossberg (eds.), *Marxism and the Interpretation of Culture*, London: Macmillan

Jameson, F. (1991), *Postmodernism, or, the Cultural Logic of Late Capitalism*, London: Verso

Kirmess, C.H. (1909), *The Australian Crisis*, London: Walter Scott Publishing Co.

Lash, S. (1990), *Sociology of Postmodernism*, London: Routledge

Lyotard, J.-F. (1979), *La Condition postmoderne: rapport sur le savoir*, Paris: Minuit

Lyotard, J.-F. (1984), *The Postmodern Condition: A Report on Knowledge*, trans. G. Bennington and B. Massumi, Minneapolis: University of Minnesota Press

Lyotard, J.-F. (1984a), 'Answering the Question: What is Postmodernism?' trans. R. Durand, Appendix to *The Postmodern Condition* (1984)

Markus, A. (1988), 'Everybody Become a Job: Twentieth Century Immigrants' in V. Burgmann and J. Lee (eds.), *A Most Valuable Acquisition*, Melbourne: Penguin

Marxism Today, (1988), Special Issue on 'New Times', October

Morris, M. (1988), *The Pirate's Fiancée: Feminism, Reading, Postmodernism*, London: Verso

Shute, N. (1950), *A Town Like Alice*, London: Heinemann

Shute, N. (1957), *On the Beach*, Melbourne: Heinemann

Shute, N. (1984), *On the Beach*, Guilford: Ulverscroft

Shute, N. (1990), *On the Beach*, London: Mandarin

Smith, J. (1976), *Nevil Shute*, Boston: Twayne Publishers

Smith, V. (1981), 'Poetry' in L. Kramer (ed.), *The Oxford History of Australian Literature*, Melbourne: Oxford University Press

Trilling, L. (1967), *Beyond Culture*, Harmondsworth: Penguin

UNESCO (1978), *Statistical Yearbook 1977*, Paris

Walker, J. (ed.) (1991), *Halliwell's Film Guide*, 8th ed., London: Harper Collins

Wilde, W.H. et al. (eds.) (1985), *The Oxford Companion to Australian Literature*, Melbourne: Oxford University Press

Williams, R. (1965), *The Long Revolution*, Harmondsworth: Penguin

Woolf, V. (1966), 'Mr Bennett and Mrs Brown' *Collected Essays*, I, London: Hogarth Press

AUSTRALIAN POPULAR CULTURE: A Bibliography

Cultural Studies: Australia

Alomes, S., 'Australian Popular Culture Revisited', *Overland*, No. 85.

Alomes, S., and den Hartog, D., *Post Pop: Popular Culture, Nationalism and Postmodernism*, Footprint (Footscray, Victoria, 1991).

Ashbolt, A., 'Against Left Optimism—A Reply to John Docker', *Arena*, 1982, Vol. 61.

Bennett, T., 'Marxist Cultural Politics: in Search of the Popular', *Australian Journal of Cultural Studies*, 1983, Vol. 1, No. 2.

Bostman, P., and Burns, C., et al (eds.), *The Foreign Bodies Papers*, Local consumption publications (Sydney, 1981).

Brett, J., 'The Chook and the Australian Unconscious', *Meanjin*, Vol. 45, No. 1.

Burgmann, J., and Lee, J. (eds.), *Constructing a Culture: A People's History of Australia since 1788*, Penguin (Ringwood, Victoria, 1988).

Craik, J., 'The Expo Experience: The Politics of Expositions', *Australian–Canadian Studies*, Vol. 7, No. 1–2.

Dermody, S., and Docker, J., et al, *Nellie Melba, Ginger Meggs and Friends*, Kibble Books (Malmsbury, Victoria, 1982).

Docker, J., *Australian Cultural Elites: Intellectual Traditions in Sydney and Melbourne*, Angus & Robertson (Sydney, 1974).

Docker, J., 'Popular Culture and its Marxist Critics', *Arena*, 1983 No. 65.

Docker J., 'Popular Culture and Bourgeois Values', in V. Burgmann and J. Lee (eds.), *Constructing a Culture: A People's History of Australia since 1788*, Penguin (Ringwood, Victoria, 1988).

Fiske, J., and Hodge, R., et al, *Myths of Oz: Readings in Australian Popular Culture*, Allen & Unwin (Sydney, 1987).

Frow, J., 'Accounting for Tastes: Some Problems in Bourdieu's Sociology of Culture', *Cultural Studies*, 1987, Vol. 1, No. 1.

Gill, G., 'Post-structuralism as Ideology', *Arena*, 1984, No. 69.

Giroux, H., and Simon, R., 'Critical Pedagogy and the Politics of Popular Culture', *Cultural Studies*, 1988, Vol. 2, No. 3.

Goldberg, S.L., and Smith, F.B., *Australian Cultural History*, Cambridge University Press (Melbourne, 1988).

Hancock, K., *Australian Society*, Cambridge University Press (Cambridge, 1990).

Johnson, L., 'The Study of Popular Cultural: The Need for a Clear Agenda', *Australian Journal of Cultural Studies*, Vol. 4, No. 1.

Kahn, J.S., 'The Culture in Multiculturalism', *Meanjin*, 1991, Vol. 50, No. 1.

Kress, G., *Communication and Culture: An Introduction*, NSW University Press (Kensington, NSW, 1988).

Milner, A., *Contemporary Cultural Theory: An Introduction*, Allen & Unwin (Sydney, 1991).

Morris, M., *The Pirate's Fiancée: Feminism, Reading, Postmodernism*, Verso (London and New York, 1988).

Morris, M., 'Cultural Studies', in P. Mellencamp (ed.), *Logics of Television*, BFI (London, 1990).

Rickard, J., 'Cultural History: The "High" and the "Popular"', in S.L. Goldberg and F.B. Smith (eds.), *Australian Cultural History*, Cambridge University Press (Melbourne, 1988).

Rowse, T., *Australian Liberalism and National Character*, Kibble Books (Malmsbury, Victoria, 1978).

Sinclair, J., Davidson, J., 'Australian Cultural Studies = Birmingham + Meanjin, OK?', Occasional paper 1, Department of Humanities, Footscray Institute of Technology, Victoria, Australia.

Spearritt, P., and Walker, D., *Australian Popular Culture*, Allen & Unwin (Sydney, 1979)

Turner, G., *National Fictions: Literature, Film and the Construction of Australian Narrative*, Allen & Unwin (Sydney, 1986).

White, R., *Inventing Australia*, Allen & Unwin (Sydney, 1981).

Whitlock, G., and Carter, D., *Images of Australia: An Introductory Reader in Australian Studies*, University of Queensland Press (St Lucia, 1992).

Australian Religion

Dicker, G.S., 'Kerygma and Australian Culture: The Case of the Aussie Battler', in V.C.

Hayes (ed.), *Towards Theology in an Australian context*, (Bedford Park, SA, 1979).

Mol, H., *Religion in Australia*, Verry (Meibourne, 1971).

Mol, H., *The Faith of Australians*, Allen & Unwin (Sydney, 1985).

Cultural Studies: Europe

Abbs, P. (ed.), *The Black Rainbow: Essays on the Present Breakdown of Culture*, Heinemann Educational (London, 1975).

Barthes, R., *Mythologies*, Paladin (London, 1973).

Benjamin, W., 'The Works of Art in an Age of Mechanical Reproduction', in his *Illuminations*, Jonathan Cape (London, 1970).

Bourdieu, P., *Distinctions: A Social Critique of the Judgement of Taste*, Routledge & Kegan Paul (London, 1984).

Chambers, I., *Popular Culture: The Metropolitan Experience*, Methuen (London, 1986).

Dunn, T., 'The Evolution of Cultural Studies', in D. Punter (ed.), *Introduction to Contemporary Cultural Studies*, Longman (London, 1986).

Fiske, J., 'British Cultural Studies', in R. Allen (ed.), *Channels of Discourse: Television and Contemporary Criticism*, University of North Carolina Press (Chapel Hill, 1987).

Hall, S., and Jefferson, T. (eds.), *Resistance Through Rituals*, Hutchinson (London, 1978)

Hall, S., and Hobson, D., et at (eds.), *Culture, Media, Language*, Hutchinson (London, 1980).

Hall, S., 'Cultural Studies and the Centre: Some Problematics and Problems', in S. Hall et al (eds.), *Culture, Media, Language*, Hutchinson (London, 1980).

Hall, S., 'Notes on Deconstructing the Popular', in R. Samuel (ed.), *People's History and Socialist Theory*, Routledge & Kegan Paul (London, 1981).

Hoggart, R., *The Uses of Literacy*, Penguin (Harmondsworth, 1958).

Johnson, R., 'The Story So Far: And Further Transformations', in D. Punter (ed.), *Introduction to Contemporary Cultural Studies*, Longman (London, 1986).

Lasch, C., *The Culture of Narcissism*, Sphere (London, 1982).

Leavis, F.R., 'Mass Civilisation and Minority Culture', in his *Education and the University*, Chatto & Windus (London, 1948).

Leavis, F.R., and Thompson, D., *Culture and Environment: The Training of Critical Awareness*, Chatto & Windus (London, 1964).

Lewis, G.H. (ed.), *The Sociology of Popular Culture*, Sage (London, 1978: Current Sociology, Vol. 26, No. 3).

McGregor, C., *Pop Goes the Culture*, Pluto Press (London, 1984).

Punter, D., *Introduction to Contemporary Cultural Studies*, Longman (London, 1986).

Swingewood, A., *The Myth of Mass Culture*, Macmillan (London, 1977).

Thompson, D. (ed.), *Discrimination and Popular Culture*, Penguin (Harmondsworth, 1964).

Williams, R., *The Long Revolution*, Chatto & Windus (London, 1961).

Williams, R., *Culture and Society 1780–1950*, Penguin (Harmondsworth, 1963).

Williams, R., *Keywords: A Vocabulary of Culture and Society*, Collins (Glasgow, 1976).

Williams, R., *Towards 2000*, Penguin (Harmondsworth, 1985).

Williamson, J., *Consuming Passions: The Dynamics of Popular Culture*, Marion Boyars (London, 1986).

Cultural Studies: America

Adorno, T., and Horkheimer, M., 'The Culture Industry as Mass Deception', in their *Dialectic of Enlightenment*, Herder & Herder (New York, 1972).

Angus, I.H., and Jhally, S. (eds.), *Cultural Politics in Contemporary America*, Routledge & Kegan Paul (New York, 1989).

Bennett, T., and Mercer, C., et al, *Popular Culture and Social Relations*, Open University Press (Philadelphia, 1986).

Fiske, J., *Understanding Popular Culture*, Unwin Hyman (Boston, 1989).

Fiske, J., *Reading the Popular*, Unwin Hyman (Boston, 1989)

Gans, H.J., *Popular Culture and High Culture*, Basic Books (New York, 1974).

Gruneau, R., (ed.), *Popular Cultures and Political Practices*, Garamond Press (Toronto, 1988)

Horkheimer, M., 'Art and Mass Culture', in M. O'Connell (trans.), *Critical Theory*, Continuum (New York, 1982).

Inge, M.T. (ed.), *Handbook of American Popular Culture*, Greenwood Press (Westport, Connecticut, 1978).

Lazere, D. (ed.), *American Media and Mass Culture: Left Perspectives*, University of California Press (Berkeley and Los Angeles, 1987).

Lowenthal, L., *Literature, Popular Culture and Society*, Pacific Books (Palo Alta, California, 1961).

Modleski, T. (ed.), *Studies in Entertainment: Critical Approaches to the Mass Media*, Indiana University Press (Bloomington, 1986).

Rosenberg, B., and White, D.M. (eds.), *Mass Culture: The Popular Arts in America*, Free press (New York, 1957).

Schudson, M., 'The New Validation in Popular Culture: Sense and Sentimentality in Academia', *Critical Studies in Mass Communication*, 1987, No. 4.

Weintraub, K., *Visions of Culture*, University of Chicago Press (Chicago, 1969).

The Everyday

Altman, D., *Paper Ambassadors—The Politics of Stamps*, Angus & Robertson (Sydney, 1991).

Carrington, K., 'Girls and Graffiti', *Cultural Studies*, 1989, Vol. 3, No. 1.

Cultural Studies, 1990, Vol. 4, No. 2, Special Issue on Ethnography and Everyday Life.

de Certeau, M., *The Practice of Everyday Life*, University of California Press (Berkeley, 1986).

Dunstan, K., *Wowsers*, Angus & Robertson (Sydney, 1974).

Factor, J., 'Drop Dead, Pizza Head: Racism in Children's Culture', Meanjin, 1984, Vol. 43, No. 3.

Halligan, M., 'From Castor to Olive in One Generation', *Meanjin*, 1990, Vol. 49, No. 2.

Hibbins, G., Fahey, J. et al, *Local History: A Handbook for Enthusiasts*, Allen & Unwin (Sydney, 1985).

Krupinski, J., and Stoller, A., *The Family in Australia*, Pergamon (Rushcutters Bay, 1974).

Reiger, K., *The Disenchantment of the Home: Modernizing the Australian Family 1880–1940*, Oxford University Press (Melbourne, 1985).

Rowe, D., and Lawrence, G. (eds.), *Sport and Leisure: Trends in Australian Popular Culture*, Harcourt Brace Jovanovich (Sydney and London, 1990).

Seal, G., *The Hidden Culture: Folklore in Australian Society*, Oxford University Press (Melbourne, 1989).

Symons, M., *One Continuous Picnic*, Penguin (Ringwood, Victoria, 1985).

Baker, S.J., *A Popular Dictionary of Australian Slang*, Robertson & Millers (Melbourne, 1941/43).

Australian Language

Baker, S.J., *The Australian Language*, Angus & Robertson (Sydney, 1945/66).

Dixon, R.M.W., *The Languages Australia*, Cambridge University Press (Sydney, 1980).

Fiske, J., 'The Australian Accent', in J. Fiske et al (eds.), *Myths of Oz*, Allen & Unwin (Sydney, 1987).

Hesling, B., *The Dinkumization and Depommification of an Artful English Immigrant*, Ure Smith (Sydney, 1963).

Morris, E.E., *Austral English: A Dictionary of Australian Words, Phrases and Usages*, Sydney University Press (Sydney, 1898/1972).

Simes, G., 'The Language of Homosexuality in Australia', in R. Aldrich and G. Wotherspoon (eds.), *Gay Perspectives: Essays on Australian Gay Culture*, Department of Economic History, University of Sydney (Sydney, 1992)

Wilkes, G.A., *A Dictionary of Australian Colloquialisms*, Sydney University Press (Sydney, 1978/1985).

Wilkes, G.A., 'Australian Colloquialisms and Colloquial Australianisms', *Southerly*, 1982, Vol. 42, No. 4.

Australian Consumerism

Cozzolino, M., *Symbols of Australia*, Penguin (Ringwood, Victoria, 1980).

Gill, G., 'The Signs of Consumerism', *Arena*, 1979, No. 53.

Joel, A., *Best Dressed: 200 years of Fashion in Australia*, Collins (Sydney, 1984).

Nava, M., 'Consumerism and its Contradictions', *Cultural Studies*, 1987, Vol. 1., No. 2.

O'Brien, J., 'The Australian Constitution and Marketing: The James Case', *Australian Studies*, 1990, No. 6.

Australian Leisure

Caldwell, G. (ed.), *Entertainment and Society*, (Report of 1976 UNESCO seminar), Australian Government publishing service (Canberra, 1977).

Caldwell, G., and Haig, B. et al (eds.), *Gambling in Australia*, Croom Helm (Sydney, 1985).

Mercer, D. (ed.), *Leisure and Recreation in Australia*, Sorrett Books (Melbourne, 1977).

O'Hara, J., *A Mug's Game: A History of Gaming and Betting in Australia*, University of NSW Press (Sydney, 1988).

van Moorst, H., 'The Policing of Leisure: Amusement Parlours as Scapegoats', Occasional paper 2, Department of Humanities, Footscray Institute of Technology (Victoria, 1982).

van Moorst, H, 'The Political Economy of Leisure', Occasional paper 5, Department of Humanities, Footscray Institute of Technology (Victoria, 1982).

van Moorst, H., *Unemployment and Leisure*, Urban and Social Research Centre, Footscray Institute of Technology (Victoria, 1982).

Wells, L., *Sunny Memories: Australians by the Seaside*, Greenhouse (Melbourne, 1982).

Australian Sport

Alomes, S., 'Politics as Sport: Reality and Metaphor in Australian Politics and Political Coverage', in S. Alomes and D. den Horteg (eds.), *Post-pop: Popular Culture, Nationalism and Postmodernism*, Footprint (Footscray, Victoria, 1991).

Andrews, B., 'The Willow Tree and the Laurel: Australian Sport and Australian Literature', in R. Cashman and M. McKernan (eds.), *Sport in History*, University of Queensland Press (St Lucia, Queensland, 1979).

Blainey, G., *A Game of our Own: The Origins of Australian Football*, Information Australia (Melbourne, 1990).

Bryson, L., 'Sport and the Oppression of Women', *Australian and New Zealand Journal of Sociology*, 1983, Vol. 19, No. 3.

Cashman, R., and McKernan, M. (eds.), *Sport in History*, University of Queensland Press (St Lucia, Queensland, 1979).

Cashman, R., and McKernan, M. (eds.), *Sport, Money, Morality and the Media*, University of New South Wales Press (Kensington, New South Wales, 1980).

Cashman, R., *'Ave a go yer Mug!': Australian Cricket Crowds from Larrikin to Ocker*, Collins (Sydney, 1984).

Corris, P., *Lords of the Ring: A History of Prize Fighting in Australia*, Cassell (Sydney, 1980).

Dunstan, K., *Sports*, Angus & Robertson (Sydney, 1974).

Fitzgerald, R., and Spillman, K. (eds.), *The Greatest Game*, William Heinemann (Melbourne, 1988).

Forsyth, C., *The Great Cricket Hijack*, Widescope (Melbourne, 1978).

Gordon, K., and Dalton, A., *Too Tough to Die: Footscray's Fightback*, Footscray Football Club (Melbourne, 1990).

Gray, O., 'Loss of a Homespun Legend', in R. Fitzgerald and K. Spillman (eds.), *The Greatest Game*, William Heinemann (Melbourne, 1988).

Hutchinson, G., *From the Outer: Watching Football in the 80s*, Penguin (Ringwood, Victoria, 1984).

Kent, H., and Merritt, J., 'The Cold War and the Melbourne Olympics', in A. Curthoys and J. Merritt (eds.), *Better Dead than Red*, Allen & Unwin (Sydney, 1986).

Lawrence, G., and Rowe, D. (eds.), *Power Play: The Commercialisation of Australian Sport*, Hale & Iremonger (Sydney, 1986).

Matthews, B., Oval Dreams: *Larrikin Essays on Australian Sport and Low Culture*, McPhee Gribble (Melbourne, 1991).

Matthews, B., 'Flying to the Footy', in his *Oval Dreams: Larrikin Essays on Australian Sport and Low Culture*, McPhee Gribble (Melbourne, 1991).

McKay, J., *No Pain, No Gain*, Prentice Hall (Sydney, 1990).

Rowe, D., and Lawrence, G. (eds.), *Sport and Leisure: Trends in Australian Popular Culture*, Harcourt Brace Jovanovich (Sydney, 1990).

Sandercock, L., and Turner, I., *Up Where Cazaly? The Great Australian Game*, Granada (Sydney, 1981).

Soldatow, S., *Politics of the Olympics*, Cassell (Sydney, 1980).

Stewart, B., *The Australian Football Business*, Kangaroo Press (Sydney, 1983).

Stoddart, B., *Saturday Afternoon Fever: Sport in the Australian Culture*, Angus & Robertson (Sydney, 1986).

Stremski, R., *Kill for Collingwood!*, Allen & Unwin (Sydney, 1986).

Carnival in Australia

Alomes, S., 'Parades of Meaning: The Moomba Festival and Contemporary Culture', *Journal of Australian Studies*, 1985, No. 17.

Ashton, P., *Waving the Waratah: Bicentenary New South Wales*, New South Wales Bicentenary Council (Sydney, 1989).

Bennett, T., 'Political and Theoretical Digressions', *Media Information Australia*, February 1991, No. 59.

Davey, M., 'Mardi Gras—Festival, Parades and Party', *Outrage*, 1992, No. 107.

Inglis, K.S., *The Australian Colonists*, Melbourne Univerity Press (Melbourne, 1974).

Roper, M., 'Inventing Traditions in Colonial Society: Bendigo's Easter Fair, 1871–85', *Journal of Australian Studies*, 1985, No. 17.

Tourism and Landscape in Australia

Australian Cultural History, special issue, Travellers, Journeys, Tourists, No. 10.

Barrett, B., *The Inner Suburbs: The Evolution of an Industrial Area*, Melbourne University Press (Melbourne, 1971).

Bennett, T., *Out of Which Past? Critical Reflection on Australian Museum and Heritage Policy*, Institute for Cultural Policy Studies, Griffith University (Griffith, Queensland, 1988).

Bonnin, M., *A Study of Australian Descriptive and Travel Writing, 1929–45*, Unpublished PhD thesis, University of Queensland (Queensland, 1980).

Davidson, J., 'Tasmanian Gothic', *Meanjin*, 1989, Vol. 48, No. 2.

Foster, J., 'Brunnings' Australian Gardener', *Meanjin*, Vol. 47, No. 3.

Fox, P., 'Memory, the Museum and the Postcolonial World', *Meanjin*, 1992. Vol. 51, No. 2.

Gale, F., and Jacobs, J., *Tourists and the National Estate*, Australian Government publishing service (Canberra, 1987).

Gilbert, A., 'The Roots of Australian Anti-Suburbanism', in S.L. Goldberg and F.B. Smith (eds.), *Australian Cultural History*, Cambridge University Press (Melbourne, 1988).

Hawkins, G., 'Too Much Fun: Producing and Consuming Pleasure at Australia's Wonderland', in D. Rowe and G. Lawrence (eds.), *Sport and Leisure: Trends in Australian Popular Culture*, Harcourt Brace Jovanovich (Sydney and London, 1990).

Hosking, S., 'I 'ad to 'av me Garden: A Perspective on Australian Women Gardeners', *Meanjin*, Vol. 47, No. 3.

Jeans, D., and Spearritt, P., *The Open-air Museum: The Cultural Landscape of NSW*, Allen & Unwin (Sydney, 1980).

Kelly, M., *Nineteenth-Century Sydney: Essays in Urban History*, Sydney University Press (Sydney, 1978).

Marcus, J., 'The Journey to the Centre: The Cultural Apropriation of Ayres Rock, in A. Rutherford (ed.), *Aboriginal Culture Today*, Dangaroo Press (Sydney, 1988).

Prato, P., and Trivero, G., 'The Spectacle of Travel', *Australian Journal of Cultural Studies*, 1985, No. 3.

Rowse, T., 'Heaven and a Hills Hoist: Critics on Suburbia', in G. Whitlock and D. Carter (eds.), *Images of Australia: An Introductory Reader in Australian Studies*, University of Queensland Press (St Lucia, 1992).

Rowse, T., 'Hosts and Guests at Uluru', *Meanjin*, 1992, Vol. 51, No. 2.

Seddon, G., and Davis, M., *Man and Landscape in Australia*, AGPS (Canberra, 1976).

Shaffer, K., 'Landscape, Representation and Australian National Identity', *Australian Journal of Cultural Studies*, 1986, Vol. 4, No. 2.

Smith, B., 'On Perceiving the Australian Suburb', in his *The Antipodean Manifesto*, Oxford University Press (Melbourne, 1976).

Stratton, J., 'Crossing the Border: Tourism as Leisure', in D. Rowe and G. Lawrence (eds.), *Sport and Leisure: Trends in Australian Popular Culture*, Harcourt Brace Jovavovich (Sydney and London, 1990).

Australian Nationalism

Alomes, S., 'The Patriot Game', *Overland*, 1982, No. 90.

Alomes, S., *A Nation at Last? The Changing Character of Australian Nationalism*, Angus & Robertson (Sydney, 1988).

Alomes, S., and Jones, C., *Australian Nationalism: A Documentary History*, Angus & Robertson (Sydney, 1991).

Carey, A., 'Social Science, Propaganda and Democracy', in P. Boreham and G. Dow (eds.), *Work and Inequality*, Vol. 2, Macmillan (Melbourne, 1980).

Castles, S. et al. *Mistaken Identity: Multiculturalism and the Demise of Nationalism in Australia*, Pluto Press (Sydney, 1990).

Cochrane, P., and Goodman, D., 'The Great Australian Journey: Cultural Logic and Nationalism in the Postmodern World', *Australian Historical Studies*, 1988, Vol. 23, No. 9.

Hutton, A., 'Nationalism in the Australian Cinema', *Cinema Papers*, 1980, No. 26.

James, P., 'The Politics of Winged Keel', *Arena*, 1983, No. 65.

James, P., 'Australia in the Corporate Image: A New Nationalism', *Arena*, 1983, No. 63.

Marcus, J. (ed.), 'Writing Australian Culture: Text, Society and National Identity', *Social Analysis*, 1990, No. 27.

Murphy, D.J., 'Queensland's Image and Australian Nationalism', *Australian Quarterly*, 1978, No. 50.

Rowe, D., Lawrence, G., 'Saluting the State: Nationalism and the Olympics', *Australian Left Review*, 1984–85, No. 90.

Internationalism

Serle, G., 'The Digger Tradition and Australian Nationalism', *Meanjin*, 1965, Vol. 24, No. 2.

Alomes, S., 'The Satellite Society', *Journal of Australian Studies*, 1981, No. 9.

Australian Broadcasting Tribunal, *The Price of being Australian*, Australian Broadcasting Tribunal (Sydney, 1988).

Bonney, B., and Wilson, H., *Australia's Commercial Media*, Macmillan (Melbourne, 1983).

Mackay, H.C., 'The Illusion of the Global Village', *the Transactions of the Menzies Foundation*, 1985, No. 9.

MacKenzie, J., *Imperialism and Popular Culture*, Manchester University Press (Manchester, 1984).

Sinclair, J., *Images Incorporated: Advertising as Industry and Ideology*, Methuen (Sydney, 1987).

Sinclair, J., 'Neither West nor Third World', *Media, Culture and Society*, 1990, No. 12.

van Moorst, H., 'Mickey Mouse Culture: Disney's Imperialist World', *The Independent Australian*, 1977, Vol. 2, No. 2.

Gendered Culture

Craik, J., 'I Must Put my Face on: Making up the Body and Marketing out the Feminine', *Cultural Studies*, 1989, Vol. 3, No. 1.

Creed, B., 'Medusa in the Land of Oz: The Female Spectator in Australia', *Camera Obscura*, 1989, No. 20–1.

Dixson, M., *The Real Matilda: Women and Identity in Australia 1788–1975*, Penguin (Ringwood, Victoria, 1976).

Edgar, P., and McPhee, H., *Media She*, Heinemann (Melbourne, 1974).

Evans, R., and Saunders, 'K., 'No Place Like Home: The Evolution of the Australian Housewife', in their *Gender Relations in Australia: Domination and Negotiation*, Harcourt Brace Jovanovich (Sydney, 1992).

Evans, R., and Saunders, K., *Gender Relations in Australia: Domination and Negotiation*, Harcourt, Brace Jovanovich (Sydney, 1992).

Gilbert, P., and Taylor, S., *Fashioning the Feminine: Girls, Popular Culture and Schooling*, Allen & Unwin (Sydney, 1991).

Lewis, G., *Real Men like Violence: Australian Men, Media and Violence*, Kangaroo Press (Sydney, 1983).

Matthews, J.J., *Good and Mad Women: The Historical Construction of Femininity in Twentieth Century Australia*, Allen & Unwin (Sydney, 1984).

Megaw, R., 'Happy Ever After: The Image of Women in Four Australian Feature Films of the 1920s', *Journal of Australian Studies*, 1980, No. 7.

Mewett, P., 'Darwin's Beercan Regatta: Masculinity, Frontier and Festival in North Australia', *Social Analysis*, 1988, No. 23.

Mitchell, S., *Tall Poppies*, Penguin (Ringwood, Victoria, 1984).

Mitchell, S., and Dyer, K., *Winning Women*, Penguin (Ringwood, Victoria, 1985).

Modjeska, D. (ed.), *Inner Cities: Australian Women's Memory of Place*, Penguin (Ringwood, Victoria, 1989).

Radner, H., This Time's for Me: Making up and Feminine Practice', *Cultural Studies*, 1989, Vol. 3, No. 3.

Shaffer, K,. *Women and the Bush: Forces of Desire in the Australian Cultural Tradition*, Cambridge University Press (Sydney, 1988).

Shute, C., 'Heriones and Heroes: Sexual Mythology in Australia, 1914–1918', *Hecate*, 1975, Vol. 1, No. 1.

Smith, J., 'Urban Aboriginal Women's Culture: A Personal Perspective', *Australian Studies*, 1989, No. 2.

Stern, L., 'Independent Feminist Filmmaking in Australia', *Australian Journal of Screen Theory*, 1978, No. 5/6.

Summers, A., *Damned Whores and God's Police*, Penguin (Ringwood, Victoria, 1975).

Australian Gay Culture

Aldrich, R., 'Australia', in W. Dynes (ed.), *The Encyclopedia of Homosexuality*, Garland Publishers (New York, 1990).

Aldrich, R., and Wotherspoon, G. (eds.), *Gay Perspectives: Essays in Australian Gay Culture*, Department of Economic History, University of Sydney (Sydney, 1992).

Burns, D., 'Cops in Toilets—Why are They There?', *Outrage*, 1992, No. 105.

Carbery, G., 'Some Melbourne Beats: A "Map" of a Subculture from the 1930s to the 1950s', in R. Aldrich and G. Wotherspoon (eds.), *Gay Perspectives: Essays on Australian Gay Culture*, Department of Economic History, University of Sydney (Sydney, 1992).

French, R., and Davis, K., *Into the Streets*, Sydney, (forthcoming).

Johnston, C., and Johnston, R., 'The Making of Homosexual Men', in V. Burgmann and J. Lee (eds.), *Staining the Wattle: A People's History of Australia since 1788*, McPhee Gribble/Penguin (Sydney, 1988).

Lee, J., 'Male Homosexual Identity and Subculture in Adelaide Before World War II', in R. Aldrich and G. Wotherspoon (eds.), *Gay Perspectives: Essays on Australian Gay Culture*, Department of Economic History, University of Sydney (Sydney, 1992).

Mitchell, P., 'Another Generation: Safe Sex and the New Breed', *Campaign*, 1991, No. 185.

Simes, G., 'Camping it up', *Sydney Star Observer*, 18 September 1987.

Simes, G., 'Beats and Bogs', *Sydney Star Observer*, 21 August 1987.

Thompson, D., *Flaws in the Social Fabric: Homosexuals and Society in Sydney*, (Sydney, 1985).

Watney, S., 'Homosexual, Gay or Queer', *Outrage*, 1992, No. 107.

Wotherspoon, G. (ed.), *Being Different*, Hale & Ironmonger (Sydney, 1986).

Wotherspoon, G., 'A Sodom in the South Pacific: Male Homosexuality in Sydney, 1788–1809', in G. Aplin (ed.), *A Different Infant: Sydney Before Macquarie*, New South Wales University Press (Sydney, 1988).

Media Politics in Australia

Barr, T., *The Electronic Estate*, Penguin (Ringwood, Victoria, 1985).

Bonney, B., and Wilson, H., *Australia's Commercial Media*, Macmillan (Melbourne, 1983).

Chadwick, P., *Media Mates: Carving up Australia's Media*, Macmillan (Melbourne, 1989).

Curthoys, A., 'The Getting of Television: Dilemmas in Ownership, Control and Culture', in A. Curthoys and J. Merritt (eds.), *Better Dead than Red: Australia's First Cold War, 1945–59*, Vol. 2, Allen & Unwin (Sydney, 1986).

Edgar, P., 'Radio and Television', in A. Patience and B. Head (eds.), *From Whitlam to Fraser*, Oxford University Press (Melbourne, 1979).

Howkins, J., 'A Shift in Perception: The Evolution of Satellites in Europe', *Media Information Australia*, 1985, No. 38.

McQueen, H., *Australia's Media Monopolies*, Widescopes (Melbourne, 1977).

Schou, K., *Structure and Operation of the Television Industry in Australia*, Australian Film, Television and Radio School (North Ryde, 1982).

Stephen, A., 'The Organisation of the Australian Advertising Industry, 1918–38', *Media Interventions* (Sydney, 1981, Interventions No. 15).

Wheelwright, E.L., and Buckley, K. (eds.), *Communications and the Media in Australia*, Allen & Unwin (Sydney, 1987).

White, P.B. (ed.), 'AUSSAT and After', Special Issue of *Media Information Australia*, 1985, No. 38.

Wilson, H., *Australian Communication and the Public Sphere*, Macmillan (Melbourne, 1989).

Windschuttle, K., The Media, Penguin (Ringwood, Victoria, 1984).

Australian Film

Abbey, R., and Crawford, J., 'Crocodile Dundee or Davy Crockett: what Crocodile Dundee Doesn't Say about Australia', *Meanjin*, 1987, Vol. 46, No. 2.

Baxter J., *Filmstruck: The Australians at the Movies, 1896 to the Present*, AFC (Sydney, 1986).

Bertrand, I., *Film Censorship in Australia*, University of Queensland Press (St Lucia, 1978).

Bertrand, I., and Collins, D., *Government and Film in Australia*, Currency Press and the Australian Film Institute (Sydney, 1981).

Bertrand, I., *Cinema in Australia: A Documentary History*, University of New South Wales Press (Kensington, 1989).

Buscombe, E., 'Film History and the Idea of a National Cinema', *Australian Journal of Screen Theory*, 1981, No. 9/10.

Collins, D., *Hollywood Down Under: Australians at the Movies*, Angus & Robertson (Sydney, 1987).

Cunningham, S., 'The Decades of Survival: Australian Film 1930–70', in A. Moran and T. O'Regan (eds.), *The Australian Screen*, Penguin (Ringwood, Victoria, 1989).

Cunningham, S., *Featuring Australia: The Cinema of Charles Chauvel*, Allen & Unwin (Sydney, 1991).

Davidson, J., 'Locating Crocodile Dundee', *Meanjin*, 1987, Vol. 46, No. 1.

Dawson, J., and Molloy, B. (eds.), *Queensland Images in Film and Television*, University of Queensland Press (St Lucia, 1988).

Dermody, S., and Jacka, E., *The Screening of Australia* Vols.1 and 2, Currency Press (Sydney, 1987–8).

Gibson, R., 'Landscape in Australian Feature Films', *Framework*, 1983, No. 22/23.

Hamilton, P., and Mathews, S., *Australian Dreams, Australian Movies*, Currency Press (Sydney, 1986).

Jacka, E, and Dermody, S., *The Imaginary Industry: Australian Film in the Late 1980s*, Australian Film, Television and Radio School (Sydney, 1988).

Larkins, B., *Chips: The Life and Films of Chips Rafferty*, Macmillan (South Melbourne, 1986).

Lawson, S., 'Towards Decolonization: Some Problems and Issues for Film History in Australia', *Film Reader*, 1979, No. 4.

Morris, M., 'Tooth and Claw: Tales of Survival and Crocodile Dundee', in her *The Pirate's Fiancée*, Verso (London, 1988).

O'Regan, T., 'Fair Dinkum Films: The Crocodile Dundee Phenomenon', in S. Dermody and E. Jacka (eds.), *The Imaginary Industry: Australian Cinema in the Late 1980s*, Australian Film, Television and Radio School (Sydney, 1988).

O'Regan, R., 'Australian Film Making: its Public Circulation', in A. Hutton (ed.), *The First Australian History and Film Conference Papers, 1982*, Australian Film, Television and Radio School (North Ryde, 1982).

O'Regan, T., 'A Fine Cultural Romance—Aspects of the Australian Film in the Late 1970s', *Australian Journal of Cultural Studies*, 1986, Vol. 4, No. 1.

Pike, A., and Cooper, R., *Australian Films 1900–1977*, Oxford University Press (Melbourne, 1981).

Shirley, G., and Adams, B., *Australian Cinema: The First Eighty Years*, Currency Press and the Australian Film Institute (Sydney, 1983).

Spear, P. (ed.), *Get the Picture: Essential Data on Australian Film, Television and Video*, Australian Film Commission (Sydney, 1989).

Stratton, D., *The Avocado Plantation*, Macmillan (Sydney, 1990).

Tulloch, J., *Legends on the Screen: The Australian Narrative Cinema 1919–29*, Currency Press and the Australian Film Institute (Sydney, 1981).

Tulloch, J., *Australian Cinema: Identities, Narrative and Meaning*, Allen & Unwin (Sydney, 1982).

Turner, G., 'Crocodile Dundee, 10BA and the Future of the Australian Film Industry', *Australian Studies*, 1989, No. 2.

Australian Television

Appleton, G., *How Australia Sees itself: The Role of Commercial Television*, Australian Content Discussion Paper, Australian Broadcasting Tribunal (Sydney, 1988).

Bailey, J.J., 'Australian Television: Why it is the Way it is', *Cinema Papers*, September-October 1979, No. 23.

Boyer, R., 'Television in Perspective', *The Australian Quarterly*, September 1957, No. 26.

Browne, G.S., 'Television: Friend or Enemy?', *Meanjin*, Winter 1954, Vol. 13, No. 2.

Collins, J., 'Watching Ourselves Watch Television, or Who's Your Agent?,' *Cultural Studies*, 1989, Vol. 3,, No. 3.

Craik, J., 'Popular, Commercial and National Imperatives of Australian Broadcasting', *Media Information Australia*, February 1991, No. 59.

Craven, I., 'Distant Neighbours: Notes on Some Australian Soap Operas', *Australian Studies*, 1989, No. 3.

Craven, I., 'Race and Ethnicity in the Drip Dramas', in W. Senn and G. Capone (eds.), *The Making of a Pluralist Australia*, Peter Lang (Bern, 1992).

Cunningham, S., 'Cultural Theory and Broadcasting Policy: some Australian Observations, *Screen*, Spring 1991, Vol. 32, No. 1.

Cunningham, S., 'Docker: Criticism, History and Policy', *Media Information Australia*, February 1991, No. 59.

Davies, A.F., 'Mass Communications', in A.F. Davies and S. Encel (eds.), *Australian Society: A Sociological Introduction*, Cheshire (Melbourne, 1970).

Davies, B., *Those Fabulous TV Years*, Cassell (Sydney, 1981).

Docker, J., 'Popular Culture versus the State: An Argument against Australian Content Regulations for Television', *Media Information Australia*, February 1991, No. 59.

Edgar, P., *Children and Screen Violence*, University of Queensland Press (St Lucia, Queensland, 1977).

Grant, G., 'Television and Us', *Overland*, July 1956, No. 7.

Grosberg, L., 'Wandering Audiences, Nomadic Critics', *Cultural Studies*, 1988, Vol. 2, No. 3.

Hagstrom, I., 'Popular Culture Undefined', *Arena*, 1982, No. 61.

Hall, S., *Supertoy: 20 Years of Australian Television*, Sun Books (Melbourne, 1976).

Hall, S., *Turning On, Turning Off: Australian Television in the Eighties*, Cassell (Sydney, 1981).

Hazlehurst, C., 'The Advent of Commercial Television', *Cultural History*, 1983–3, No. 2.

Holmes, C., 'Television in Australia: A Survey', *Meanjin*, April 1958, Vol. 17, No. 1.

Hutchinson, G., 'Graham Kennedy: The Funny Melbourne Television Phenomenon', *Meanjin*, 1986, Vol. 45, No. 2.

Inglis, K.S., and Brazier, J., *This is the ABC: The Australian Broadcasting Commission*, 1932–83, Melbourne University Press (Melbourne, 1983).

Jacka, E., *The ABC of Drama, 1975–90*, Australian Film, Television and Radio School (North Ryde, 1991).

James-Bailey, J., *Australian Television: Historical Overview*, Australian Film Television and Radio School (Sydney, 1979).

King, N., and Rowse, T., 'Typical Aussies: Television and Popularism in Australia', *Framework*, 1983, No. 22/23.

Lashwood, H., 'Television and Australia', *Meanjin*, Summer 1954, Vol. 13, No. 4.

McCallum, M. (ed.), *Ten Years of Television*, Sun Books (Melbourne, 1986).

Moran, A., *Images and Industry: Television Drama Production in Australia*, Currency Press (Sydney, 1985).

Moran, A., *Australian Television Drama Series, 1956–81*, Australian Film, Television and Radio School (North Ryde, 1989).

Palmer, P., *The Lively Audience: Children in Front of the Television Set*, Allen & Unwin (Sydney, 1986).

Palmer, P., *Girls and Television*, NSW Ministry of Education (Sydney, 1986).

Pingree, S., and Hawkins, R., 'US Programs on Australian Television: The Cultivation Effect, *Journal of Communication*, 1981, Vol. 31, No. 7.

Radway, J., 'Reception Study: Ethnography and the Problems of Dispersed Audiences and Normadic Subjects', *Cultural Studies*, 1988, Vol. 2, No. 3.

Roddick, N., 'Strewth! A Beginner's Guide to Australian Television', *Sight and Sound*, Autumn 1985, Vol. 54, No. 4.

Sadlier, K., 'Down and Going Under', *Screen International*, September 1990, No. 775.

Sadlier, K., 'Australia: Down but Not Under', *Screen International*, Special MIFED Issue, Spring 1991.

Semmler, C., *The ABC: Aunt Sally and Sacred Cow*, Melbourne University Press (Melbourne, 1981).

Spear, P. (ed.), *Get the Picture: Essential Data on Australian Film, Television and Video*, Australian Film Commission (Sydney, 1989).

Stewart, D., *The Television Family*, Institute of Family Studies (Melbourne, 1983).

Stone, D., 'How Television Makes use of Minority Groups', *Sunday Age*, 28 October 1990.

Tulloch, J., and Moran, A., *A Country Practice: Quality Soap*, Currency Press (Sydney, 1986).

Tulloch, J., *Television Drama: Agency, Audience and Myth*, Routledge & Kegan Paul (London, 1989).

Tulloch, J., and Turner, G. (eds.), *Australian Television: Programs, Pleasures and Politics*, Allen & Unwin, (Sydney, 1989).

Watts, R., 'Social Ventriloquism in Defence of Media Culture, *Arena*, 1984, No. 68.

Webb, L., 'The Social Control of Television', *Public Administration* (Sydney), September 1960.

Australian Radio

Bridges, and N., Crook, F., *Wonderful Wireless*, Methuen (Sydney, 1983).

Counihan, M., 'The Foundation of a Broadcasting Audience: Australian Radio in the Twenties', *Meanjin*, 1982, Vol. 41, No. 2.

Johnson, L., 'Sing 'em Muck, Clara: Highbrow versus Lowbrow on Early Australian Radio', *Meanjin*, 1982, Vol. 41, No. 2.

Johnson, L., *The Unseen Voice: A Cultural Study of Early Australian Radio*, Routledge & Kegan Paul (London, 1988).

Kent, J., *Out of the Bakelite Box*, Angus & Robertson (Sydney, 1983).

Law, M., 'Public Radio—Where is it Headed, and Will it get There?', *Media Information Australia, 1986, No. 41*.

Newsom, J., 'Development of Local/Community Radio in Australia', *Combroad*, 1989, No. 82.

Potts, J., *The Price you Pay: Radio Advertising in Australia 1939-1945*, MA thesis, New South Wales Institute of Technology (Sydney, 1984).

Potts, J., *Radio in Australia*, University of New South Wales Press, (Sydney, 1990).

Ryan, N., 'Public Broadcasting in the Twilight Zone', 1983, No. 42.

Australian Popular Music

Australian Broadcasting Tribunal, *Australian Music on Radio*, Australian Broadcasting Tribunal (Sydney, 1986).

Beilby, P., and Robertson, M., *Australian Music Directory 1981–82*, Australian Music Directory (North Melbourne, 1981).

Bennett, T. (ed.), *Rock Music: Politics and Policy*, Institute for Cultural Studies, Griffith University (Nathan, Queensland, 1989).

Birch, A., 'The Politics of Popular Music', *Meanjin*, 1984, Vol. 43, No. 4.

Bissett, A., *Black Roots White Flowers: A History of Jazz in Australia*, Golden Press (Sydney, 1979).

Breen, M. (ed.), *Missing in Action: Australian Popular Music in Perspective*, Verbal Graphics (Kensington, Victoria, 1987).

Bryden-Brown, J., *J. O'K.: The Official Johnny O'Keefe Story*, Doubleday (Sydney, 1982).

Caswell, R., *Shout: The Story of Johnny O'Keefe*, Currency Press (Sydney, 1986).

Hayward, P. (ed.), *From Pop to Punk to Postmodernism: Popular Music from Australian Culture from the 1960s to the 1990s*, Allen & Unwin (Sydney, 1992).

McGrath, N., *The Australian Encyclopaedia of Rock*, Outback Press (Collingwood, Victoria, 1978).

McGregor, C., *People, Politics and Pop*, Ure Smith (Sydney, 1968).

McGregor, C., *Soundtrack for the Eighties*, Hodder & Stoughton (Sydney, 1983).

Mislom, W., and Thomas, H., *Pay to Play*, Penguin (Ringwood, Victoria, 1986).

Rogers, B., and O'Brien, D., *Rock n' Roll Australia: The Australian Pop Scene 1954–64*, Cassell (Sydney, 1975).

Walker, C., *Inner City Sound*, Wild and Woolley (Glebe, NSW, 1982).

Walker, C., *The Next Thing: Contemporary Australian Rock*, Kangaroo Press (Kenthurst, NSW, 1984).

Watson, E., *Country Music in Australia* Vol. 1, Rodeo Publications (Sydney, 1975).

Watson, E., *Country Music in Australia* Vol. 2, Angus & Robertson (Sydney, 1983).

Zion, L., 'Pop Music and Australian Culture: Some Considerations', *Melbourne Historical Journal*, 1982, No. 14.

Zion, L., 'Rock and Opera: Selling the Product', *Arena*, 1984, No. 68.

Zion, L., 'The Sound of Australian Music', in V. Burgmann and J. Lee (eds.), *Constructing a Culture: A People's History of Australia since 1788*, McPhee Gribble and Penguin (Fitzroy and Ringwood, 1988).

Australian News

Edgar, P., *The Politics of the Press*, Sun Books (Melbourne, 1979).

Edgar, P. (ed.), *The News in Focus*, Macmillan (Melbourne, 1980).

Gerdes, P., and Charlier, P., *TV News—That's the Way it Was*, Australian Film and Television School (Sydney, 1985).

Greenfield, C., and Wiliams, P., 'Bicentennial Preliminaries: Aboriginal Women, Newspapers and the Politics of Culture', *Hecate*, 1987/88, Vol. 13, No. 2.

Meadows, M., and Oldham, C., 'Racism and the Dominant Ideology: Aborigines, Television News and the Bicentenary', *Media Information Australia*, 1991, No. 60.

Mickler, S., 'Visions of Disorder', *Cultural Studies*, 1992, Vol. 6, No. 3.

Seal, G., 'Azaria Chamberlain and the Media Charivari', *Australian Folklore*, March 1987.

Windschuttle, E. and Windschuttle, K. (eds.), *Fixing the News: Critical Perspectives on the Australian Media*, Cassell (Sydney, 1981).

Australian Reading

Arthur, K.O., *Recasting History: Australian Bicentennial Writing*, Murdoch University External Studies Unit (Perth, 1990).

Borchardt, D.H., and Kirsop, W. (eds.), *The Book in Australia: Towards a Cultural and Social History*, Historical Bibliography Monograph 16, Australian Reference Publications (Melbourne, 1988).

Lawson, S., *The Archibald Paradox: A Strange Case of Authorship*, Penguin (Ringwood, Victoria, 1987).

Long, E., 'Reading Groups and the Postmodern Crisis of Cultural Authority', *Cultural Studies*, 1987, Vol. 1, No. 3.

McKenzie, D.F., 'The Sociology of a Text: Orality, Print and Literacy in Early New Zealand', *The Library* (6th series), 1984, Vol. 6, No4.

Representing Aboriginality in Popular Culture

Avery, J., 'Two Laws, *Cinema Papers*, 1982, No. 39.

Beckett, J.R. (ed.), *Past and Present: The Construction of Aboriginality*, Aboriginal Studies Press (Canberra, 1988).

Bostock, L., *The Greater Perspective: Guidelines for the Production of Television and Film about Aborigines and Torres Strait Islanders*, SBS (Sydney, 1987).

Brown, K., 'Racial Referents: Images of European/Aboriginal Relations in Australian Feature Films 1955–84', *Sociological Review*, 1988, Vol. 36, No3.

Dougal, J., and Lucas, R., 'Picturing the Real? The Representation of Aborigines in the Media', *Metro*, 1988, No. 77.

Goodall, H., and Jacubowicz, A. (et al), *Racisim, Cultural Pluralism and the Media*. Report for the Office of Multicultural Affairs, by the University of Technology, Sydney (Sydney, 1990).

Harding, J., 'Canons in the Cinema', *Cinema Papers*, 1992, No. 87.

Hicking-Hudson, A., 'White Construction of Black Identity in Australian Films about Aborigines', *Literature Film Quarterly*, 1990, Vol. 4, No. 18.

Hodge, B., and Mishra, V., *Dark Side of the Dream: Australian Literature and the Postcolonial Mind*, Allen & Unwin (Sydney, 1990).

Jennings, K., 'Ways of Seeing and Speaking about Aboriginal Women: Black Women and Documentaries', *Hecate*, 1987/88, Vol. 13, No. 2.

Jennings, K., 'Myths and Memories: Aboriginality in Australian Films', *Bulletin of the Olive Pink Society*, 1989, Vol. 1, No. 1.

Langton, M., *Well I Heard it on the Radio and I Saw it on the Television...An Essay for the AFC on the Politics and Aesthetics of Film-making By and About Aboriginal People and Things*, AFC (Sydney, 1992).

Malone, P., *In Black and White and Colour: A Survey of Aboriginality in Australian Feature Films*, Nelen Yubu Missiological Series No. 4 (Northern Territory, 1987).

Maynard, S., 'Black (and White) Images: Aborigines and Film', in A. Moran and T. O'Regan (eds.), *The Australian Screen*, Penguin (Ringwood, Victoria, 1989).

Michaels, E., 'Hundreds Shot at Aboriginal Community: ABC Makes Television Documentary at Yuendumu', *Media Information Australia*, 1986, No. 45.

Mickler, S., *Gambling on the First Race: A Comment on Racisim and Talkback Radio—6PR, the YAB and the WA Government*, Louis St John Johnson Memorial Trust Fund, and the Centre for Research in Culture and Communications, Murdoch University (Murdoch, 1992).

Moore, C., and Muecke, S., 'Racism and the Representation of Aborigines in Film', *Australian Journal of Cultural Studies*, 1984, Vol. 2, No. 1.

Muecke, S., *Textual Spaces: Aboriginality and Popular Culture Studies*, New South Wales University Press (Kensington, 1992).

Pike, A., 'Aboriginals in Feature Films', *Meanjin*, 1977, No. 26.

Turner, G., 'Breaking the Frame: The Representation of Aborigines in Australian Film', in A. Rutherford (ed.), *Aboriginal Culture Today*, Dangaroo Press (Sydney, 1988).

Aboriginal Uses of Popular Forms

Aboriginal and Torres Strait Islander Commission, *Aboriginal and Torres Strait Islander Broadcasting*, Aboriginal and Torres Strait Islander Commission and the Department of Transport and Communication.

Baird, L., 'I've Always Wanted to be in Radio—But How?', *Media Information Australia*, 1986, No. 41.

Balodis, J., 'A Dream of Aboriginal Radio Complete', *Scan*, 19 October–8 November 1981.

Balodis, J., 'Aboriginal Radio Takes Off', *Scan*, 6 December 1982–6 February 1983.

Bellamy, L., 'Black and White Television from the Heart', *Age*, 'Green guide', 22 October 1987.

Breen, M. (ed.), *Our Place, Our Music: Aboriginal Popular Music in Perspective*, Aboriginal Studies Press for the Institute of Aboriginal Studies (Canberra, 1989).

CAAMA Group, *An Introduction to the CAAMA Group of Companies*, CAAMA (Alice Springs, 1989).

Corker, J., 'An Aboriginal Commercial Television Station', *Legal Service Bulletin*, June 1986.

Department of Aboriginal Affairs, 'Aborigines Move into Radio', *Aboriginal Quarterly*, 1979, Vol. 2, No. 2.

Dutchak, P., 'Black Screen', *Cinema Papers*, 1992, No. 87.

Horne, T., 'Modern Message Stick', *Duran Duran*, 1985, No. 28

Katz, E., 'Can Authentic Cultures Survive New Media?', *Journal of Communication*, 1977, Vol. 27, No. 2.

Lewis, K., 'A Radio Station for Aborigines', *Identity*, April 1974.

Meadows, M., 'The Jewel in the Crown', *Australian Journalism Review*, 1988, No. 10.

Michaels, E., and Granites, L.J., 'The Cost of Video at Yuendumu', *Media Information Australia*, May 1984.

Michaels, E., and Toyne, P., 'The Cost of not Having a Telephone', in E. Michaels (ed.), *Working Papers in Aboriginal Communications, 1983–84*, AIAS (Canberra, 1984).

Michaels, E., *The Life History of an Aboriginal Videotape*, Working Paper, Remote Television Project, AIAS (Canberra, 1984/5).

Michaels, E., 'The impact of Video, Television and Satellites in Aboriginal Communities', in B. Foran and B. Walker (eds.), *The Application of Science and Technology to Aboriginal Development in Central Australia*, CSIRO (Canberra, 1986).

Michaels, E., *The Aboriginal Invention of Television in Central Australia 1982–85*, Aboriginal Studies Press (Canberra, 1986).

Michaels, E., 'Hollywood Iconography: A Warlpiri Reading', in P. Drummond and R. Paterson (eds.), *Television and its Audience: International Research Perspectives*, BFI (London, 1988).

O'Regan, T., *Communication and Tradition: Essays after Eric Michaels*, special issue of Continuum, 1990, Vol. 3., No. 2.

Wilmot, E., 'Aboriginals, AUSSAT and Satellite Broadcasting', *Media Information Australia*, 1985, No. 38.

Wilmott, E. et al, *Out of the Silent Land: Report of the Task Force on Aboriginal and Torres Strait Islander Broadcasting and Communications*, AGRS (Canberra, 1984).

Notes on Contributors

Dr Stephen Alomes is a senior lecturer in Australian Studies at Deakin University, Geelong. His books include *A Nation at Last?* (1988) and (with Catherine Jones) *Australian Nationalism* (1991). A football, as well as history, graduate of the University of Tasmania, where he retreated from the wing to the back pocket, he now takes high marks in the lounge-room.

Nicholas Brown is an Australian Research Council Post-doctoral Fellow in the Department of History at the Australian National University. In 1991 he established an Australian Studies course at the ANU. Under the working rubric, 'Governing Prosperity', he is currently assessing the interaction between intellectuals and social change in Australia from the 1940s to the 1970s.

Ruth Brown is an expatriate New Zealander who live in Sussex, UK, where she has an asparagus farm and teaches part-time with the University of Sussex Centre for Continuing Education.

Ian Craven teaches Film and Television Studies at the University of Glasgow, Scotland. He serves on the Executive Committee of the John Logie Baird Centre, and was a founder member of the European Association for Studies on Australia. He is co-author of *The Hollywood Cinema: An Introduction* (Basil Blackwell, 1993) and has contributed articles on Australian film and television to many journals. He is currently preparing a study of the South Australian Film Corporation.

Kay Ferres teaches Women's Studies and cultural history in the Faculty of Humanities, Griffiths University. She is currently writing a biography of Rona Campbell Praed, and has edited *The Time to Write: Australian Women Writers 1900–1930* to be published by Penguin in December 1993.

Kevin Foster is a graduate of Manchester, Saskatchewan, and Monash Universities. He is currently a lecturer in the Department of English and Communication Studies at the University of New England, Armidale, New South Wales. His previous publications include articles on the cultural construction of the Falklands and Gulf Wars, African autobiography and the Spanish Civil War.

Christine Higgins is a lecturer in English and Australian literature in the School of Humanities, at Queensland University of Technology. Her current research involves an exploration of the uses of Gothic tropes and archetypes in the reporting of violent crime in the Queensland press.

Stephen Knight is Professor of English at De Montfort University, Leicester, having previously been Professor of English at the University of Melbourne. He is the author of reviews and articles on crime fiction and other topics, and edited *Dead Witness* (Penguin, Melbourne, 1989), a historical anthology of short Australian crime stories.

Andrew Milner is Associate Professor and Director of the Centre for Comparative Literature and Cultural Studies at Monash University. He is the author of *John Milton and the English Revolution* (1981), *The Road to St Kilda Pier* (1984), *Contemporary Cultural Theory* (1991) and *Cultural Materialism* (1993), and co-editor of *Postmodern Conditions* (1988) and *Discourse and Difference* (1990)

Dr Xavier Pons teaches Australian Studies at the University of Toulouse-Le-Mirail (France). His latest book, *A Sheltered Land?*, will be published in 1994 by Allen & Unwin.

Graham Seal is Director of the Centre for Australian Studies at Curtin University of Technology, Perth, Western Australia. He is author of *The Hidden Culture: Folklore in Australian Society* (OUP, 1989) and joint editor with Gwenda Beed Davey of the *Oxford Companion to Australian Folklore* (OUP, 1993).

George Seddon is a Professor Emeritus of Environmental Science at the University of Melbourne and Honorary Senior Research Fellow in the Centre for Studies in Australian Literature at the University of Western Australia. His better known books include *Swan River Landscapes* (UWA Press, 1970), *A Sense of Place* (UWA Press, 1972), *Man and Landscape in Australia* (Aust. Govt. Printer, 1976) and *A City and its Setting* (Fremantle Arts Centre Press, 1986). His next book, *Snowy River*, is on environmental history, in press with Allen & Unwin.

James Walter is Professor of Australian Studies at Griffith University, Brisbane. He has recently returned to Australia after a term as Head of the Sir Robert Menzies Centre for Australian Studies, University of London.

Robert White is Professor of English at the University of Western Australia. He makes occasional forays into Australian studies, but he is better known for his works on Shakespeare. *Furphy's Shakespeare* (Centre for Studies in Australian Literature, Perth) brings together in unholy wedlock the two areas.